THE TURIN SHROUD:

PHYSICAL EVIDENCE OF LIFE AFTER DEATH?

(With Insights from a Jewish Perspective)

MARK NIYR

www.bookstandpublishing.com

Published by
Bookstand Publishing
Morgan Hill, CA 95037
4695_14

ISBN 978-1-63498-808-7

LICENSING PERMISSIONS
FOR USE OF THIS WORK

The Turin Shroud: *Physical Evidence* of Life After Death? (With Insights from a Jewish Perspective) by Mark Niyr is licensed under the terms of the **Creative Commons Attribution 3.0 Unported (CC BY 3.0) License**. ("Unported" indicates that it is an international license.) To view a copy of this license for those interested to reuse this work, visit the following *URL*: https://creativecommons.org/licenses/by/3.0/. (At the bottom of the website, you may click a link to translate the license information into different languages.)

CONTENTS

FOREWORD

I would like to welcome the reader to the new and dynamic intersection of science and religion. Historically, this has been considered a rather narrow intersection with very little in common between the two disciplines, in which one is usually based on measurements, observations, and experiments, while the other is often based on faith and on things that are unseen and intangible.

However, in the last forty years scientists from some of the most prestigious institutions in the world began to rigorously study the Shroud of Turin. This burial cloth is now said to be the most scientifically studied relic in history. Yet, we're just beginning to acquire some of the vast amount of information that has been uniquely encoded within this more than 14-foot-long and 3 1/2-foot-wide (4.34 m x 1.10 m) linen cloth. Scientists of all backgrounds such as physics, chemistry, biology, engineering, medicine and anatomy have been attracted to this subject, as have theologians, Christians, Jews, Muslims, atheists, agnostics (which was my origin over 37 years ago), as well as those from other religious or philosophical persuasions. In addition, Shroud research and investigations have necessarily involved those from the general fields of archaeology, history, law, botany, optics, computer science, forensic science, medical jurisprudence, and so many more.

Many of these Shroud experts now realize that the intersection between science and religion has not only become longer and wider, but it is rapidly expanding as their research expands. These and other experts are understanding that the information gained from each of these disciplines is adding to the common knowledge of humanity and that it could benefit all people throughout the world. This knowledge is not only allowing people to acquire a new perspective but to answer some of the most fundamental and universal questions in human history.

So, please continue to read and enjoy the new perspective and information contained in this excellent book on the Shroud of Turin.

Mark Antonacci
Attorney at Law

INTRODUCTION TO THE BOOK

My father flew numerous combat missions for the United States during World War II and the Korean War. He retired from the U.S. Air Force shortly afterward as a Captain. His colleagues and crew developed a very close-knit bond from those experiences. They kept in touch with each other on a regular basis during the following decades. One evening, one of those colleagues phoned my father and informed him that he was going to die soon. He had been taking blood transfusions and his body was starting to reject them. He confided to my father that he did not know what to think about God. If possible, where could he find credible answers about God? I offered my father an initial rough draft of this writing about the Shroud of Turin so that he could pass it along to his close friend whose life was soon to end. A week or two later that friend phoned my father and very gratefully thanked him for the paper. He explained that it gave him the answers he was longing for. Within a couple months he passed away.

It may be that you know of someone who is facing death and needs assurance or answers about God. One day you personally will also be facing your own death. Perhaps this topic regarding the Turin Shroud could provide credible scientific answers and comfort during those final days. Keep this in mind for your own family members, relatives, friends, neighbors, and associates which God has brought into your life for a purpose. One important aspect about the Shroud is that it can speak to people who would not normally have *any* regard for the Bible. Uniquely, the Turin Shroud is an intriguing *scientific journey* investigating one of the greatest mysteries of the world. It has captivated the curiosity of atheists, agnostics, and people from a variety of religions. In fact, many of the scientists who investigated the Shroud were from a diversity of religions as well as atheists and agnostics.[1] Those who are superficially aware about the Shroud (yet know little about it) are essentially ignorant. The real impact of its message can *only* (or truly) be fathomed from its impressive details.

Hopefully, this book will elicit insights which a casual observer might not think to consider, and likewise enable non-scientists to grasp the significance of the findings that so astounds the scientific community concerning the Shroud of Turin. Regarding myself, I am a Jew. My hope, therefore, is to also draw readers into the Jewish perspective which can transport them back in time to that the first century world: a world which surrounded the biblical background and context of the Shroud's story. The Jewish perspective enlightens answers to important questions which have been brought up regarding the Shroud. (All facts presented in this publication have been meticulously documented with hundreds of reference notes. They also provide a source for additional information.)

Mark Niyr, Author

Chapter 1

SCIENTIFIC INVESTIGATION OF THE SHROUD

Is it possible there might be *physical evidence* of life after death? *Physical evidence?* What if scientists throughout the world could examine, test, and scrutinize the physical evidence from numerous scientific perspectives? What if some scientists hoped to disprove it, while others just wanted to know the answer? What if they could lavish their efforts over many decades in order to meticulously pursue this research? Would you like to review their findings so you could draw your own conclusion?

What is the most scientifically studied archeological relic in history? Some people might guess that would be the Rosetta Stone (which unlocked the interpretation of Egyptian hieroglyphs). However, the answer is unquestionably the Shroud of Turin. Hundreds of thousands of scientific hours of analysis, research, and testing has been devoted to the Shroud.[2] In the process, international scientists have employed some of the most sophisticated scientific equipment and technology in the world, involving such prestigious institutions as (to name a few) Los Alamos Scientific Laboratory, Jet Propulsion Laboratory, U.S. Air Force, Sandia Laboratory, Zurich Criminal Police, and universities such as Harvard, Yale, Cambridge, and Oxford. Never before had such an impressive body of scientists of the highest caliber, from such a diverse range of scientific disciplines and professional fields, from all parts of the world, brought together such extensive research to bear on a relic of antiquity. Their evidence (published in numerous peer-reviewed scientific journals, academic, and professional publications throughout the world) is extensive and compelling.[3]

> "The Shroud of Turin is the single, most studied artifact in human history" — Journal of Research of the National Institute of Standards and Technology, U.S. Department of Commerce.[4]

Some readers who have already heard about the Shroud of Turin may think that everyone else is already aware of it. The fact is that the vast majority of people are completely unaware of the existence of the Shroud. Furthermore, most of those who have heard about the Shroud know very little about it.[5] Even amongst those who are aware, only a small fraction of them are familiar with many of the significant details brought to light with this publication (which here includes the latest scientific test results for dating the age of the Shroud cloth).

Chapter 2

STURP:
THE SHROUD OF TURIN
RESEARCH PROJECT

The Shroud of Turin is a linen cloth (14 feet 3 inches long by 3 feet 7 inches wide, or 4.34 m x 1.10 m)[a] which is purported to be the burial cloth that wrapped the body of Jesus of Nazareth in the tomb.[6] Concerning the name "Jesus," the actual name given to the Nazarene (the name by which he was known among those who lived during his time) was the Hebrew name "Ye-**SHU**-a" (ישוע). Interestingly, the English name Jesus does not mean anything. It is merely a transliteration of letters from Hebrew to Greek to English. However, in the Hebrew language of the Jews, the name "Yeshua" conveyed a very definitive meaning: it literally translates, "salvation." His name is the masculine form of the Hebrew word "yeshu'ah".[7] It is thought provoking to consider that the only man whose life would one day split the calendar of the world (B.C. to A.D., or B.C.E. to C.E.) would be assigned a name—*prior to his birth*—that would presage his life's mission: "salvation." (The book of Matthew reports how an angel assigned this name to him *before his birth* to foretell his future calling: "you shall call His name **Yeshua**, for He will **save** His people from their sins"—Matt. 1:21 TLV.) Every time his name was spoken (even by his enemies), it declared his mission: "salvation." Therefore, with due respect, the remainder of this text will refer to the actual Hebrew name *Yeshua*, rather than the English name Jesus. The Hebrew name *Yeshua* also serves as a reminder of him being a Jew.

---

[a] Why is the Shroud an odd size (14'x3" by 3'x7")? Actually, this is not an odd or random size. Rather it is a logical size from a Jewish perspective. For many centuries, including the 1st century, the Jewish community measured size by the Jewish "cubit." When measuring the Shroud using the Jewish "cubit" of measurement, the Shroud is found to be an even 8 x 2 size in cubits.

National Geographic Magazine captivated the attention of the world when they published a feature article regarding a team of 26 international scientists and specialists who were granted permission to perform the first ever scientific experiments and analysis of the Shroud in Turin, Italy.[8] [b] (They brought with them *seven tons* of scientific equipment!) Eventually, this team grew to a total of 33 international members from a wide variety of scientific disciplines, bearing credentials at high level posts from 20 major research institutions. The name of this project was called the *Shroud of Turin Research Project* (acronym: STURP).[9]

What prompted such scientific intrigue surrounding the Shroud? There is an image of a crucified man on this burial shroud that has mystified and astounded scientists. Such an impressive array of international scientists would not have volunteered this extensive sacrifice of their time, effort, and personal expense if the investigation was not worthy of their effort. They meticulously planned the project more than a year in advance with numerous international meetings. The entire endeavor was undertaken from their own initiative out of scientific inquiry. Accordingly, it is well worth taking time from our busy lives to consider some of the highlights that compelled this extensive scientific research.

At first, many of the scientists thought they could readily refute the Shroud's image as an artistic forgery.[10] However, the more scientific tests that were performed, the more astonishing details came to light, prompting more extensive research, which then in turn revealed yet further stunning discoveries. The results from this research hold far-reaching repercussions. It has opened new insights which all prior generations were scientifically unable to grasp or perceive. Furthermore, it has brought to fore some of the most fundamental questions and issues of life.

---

[b] Visit this *National Geographic* article and its gallery of enhanced Shroud photos: http://home.kpn.nl/britso531/Nat.Geographic.June1980.pdf.

Your Decision: You Make the Call

People often rely on the opinions of others to decide what to think about a matter. Do not let other people, or the media, manipulate your opinion. Here is *your* chance to examine the evidence of scientific research for *yourself* so *you* can draw *your own* conclusion and make *your own* assessment. Use *your own* inductive logic to weigh what "seems most logical and plausible" to *you*.

During the time of *Yeshua*, people responded with differing reactions concerning his miracles: some disbelieved and rejected, some doubted, some were non-committal (i.e. remaining *agnostic*), some were indifferent and could care less, but some were deeply appreciative: "glorifying God," giving "praise to God" (Luke 18:43 NASB), and "rejoicing over all the glorious things being done by Him" (Luke 13:17 NASB). Have you ever wondered what your reaction might have been had you been there? Which of those responses might have been yours? Here then is an opportunity for you to draw *your own* verdict and provide *your own* response to what may (or may not have been) one of *Yeshua's* very miracles (left behind for 2,000 years for our generation to research with our modern scientific technology). The Shroud may be authentic, or it may not be. What will *you* decide? What will be *your* opinion?

   (a) Is the image on the Shroud an accident of nature?
   (b) Is the image an artistic forgery: a hoax?
   (c) Or, is the image authentic—a miracle left behind from the historical *Yeshua* of Nazareth, some 2,000 years ago? *You* decide for yourself.

Of course, belief in *Yeshua* may be based on other traditional sources. In that regard, the Shroud may (or may not) provide additional confirmation. However, the fact is that *Yeshua* himself often cited his works (his miracles) as an important credential bearing witness to who he was. What will your response be? What will be your opinion?

17

Now when John [a.k.a. John the Baptist] heard in prison about the **works** of the Messiah, he sent word through his disciples and said to *Yeshua*, "Are You the Coming One [i.e. the Messiah], or do we look for another?" *Yeshua* replied, "Go report to John what you hear and see: the blind see and the lame walk, those with *tza'arat* [i.e. leprosy] are cleansed and the deaf hear, and the dead are raised and the poor have good news proclaimed to them. Blessed is the one who is not led to stumble because of Me (Matt. 11:2-6 TLV, emphasis added).

Have you ever wondered what might have resulted if scientists had been given the opportunity to examine one of the alleged miracles of *Yeshua*? The Shroud may provide just such an opportunity. Will it pass the scientific test?

Chapter 3

A BRIEF HISTORY OF THE SHROUD

If the Shroud is the historical burial cloth of the crucified *Yeshua*, then its first recorded history took place in Jerusalem, such as recorded in the Gospel of Matthew:

> When evening had come, a rich man named *Yosef* [Joseph] from *Ramatayim* [Arimathea] came. He himself was also a disciple of *Yeshua*. This man went to Pilate, and asked for *Yeshua's* body. [Deut. 21:23] Then Pilate commanded the body to be given up. **Yosef** [Joseph] **took the body and wrapped it in** a clean **linen cloth** [Grk. *sindon*, i.e. shroud; "*linen cloth*, esp. that which was fine and costly, in which the bodies of the dead were wrapped"[11]]. Then he laid it in his own new tomb, which he had hewn out in the bedrock. And he rolled a large stone to the opening of the tomb, and departed (Matthias [Matthew] 27:57-60, MW, emphasis added).

The first extra biblical account of the shroud's history comes from many ancient Syriac manuscripts (which are noticeably corrupt). They relate stories regarding a disciple of the Christ named Thaddaeus (or Syrian name *Addai*) who came to Edessa (modern day Urfa, Turkey) during the first century. As a result, Edessa's King Abgar (V) became a believer along with numerous people from that region. Some of these documents relate how a cloth with an image played a role amid this.

Later, during the 1840s, many supplementary Syriac manuscripts were recovered from the desert of Lower Egypt at the Nitrian Monastery. They also related additional references to an "Image of Edessa" cloth and the evangelization of that region. Followers of the

Jewish Messiah flourished at Edessa during the reign of King Abgar (V) and his son Ma'nu V (A.D./C.E. 50-57) until Ma'nu VI ascended the throne. King Ma'nu VI returned to traditional pagan religion and severely persecuted these followers. At that point, the cloth disappeared for centuries.[12] Early Christian historian Eusebius from the fourth century also quoted portions of King Abgar's (V) conversion from the Syriac manuscripts (but omitted references about the cloth).[13]

During the 6th century (year 525), a shroud cloth was recovered from a hidden niche above Edessa's western gate. It was found during reconstruction of the city of Edessa following a devastating flood. This gate was located at one of the highest parts of the city, and the height of the gate had apparently spared the cloth from damage by the flood. When the shroud cloth was rediscovered, there was also found with it a brick-red tile that bore a twin image of the shroud face. That tile became known as the *Keramion*.[14] Parthian rulers were known to display images of their gods above the city gates. Shroud historian Ian Wilson makes the case that this tile may have been mounted above the city gate by one of the kings of Edessa who became a believer in the Christ. Then once the persecutions of King Ma'nu (VI) broke out, someone may have pried out the tile to conceal the cloth within the brickwork above the gate and then remounted the tile, face inward, to hide the cloth inside above the gate.[15] Upon its 6th century discovery, this shroud cloth was then hailed as *acheiropoietos* (i.e. having an image not formed by the hands of man).[16] The shroud, henceforth, became known as *"the Image of Edessa."*[17]

During the centuries prior to the Edessa cloth discovery, illustrations of the Nazarene varied widely but typically portrayed him as clean shaven with short hair. However, the 6th century rediscovery of this "Image of Edessa" brought about a decisive change to the world's artistic profiles of the face of the Nazarene from that time onward.[18] For example, artistic portraitures then began to adopt various peculiarities (which resembled the image of the Turin Shroud)—such as, long hair (not short hair), a mustache and beard (not clean shaven), a hairless area above the chin, an extremely *unique* forked split in the beard below the chin, and a distinct transverse line below the chin across the neck (matching a crease line in the Shroud cloth).[19] Many such anomalies found from the art after the 6th century Edessa discovery served no logical or artistic purpose. They were evidently simply copied from the "Image of Edessa" — yet they matched unique peculiarities found with the Shroud of Turin. The discovery of the "Image of Edessa" thus set off a new distinctive trend resulting in more consistent artistic renditions of the Nazarene, and also bearing similarities with the Turin Shroud.

During the year 943, a Byzantine historian reported that the Savior's features were imprinted on a cloth.[20] In that same year (943), the Byzantine emperor determined to bring the cloth from Edessa to Constantinople (modern day Istanbul, Turkey). In what must have been one of the most unusual military events in history, his army surrounded Edessa (which had been conquered by Moslems) and promised the emir that the city would be spared, that 200 high-ranking Moslem prisoners would be set free, that 12,000 silver crowns would be paid, and that the city of Edessa would be guaranteed perpetual immunity — all in exchange for the "Image of Edessa" cloth. From year 944 until 1204, the cloth then resided in Constantinople, where it was then called the "*Mandylion*."[21]

The French 4th crusade besieged Constantinople on occasions between 1203 and 1204.[22] Crusader Robert de Clari wrote about "seeing in the Church of St Mary at Blachernae 'the *sydoines* [shroud] in which our Lord had been wrapped' adding, 'on every Friday this raised itself upright . . . so that one could see the figure of our Lord on it.'"[23] Subsequent events led to a new attack by the crusaders, who ransacked the city. The shroud cloth then disappeared again for nearly 150 years.

The next historical citing of the shroud cloth was from the village of Lirey in France during the 1350s. At that time there were public expositions of the shroud in Lirey which drew large crowds of pilgrims from various nations who could obtain souvenir medallions portraying the shroud.[24] (There exists a letter allegedly written to Pope Innocent III of Rome [back in August 1205] which complained that the French crusaders had looted the relics from Constantinople — including specifically the linen which wrapped "our Lord Jesus" after his death.[25] This could explain how the shroud eventually ended up in France after being looted by the French 4th crusade.) The shroud was then displayed at expositions in Lirey, France during the 1350s. One of the pilgrim souvenir medallions from the Lirey expositions of the shroud still exists today in the Cluny Museum in Paris, France. This is highly significant because the Lirey Medallion displays an embossed depiction of the *entire* shroud. *It is the earliest historical portrayal of the shroud that offers a visual illustration of the complete shroud, thus revealing the appearance of what the shroud looked like at that time (during the 1350s) — and it is an unmistakable replica of the Shroud which exists today in Turin, Italy.* It further exhibits a weave pattern on the back of the medallion to represent the unique weave pattern of the Shroud cloth. On the lower right, the Lirey Medallion presents three shields within a shield which was the "coat of arms" symbol of the owner of the Shroud (Geoffrey I de Charny, lord of Lirey, France) who died soon thereafter on the battlefield of Poitiers on September 19, 1356). **Thus, for the first time in recorded history we have a *full visual confirmation* that the Shroud (which today resides in Turin, Italy) is the same Shroud that existed in Lirey, France during the 1350s.**[26]

Chapter 4

THE IMAGE:
CHARACTERISTICS LIKE
A PHOTOGRAPHIC NEGATIVE?

To the natural eye, the image on the Shroud looks like a faint blur. Its form appears as though someone had applied a wet, blunt sponge to the cloth with some light coloring to fashion its features. Eventually, in 1898, Italian photographer Secondo Pia took the first-ever photograph of the Shroud. He did not expect that his photo would differ from the faint, fuzzy image he had examined while surveying the cloth. Shroud historian Ian Wilson reports that when Secondo Pia developed his negative plate from the first-ever photograph, he was stunned and shocked. He almost dropped and shattered the negative plate. Instead of the expected spongy, blurry image which he had surveyed, the developing negative plate resolved into a lifelike, vivid, sharply focused, positive photographic-like depiction![27] This meant that the image on the Shroud somehow bore characteristics like a photographic *negative*, which upon being photographed, produced a *positive-like* photographic result on the *negative* plate (instead of the expected negative image on the negative plate). How could that be? The confirmed existence of the Shroud dates back to at least the 1300s, whereas photography and the concept of photonegativity would not be invented until 500 years later (in the early 1800s). French physicist Joseph Nicephor Niepce made the first negative on paper in 1816, and the first known photograph in 1826.[28] With this photographic likeness of the Shroud, what had previously been the faint, blurry, spongy appearance on the Shroud now leaped out from the photographic negative with sharply defined focus, with precise depth shadowing, reversed light/dark contrast, and reversed left/right positioning—exactly what happens when a negative is transformed into a positive with photography. New details that had previously been invisible to the natural eye now became visible on the photographic negative.[29]

How could a medieval craftsman from the 1300s produce a *photo-like* negative *500 years before the invention of photography and photo-negativity*? How could the artist include details that would remain invisible to the naked eye for 500 years until the invention of photography? Suppose the medieval artist did somehow invent the concept of photo negativity by himself (something that no one else in history would conceive of for next five centuries), how could the medieval artist monitor that the outcome would transform into this astonishing lifelike, positive image? The medieval forger would have no way to see this transformation effect. No cameras would be available for the forger to view this photographic effect until 500 years later. Take a moment to look over the photo on the front cover of this book. Suppose you were the medieval artist. When you examine the photo on the cover, if you had no concept of photography, would you ever imagine that the blurry view of the Shroud seen by the naked eye (on the left side of the front book cover) would transform itself into the photographic-like image (displayed on the right side of the book cover photo) once it was revealed centuries later by the invention of photography?

The tendency for us is to ponder these matters from our modern-day perspective. Try as best you can not to be biased by the fact that you are already familiar with photography. Rather, try to think from a medieval perspective when there was no concept of photography or photo negativity. Applying inductive logic pertaining to this photographic feature, what is your appraisal? What seems most plausible to you? (1) Does this appear to be an accident of nature? Or (2), does this most likely seem to be the work of a medieval forger from the 1300s? Or (3), does this photo-like negative image most likely indicate an authentic relic? Questions like this ultimately prompted scientists decades later to rigorously investigate the Shroud. What is your honest appraisal regarding this? (Please stop to decide your evaluation for just this one particular aspect of the Shroud before reading further. You will be invited to give your opinion on many separate aspects about the Shroud as we continue. Some aspects may favor and other aspects may go against the Shroud's authenticity. Please evaluate each aspect separately with your own personal conclusion.)

Note: there are no other examples in history of a burial cloth revealing an image. Throughout the centuries, archeologists have uncovered thousands of ancient burial cloths. But none of them have left any sort of image.[30])

Dead bodies begin to decompose after a couple days. However, there is no evidence of stains of decomposition from the body found on the Shroud.[31] Photos reveal the body to be in a state of stiffened, ridged rigor mortis such that the buttocks are round (not flattened from gravity of the body's weight). One foot had been placed over the other and then nailed through both feet with a single spike into the beam. On the Shroud, the feet remain stiffened in this downward pointing posture with one top foot, leg, and heel elevated higher than the other.[32] When the crucified man died, his head had fallen somewhat toward his chest and was tilted slightly to his right.[33] The fact that the image on the Shroud shows the body still hardened stiff by rigor mortis with one leg and heel raised up off the ground, the head raised up off the floor (with the chin tilted right), and the buttocks round (not flat), shows that this image had to be made over a short period of time *before* the effects of rigor mortis wore off. Once rigor mortis starts to wear off, then the raised leg would have collapse down to the floor, the head would have fallen backward toward the floor (no longer tilled upward toward the chest), and the round buttocks would have been flattened by gravity. Since rigor mortis typically lasts only up to two or a part of three days, this would not have left much time for an image to develop on the Shroud by an accident of nature. Scientists who later researched the Shroud have not treated the "accident of nature" hypothesis as a plausible explanation for the origin of the

Shroud's image. Thus, the scientists have only considered two alternatives as plausible: (1) either the image is the result of an artistic forgery, or (2) the Shroud's image is an authentic relic which baffles scientific explanation.

As we traverse these chapters you may notice a repeated motif. The Shroud itself bears a variety of features discovered by the scientists that predate (?) the history of scientific knowledge itself by many centuries, or even thousands of years. And all these discoveries from the Shroud that predate the history of scientific knowledge revolve around one common theme. Namely, what? A crucified man's image on a burial cloth? Of all things, why would that be the one artifact bearing features that predate scientific knowledge?

Chapter 5

HIDDEN INSIGHTS REVEALED FROM THE SHROUD

T he Shroud reveals hidden insights bearing exquisite detail. However, many of these facets lie beyond the grasp of a casual observer. They would not be recognized until the aid of modern science and technology. The generation living near the turn of the 21st century is the first generation to discover these hidden features which had gone undetected for centuries.

We will begin by reviewing the underlying story of the Shroud from some of its more obvious themes. With remarkable detail, the injuries to the body on the Shroud match the account in the Bible of *Yeshua's* suffering and crucifixion. There are some elements which are unique to *Yeshua's* situation, and *atypical* of normal crucifixions.

With regard to the evidence found on the Shroud, it is interesting to note that if this is truly the historical *Yeshua* that appears on the Shroud, then not only do we have a photographic-like image of him (made 1,800 years before the invention of photography), but its details (examined with modern technology) further enlighten us with new insights about his sufferings that were never known before.

There is no art from the ancient world or medieval times that would remotely match the photographic quality of this image. Every wound and depiction of the body is physiologically and anatomically flawless, down to the minutest detail. It bears precision of detail not understood until centuries after any medieval forger.[34]

He [i.e. Pilate, the Roman governor over Judea] went out again to the Judean leaders. He said to them, "I find no case against him [i.e. against *Yeshua*]. But it's your custom that I release someone for you at Passover. So do you want me to release to you the King of the Jews?"

They shouted back, "Not this One, but *Bar-Abba!*" Now *Bar-Abba* was a revolutionary.

Then Pilate took *Yeshua* and had Him **scourged** (John 18:38 – John 19:1 (TLV), emphasis added.

There are more than one hundred dumbbell-shaped scourge wounds visible over virtually the entire body. They correspond precisely with the injuries inflicted by scourging with the ancient Roman flagrum whip.[35] If the man on the Shroud is *Yeshua*, then the Shroud also reveals additional details that were not reported in the Bible. The photographic-like image of the Shroud exhibits bruising and swelling on the body, and also on the nose of the Shroud victim. There is swelling on the cheeks, swelling near the right eye, and indications of dislocated nose cartilage (from facial beatings?). There are more than thirty pierce blood trails on the top, middle, and back of the head and sides of the forehead that would suit a disparaging crown cap of thorns.[36]

Then the governor's soldiers took *Yeshua* into the Praetorium and gathered the whole cohort around Him. They stripped Him and put a scarlet robe around Him. And after braiding a **crown of thorns**, they **placed it on His head** and put a staff in His right hand. And falling on their knees before Him, they mocked Him, saying, "Hail, King of the Jews!" They spat on Him, and they took the staff and **beat Him over and over on the head** [i.e. while wearing the crown cap of thorns]. When they finished mocking Him, they stripped the robe off Him and put His own clothes back on Him. And they led Him away to crucify Him (Matt. 27:27-31 TLV, emphasis added).

28

Biblical accounts inform us that *Yeshua* began his trek upward toward the execution site while bearing the crossbar used for his crucifixion (John 19:17). However, as a result of the prior severe scourging and beatings, *Yeshua* apparently could not complete the task. Thus, the Bible informs us that Romans soldiers forcefully conscripted a man from Cyrene named *Shim'on* (Simon) to finish carrying *Yeshua's* crossbeam for the remainder of the journey (Matt. 27:32). The Shroud shows evidence of this with two wide excoriated areas across the shoulder blades consistent with the man bearing a large, rough object.[37] Corresponding to this, the Shroud also reveals scratches, lesions, and abrasions on the knees as well as traces of dirt on the knees, and dirt and scratches on the nose in those areas of the Shroud, suggesting that the victim had fallen on his face before being crucified.[38]

The Bible reports that when *Yeshua* was crucified, each of his hands were nailed to the beam (John 20:24-28). Throughout history, artistic renditions of the crucifixion show the nails centered in the middle of the palms, not through the wrists as viewed from the Shroud.[39] However, it is now known that it is impossible for nails to support the body's weight from the palms of the hands. Nails in the palms would simply tear away through the flesh from the weight of the body. Only since the 20th century (from medical experiments after 1930) have scientists established this fact. Archeological discoveries since the 1960s have confirmed that crucified victims were indeed nailed through the wrist or lower forearms (not through the palms of the hands).[40] Therefore, artistic depictions of nails in the palms of the hands are anatomically erroneous. However, most people are unaware that the Greek language of the Messianic Writings (i.e. New Testament) when referring to these nail wounds employed a Greek word for "hand" (Gk *cheir* / John 20:25) which includes not only the hand, but also down through the forearm.[41] Here again the Shroud is found to be anatomically correct in a way that surpassed medieval knowledge. There are no art depictions from medieval times, nor prior to the 17th century, showing the nails in the wrists. All art illustrations prior to the 17th century show the wounds in the palms of the hands.[42] [c] This suggests that a medieval forger would not have been aware of this fact. The image of the Shroud reveals that the nails were driven either into the "thenar furrow" of the hand (the extreme bottom of the hand, angled down to exit the wrist area) or through the radial (thumb) side of the wrist. We can only see the back of one hand, but nonetheless, the nail exited the radial (thumb) side of the wrist. Either way, the nail would not break any bones and would support a couple hundred pounds of body weight. STURP forensic examiner Frederick Zugibe, M.D., Ph.D., pointed out that a nail in this location would strike (and continuously irritate) "the median nerve resulting in one of the most exquisite pains ever experienced by man—known medically as causalgia (*cau-sal-gia*)."[43] It is also possible that the nail may have entered a location called the "Space of Destot," which also could receive a spike without breaking any bones, and could readily support the weight of a body. A nail through the wrist could stimulate the median nerve causing the thumbs to contract toward the palms (as found on the Shroud.[44]

There is an ellipse *pierce wound* on the victim between the fifth and sixth ribs on the right *side of the chest* which drew a *post-mortem* blood flow as well as a gush of *watery fluid*.[45] The Bible describes precisely this same type of a lance pierce wound to the ribs occurring with *Yeshua* while on the cross *after* his death.

> So the soldiers came and broke the legs of the first [victim] and then the other who had been executed with *Yeshua*. Now when they came to *Yeshua* and saw that He was already dead, they did not break His legs. But one of the soldiers pierced His side with a

---

[c] Fold marks on the Shroud may indicate that when the Shroud was typically displayed publicly throughout the centuries it was likely folded in such a manner that only the face appeared (not the hands). The face was the part that was easiest to see with the natural eye.

spear, and immediately **blood** and **water** came out (John 19:32-34 TLV, emphasis added).

The pierce wound between the ribs on the Shroud likewise exhibits a *post-mortem* blood flow with a *gush of water*. Had the man on the Shroud been alive when the pierce wound was inflicted, the blood from the side wound would have splattered from breathing (as air escaped from the lung). Instead, the blood from the side wound of the Shroud victim merely oozed out with no sign of breathing or heart beating. This was clearly a post mortem blood flow.

The abnormally expanded rib cage and enlarged pectoral muscles draw in toward the collarbone betray strenuous efforts to breathe.[46] In order to breathe from the hanging position, the crucified victim would have to exhale by painfully pushing off the nail spike driven through the feet, raising the shoulders by pulling on the nails from the wrists, and then expanding the ribcage.[47] Blood trails from the Shroud carefully map together these themes. Dual blood trail streams run parallel along the wrists to the elbows at 65 and 55 degrees— evidence that the wrists were nailed to a cross beam which required this seesaw effort of raising up and down from the wrist spikes (combined with pushing off the foot spike) in order to exhale for each breath of air (and to shift the pain).[48]

Throughout the Shroud, diverse, anatomically precise, blood streams dovetail in synchronization showing the different positions of the body, including postmortem blood trails. Scientists from around the world have confirmed that the blood on the Shroud is real human blood of the rare "AB" type. (Only three percent of the world has this blood type, but disproportionably 18% of the Jewish population has this blood type.[49]) All this lends more evidence restricting the identity of the victim. The evidence indicates he was likely a Jew, not a Gentile. His physical features and hair style seen on the Shroud, including a rear pigtail (which are found most uniquely among buried Jewish men of antiquity) combine to support a Jewish identity of the victim.[50]

If the man on the Shroud is the *Yeshua* recorded in the Bible, then, though undeserving of death, he willingly subjected himself to this suffering—to make atonement for sin. If this is the *Yeshua* of the Bible on the Shroud, then notice how his body is exposed essentially naked. This is not the image of boastful power and arrogance displayed by political rulers throughout human history; rather this is an image of humility and sacrificial love by God's chosen King—the Messiah. If this is the *Yeshua* of the Bible found on the Shroud, then observe the torments he endured. Does God care if we experience suffering? Does God care that we experience death? Does God care if some of us pass into eternal judgment? Sometimes we may think of God as somewhere up in heaven, completely detached, unaffected, impervious, and insulated from all our sufferings here on earth. Yet here (as it may be) is the *Yeshua* of the Bible, found on the Shroud *voluntarily* bearing *complete and total empathy* with our sufferings: his body racked by tortured afflictions specifically targeted to **EVERY** *sector of his body* (from **head to foot**/crown of thorns to spike in feet, **from front to back**/over 100 scourge wounds over nearly every part of the body, from **left to right**/spikes in each wrist, pulling and pushing on spikes to struggle for each breath of air, the torso **pierced in the chest**), and also viewed *personally empathizing with our experience of death*. Is all this just something haphazard? These afflictions display like a virtual billboard of empathy with our sufferings. In fact, it might even be said that the Messiah went to such length to express his empathy with our sufferings so as *to personally experience every person's divine judgment*—even for those who would eventually reject him and his atoning sacrifice. Thus, if a person dies and passes into divine judgment, the Biblical *Yeshua personally bore, fully empathized,* and *actually experienced* that person's personal divine judgment on behalf of that person. He did so with love while providing himself as the atoning sacrifice for *our* sin. And finally, since the Bible mentions that God "inhabits eternity" (Isa. 57:15), could it be possible that *Yeshua* might have endured an ***eternity*** of judgment for each person's sins? What a horrendous price that would be. What complete empathy he bore with our human sufferings: **God does care**.

(The Bible may offer a hint [a Hebrew "*remez*"] that *Yeshua* potentially experienced an *eternity* of judgment for our sin when it states that *Yeshua* is "the Lamb who was **slain from the creation of the world**" [Rev. 13:8 NIV, emphasis added].)

Chapter 6

MICROSCOPIC DISCOVERIES
AND ULTRAVIOLET LIGHT

There are more than one hundred scourge wounds over nearly the entire body of the Shroud victim. The scourge marks resemble the effect of the Roman flagrum—typically a whip with an array of leather thongs, each one fastened at the end with small dumbbell-shaped metals. When the flagrum strikes, it tears away into the flesh, ripping out an array of vicious wounds. This begins a process called syneresis (si-**ner**-uh-sis) where blood clots begin to form. As the red blood cells retract together and coagulate to form a blood clot, the blood serum is squeezed out of the blood cells into the surround area of the clot. The scientists took high resolution enlarged photos of these wounds on the Shroud and examined them with microscopes. What they discovered is that *every* scourge mark bore detailed, *microscopic depressed centers*, with *elevated edges* which had not been visible to the naked eye until seen from a microscope. The scientists also took photos of the scourge wounds under ultraviolet light. When the scourge wounds were placed under ultraviolet lighting, the previously invisible blood serum surrounding the wounds lit up and fluoresced. This confirmed the presence of real blood serum surrounding each wound. The blood serum was also chemically tested and verified by chemists/scientists John Heller and Alan Adler.[51]

Such details of the scourge marks are *not visible to the naked eye*. A medieval forger would not have been able to see the microscopic detail of each scourge wound, nor see the blood serum surrounding each wound that was revealed only by ultraviolet light. Nor would he possess the anatomical knowledge to try to depict them. This only became visible with the aid of microscopes and ultraviolet lighting.

34

Ultraviolet light and microscopic technology were unknown during medieval times. It was not until centuries later that they were invented.[52] *Microscopes were not invented until the early 1600s in the Europe[53]--about 300 years after the Shroud's 1350s A.D./ C.E. public display in Lirey, France* (the event from which we have visual confirmation that today's shroud in Turin, Italy is the same Shroud that once resided in Lirey, France during the 1300s). *Ultraviolet light was not discovered until another two centuries after the microscope (year 1801)* by Johann Wilhelm Ritter.[54] How could the forger create microscopic detail that he could not see? How could the medieval forger even think to add blood serum halos around each scourge wound when blood serum was invisible to a human eye? Blood serum could not be seen by the human eye until the discovery of ultraviolet light (five centuries later—year 1801). If just one of the more than one hundred scourge marks revealed a microscopic unrealistic physiological reaction, then Shroud would be exposed as a hoax.

What is your opinion regarding these findings? Does the scientific discovery of scourge wound features bearing anatomically flawless detail visible only since the invention of the microscope, as well as invisible blood serum (unknown during medieval times which could not be seen until the discovery of ultraviolet light) surrounding over one hundred scourge marks most logically point to a hoax forgery by a medieval artist from the 1300s? Or, do these attributes more likely attest to an authentic, non-crafted relic? Draw your conclusion.

Chapter 7

A THREE-DIMENSIONAL IMAGE?

Once technology developed to the point of being able to produce simulated three-dimensional elevations from brightness maps with a VP-8 Image Analyzer,[55] physicist John Jackson and Bill Mottern (an image specialist at Sandia Laboratory) made arrangements for a test to be made at Sandia Laboratory to observe what would happen if the Shroud's image was processed by a VP-8 Image Analyzer. They were stunned by the result: *the Shroud gave off a correctly proportioned three-dimensional display of its image!*[56] When a normal photograph is processed by the VP-8 Image Analyzer, the image is collapsed and distorted. Yet, when viewing the Shroud from the Image Analyzer, it rendered a striking 3-D display, such that from the screen monitor they could explore the body's three-dimensional form and follow it as though traversing a range of mountains from a moving helicopter.[57] A two-dimensional Shroud cloth had conferred this three-dimensionally encoded information. How could that be?

Indeed, it is the scientists that truly recognize how "astonishing" and "mind-blowing" these discoveries were—far more than the average person who is not a scientist. For example, with a normal photograph of the front of a face, the view is restricted to that frontal perspective. But with the Shroud's 3-D image, there is not only the frontal view, but the face may also be observed from either side facial profiles in 3-D—such as viewing from the left side profile and then over across to the right side profile of the face.[58] It is mind-boggling to think that a flat two dimensional cloth could confer a three dimensional image.

Engineer Peter Schumacher (who pioneered the production and delivery of the VP-8 Image Analyzer) wrote a paper delivered at the

Shroud of Turin International Research Conference in Richmond, Virginia, regarding his initial encounter with this:

> A "true-three-dimensional image" appeared on the monitor. . . . The nose ramped in relief. The facial features were contoured properly. Body shapes of the arms, legs, and chest, had the basic human form. This result from the VP-8 had never occurred with any of the images I had studied, nor had I heard of it happening during any image studies done by others.
>
> I had never heard of the Shroud of Turin before that moment. I had no idea what I was looking at. However, the results are unlike anything I have processed through the VP-8 Analyzer, before or since. Only the Shroud of Turin has produced these results from a VP-8 Image Analyzer isometric projection study.[59]

Schumacher added:

> One must consider how and why an artist would embed three-dimensional information in the grey shading of an image. In fact, no means of viewing this property of the image would be available for at least 650 years after it was done. One would have to ask . . . "Why isn't this result obtained in the analysis of other works? . . . Why would the artist make only one such work requiring such special skills and talent, and not pass the technique along to others? How could the artist control the quality of the work when the artist could not "see" grey scale as elevation? . . .
>
> The VP-8 Image Analyzer's isometric display is a "dumb" process. That means it does one process on whatever "data" is sent to it. . . . Like a photographic negative, the process is not "involved" in the result. It is simply photons in and voltage out. The Shroud image induces the three-dimensional result. It is the only image known to induce this result.[60]

Not only the front (ventral) side of the body is three-dimensional, but also the back (dorsal) side of the body. What is found on the dorsal (back) side is of particular significance. The buttocks are not flattened by gravity from the weight of the body. They are fully round—defying gravity. This is due to the body's stiffened, ridged state of rigor mortis. Rigor mortis can only last for a limited time—during the first two or three days after death. This duration of rigor mortis precisely correlates with the time frame reported between the burial and resurrection of *Yeshua*.

Bear in mind: photographs do not render three-dimensional information. Photographs only convey light, darkness and color. Here with the Shroud we have a two-dimensional cloth that is embedded with three-dimensional encodement (the "grey scale") which communicates the distance between the cloth and the body at every pin point location between the body and the Shroud. Unlike a photograph, the Shroud provides left, front, and right profiles of the face as well as with the front and back of the body when the "grey scale" is decoded.

Now imagine trying to encode this life-size three-dimensional image onto a two-dimensional cloth. You would not be able see any effect of what you were trying to do to the cloth to induce a 3-D outcome, nor could you see its final result until centuries later (when the encodement could finally be translated to interpret the code into its three-dimensional depth).

Your opinion pertaining to the three-dimensional image of the Shroud: Is the 3-D effect most probably a fabrication by a medieval artist from the 1300s who could not see the 3-D effect until many centuries later? Or, is this evidence most indicative of an authentic relic? You decide. (See notes for additional comments about the 3-D image.[61])

(For further very important information related to the 3-D image, be sure to read chapter 23 part 1.)

By year 2006, the first 3-D holograph of the Shroud image was produced. It was later filmed into a video by scanning across the 3-D image from side-to-side profiles. This was accomplished by Dr. Petrus Soons and Bernardo Galmarini in conjunction with Dutch Holographic Laboratory in the Netherlands. **Readers are encouraged to view videos of the three-dimensional image where they can examine the body from side to side profiles. The visual results are all the more striking and impressive when viewed with 3-D glasses.[d] Keep in mind that the actual image is life-size (not small like your computer screen). To watch the videos, visit the Internet URL addresses below from your PC (they cannot be accessed from your cell phone). If you do not find the videos, then exit completely out. Next go to youtube.com directly, and then from there enter the URL address (into the youtube search bar, not the address bar) and try again.**

(1) https://www.youtube.com/watch?v=G9K3yw0oKr4
(2) https://www.youtube.com/watch?v=y_of-ou4BFs
(3) http://shroud3d.com/conversion-process-of-2d-to-3d/3d-movies-of-head-body

The image is best seen when observed from your PC or laptop. **Darken your room.** Be sure to watch it in **"full screen"** mode. **These holographic 3-D images were decoded** *exclusively* **from the three-dimensional encodement ("grey scale") embedded within the Shroud cloth itself. The "grey scale" of the Shroud's image conveyed the distances between each pin point location of the body to its corresponding point on Shroud.[62]**

The inventor of holography was Dennis Gabor who in 1947 originated its concept and eventually won the Nobel Prize for Physics for his invention in 1971.[63]

---

[d] 3-D glasses may be purchased from Amazon.com.

Chapter 8

WHAT MAKES THE IMAGE APPEAR ON THE SHROUD?

Investigation was undertaken by the STURP scientists to ascertain what material made the image appear on the Shroud. They wanted to confirm if there was some ingredient like paint, pigmentation, or dye placed on the Shroud to form its image. The scientific research concluded that no substance of any kind was added to the Shroud which produced its image.[64] Instead, what they discovered is that the image exists exclusively due to changes to the cellulose fibers of the Shroud cloth itself which became denatured in the image area (as compared to fibers elsewhere on the Shroud).[65] All the various theories which try to claim that the image was made by paint pigmentation, staining, oils, or some form of pre-photographic chemicals either ignore or deny this thoroughly proven fact.

Chapter 9

SUPERFICIALITY OF THE IMAGE

An unexpected discovery by the scientists was finding that the straw-yellow image on the Shroud is *extremely* superficial. Each linen thread is composed of vastly smaller fibers, many of which are too microscopic to be seen by the natural eye.[66] The fibers are 10 to 20 times thinner than a human hair.[67] No fiber deeper than the top two or three fibers of a thread has been affected wherever the image exists.[68] There is no coloration on any fiber that is covered above by a colorized fiber. Another surprising disclosure revealed that all colored fibers are approximately the same color and darkness throughout the image.[69] Furthermore, the Shroud image is so light and so superficial that only the external surface circumference of a colored fiber has been colored (the inside of the fibers remain white, not straw-yellow).[70] The color does not penetrate deeper than 0.2 microns (millionths of a meter) of the surface of a typical 20-micron diameter fiber, or one-hundredth of the diameter of an individual fiber (of which there are typically 200 such fibers in a single linen thread)![71]

This startling superficiality of depth of coloration is consistent throughout the *entire* image on the Shroud. Now, imagine trying to scorch an image on a cloth by heating a metal statue and then wrapping a cloth over it. That would violate the consistency of superficiality found throughout the entire Shroud image. Such scorching would go vastly deeper into the fibers, and the depth of the scorching would not be *uniformly consistent* like the depth of coloration on the Shroud.[72] Scorching by draping a cloth over a hot statue would inevitably result in varied depths of scorching at various location points, such as where the weight of the cloth would bear more pressure upon certain location points (such as the tip of the nose of a hot metal statue). Another problem for a forgery is that the Shroud image includes areas of the body that did not touch the cloth.[73] How could parts of the body not touching the cloth create an image? Why would parts of the body not touching the cloth also consistently penetrate exactly the same superficial depth—precisely the same depth as parts of the body that did touch the cloth? Consider the parts of the body not touching the cloth: If a cloth was scorched on a hot metal statue and the parts of the nose that did not touch the cloth were scorched by pressing down along the sides and bottom of the hot statue's nose, then when the cloth is opened flat, the nose would appear widened and distorted. Fine points like this indicate that whatever made the image did so in a straight-line vertical path between the body and the cloth, without pressing the cloth into the indented parts of the body that would not touch a draped cloth.[74]

Now imagine the difficulties an artistic forger would encounter when trying to craft this. Whenever the forger approaches closer than six to ten feet away from the Shroud, the very faint straw-yellow image blends away and disappears into the lighter straw-yellow background of the cloth.[75] Once the forger approaches *within reaching distance* of the cloth (less than six to ten feet away), he literally cannot see the image he is making on the cloth. Also, when the forger does scorch his image, he cannot let the scorch go any deeper than the superficial surface of a fiber (these fibers being 10 to 20 times thinner than a human hair). While consistently scorching (probably from a distance of six to ten feet away so he can see what he is doing), the medieval forger must produce an image of photographic quality, with photonegativity, and three-dimensional encodement. In addition, from six to ten feet away he must also produce anatomically flawless scourge wounds that bear microscopic detail (invisible to the natural eye until 500 years later with the invention of microscopes).[76] What if the forger made a mistake on the Shroud? How could he make a correction that would remain so superficial in depth?

Knowing that there are typically 200 fibers in just a single linen thread, and that such fibers are microscopic (ten to twenty times thinner than a human hair), and that only the very outermost surface of such fibers are colorized (the outer surface being 0.2 microns of a typical 20-micron diameter fiber, or one-hundredth of the of the diameter of a microscopic fiber), and that the inside of each fiber remains completely unaffected, white not colorized, a forger may consider it to be a fantastic accomplishment just to successfully colorize one fiber so superficially—much less to render an entire, life-size Shroud image that way.

Your verdict: Is the superficiality of the image best explained as the craftsmanship of a medieval forger? Or, is the superficiality of the image more likely evidence of an authentic relic?

Chapter 10

NON-DIRECTIONALITY OF THE IMAGE

T he Shroud image was also tested at the Jet Propulsion Laboratory by Don Lynn and Jean Lorre (who were image processing specialists for various NASA space mission projects to planets such as Venus and Saturn).[77] They performed research using imaging equipment known as a microdensitometer. This equipment performed digital image processing analysis on the Shroud image. The device fed small areas of the image one tiny section at a time through a microscope lens to a detector which measured the amount of light transmitted for optical density. Each optical density of approximately one pixel was computed and expressed as a digital number. The processing facility had *hundreds of thousands of algorithms* which could be selected to perform numerous analytical functions on the data.[78]

The result is that the microdensitometer revealed new microscopic details that had previously been invisible to the natural eye. It also brought to light another major discovery that impressed the scientific world: namely, the image was *microscopically directionless*. Except for the weave pattern of the cloth fibers, the image was completely devoid of any two-dimensional directionality. A human artisan, for example, would have left directionality upon the image (such as up and down, or side to side movement like brush strokes). Any directionality on the Shroud's image would have been exposed by the microdensitometer. Instead, the image was confirmed to be *microscopically directionless*. This finding contra indicated the possibility that a human hand had applied the image.[79]

Your appraisal: Does the microscopic non-directionality of the image best indicate the skill of a medieval artist? Or, does this bear witness to a genuine relic not made by human hands?

Chapter 11

INVESTIGATION OF THE BLOOD MARKS

There are more than one hundred dumbbell-shaped scourge wounds which have been identified on the Shroud. But physicians and scientists were surprised once they discovered the anatomical accuracy of these wounds. They exist on the Shroud precisely as they would exist on actual skin of a body, and yet they have been transferred with microscopic, undisturbed precision onto the textured, fibrous material of the Shroud cloth, without evidence of smearing, or disruption, including jelly-like coagulated blood, and with microscopic sharply defined indented centers, upraised edges, and serum halos surrounding their boarders. This quality of detail could not be seen by the naked eye. Even to this day, no artist, physician, or scientist has ever yet been able to reproduce, or otherwise transfer such microscopic precision of wounds from a body to a different object to date—much less to accomplish this flawlessly for over one hundred scourge wounds.[80]

Yet, there remain further formidable problems facing the medieval forger. Overall, there are 130 or more blood trails on the cloth. They correlate in synchronization, reflecting the variant positions that the body was in at different times as well as the diverse medical conditions of the body at various points of time. When a body undergoes traumatic shock, it can induce hemolysis (the break down of red blood cells so that hemoglobin is released into the fluid and plasma). As blood passes through the liver, bilirubin is picked up. The blood on the Shroud has high levels of methemoglobin and high levels of bilirubin which dries and ages leaving the surprising red colored blood found on the Shroud (rather than the normal dark brown or black color of old blood).[e] [81] This rare blood condition of bilirubin occurs when a person suffers tremendous violence and undergoes a state of traumatic shock.[82] The rivulets of blood on the Shroud also carry distinct characteristics, such as being either *venous* or *arterial* blood in the correct locations for each type of blood.[83] (Knowledge of the difference between *venous* vs. *arterial* blood was not discovered until 1593 by Andrea Cesalpino--centuries after the 1350s.[84])

The blood streams exhibit the varied states of condition the man was in at different times, as well as positions of the body during the time of bleeding—such as (1) parallel blood trails from pierced wrists down to the elbows at 55 and 65 degrees [f] (from the horizontal axis) resulting from the up and down seesaw struggle on the cross to catch each breath of air, (2) thicker blood streams once blood coagulation progressed, (3) hemolytic blood with bilirubin, (4) blood serum, (5) post-mortem blood flows, (6) post-mortem watery fluid from a lance-like pierce wound to the pleural cavity on the right side of the chest (like as recorded from the pierce side wound in the Gospel of John 19:34, (7) this pierce wound between the 5th and 6th ribs on the right side of the chest also bears a post-mortem blood flow from the right auricle (which fills with blood upon death) such that the blood oozed out by gravity without a pumping heart, or splattering from breathing, and (8) distinct arterial versus venous blood trails from their correct anatomical locations.[85]

A forger would have to apply this complex variety of blood marks, bearing the anatomically precise detail and chemistry found on the Shroud, including its diverse characteristics (which were unknown

---

[e] Additional experiments by Dr. Carlo Goldoni have also demonstrated that blood exposed to neutron radiation followed by ultraviolet light (such as sunlight) likewise results in bright red blood marks rather than the normal dark brown-black of old blood. See chapter 16.

[f] The angle of the blood trails (55 to 65 degrees) from the wrists to the elbows confirms that there was a cross beam attached to the crucifixion stake.

during medieval times), using *real* human blood (hemolytic blood would essentially require blood from an actual tortured victim)—all of it correlating in synchronization to reflect the different positions of the body and medical conditions at different points of time. Again, no mistakes could be made, or it would expose the Shroud as a fraud.[86] Ask yourself. If you were the medieval forger, and no one at that time had ever heard of *arterial* versus *venous* blood, would you be able to distinguish the difference between them and know where on the body to apply each? Meanwhile, though efforts have been made, no scientist, physician, or artist using any method has ever yet been able to depict or transfer such complex and perfect blood marks from a body to another surface (or cloth) as exhibited on the Shroud.[87] Although a medieval forger would certainly do his best, he would be unaware of the future precision of scrutiny of modern-day science, by which forensic pathology can rigorously analyze and expose any tampering of evidence. Medical illustrations from the 15th century underscore how poorly blood flows were understood at that time.[88]

What is your evaluation pertaining to the medical variety of blood markings on the Shroud? Do the assorted blood depictions augur in favor of a medieval understanding of blood depictions during the 1300s, or is this more credibly a bona fide relic?

Chapter 12

BUTTONS OVER THE EYES?

A momentous discovery ensued one day while Ph.D. Physicist John Jackson, together with Ph.D. Eric Jumper from the Dept. of Aeronautics and Astronautics, Air Force Institute of Technology, and Bill Mottern, image specialist at Sandia Laboratory were reviewing the three-dimensional image of the Shroud from the VP-8 Image Analyzer. They never would have noticed this discovery had it not been for the VP-8 analyzer. What caught their attention was something akin to three-dimensional buttons appearing over each eye of the Shroud victim. What was this? Naturally, this roused the curiosity of researchers to more extensively scrutinize the matter. Professor Francis Filas of Chicago made the eventual discovery that these were apparent coins placed over the eyelids. Upon rigorous examination from Log E Interpretations Systems at Overland Park, Kansas, it was successfully demonstrated that the coins bore three-dimensional quality with embossed letters. The letters are about 1.5 millimeters high. Others later would confirm these findings.[89] The coins were best apparent from enlarged photographs of the face made by film emphasizing contrast when the Shroud was stretched taut. It became evident that these buttons exhibited both letters and a symbol.[90] Further research by Professor Filas discovered that the letters and the symbol matched some lepton coins minted for Pontius Pilate between the years 29 and 32 (A.D./C.E.).[91] (Pontius Pilate was the Roman Prefect [i.e. governor] of Judea who presided over the Roman trial and crucifixion of *Yeshua*.) The presence of the lepton coin characteristics were seen over both eyes, but were most clear from the coin over the right eye. An array of four letters ("UCAI") had remained on the coin. It was an abbreviation of the Greek inscription: "Of Tiberius Caesar" (TIBEPIO**UKAI**CAPOC). Some of these Pontius Pilate coins still exist today. However, numismatists had never noticed before (until observed on the Shroud) that the abbreviation was misspelled! The correct spelling should have been "UKAI" (instead of "UCAI" found on the Shroud). At first, some people insisted that the misspelling was evidence that the Shroud was a fraud. However, subsequent research identified several surviving Pontius Pilate coins still in existence bearing that exact misspelling ("UCAI"). (The error in minting was likely a phonetic misspelling because both spellings evoke the same hard "K" sound when pronouncing *"Caesar"* in Latin and *"Kaisaros"* in Greek.)[92]

Another characteristic of the coin is that the letters appeared above a *lituus* symbol (an astrologer's staff with a handle arranged similar to a horizontally reversed/inverted question mark). The lituus symbol of the astrologer's staff was an official Roman government emblem found on *all* coins minted for Pontius Pilate from years 29 through 32 (A.D./C.E.).[93] Pilate's usage of the lituus staff as his official Roman government emblem was unique within the Roman Empire. Since the reign of Pilate, the lituus symbol was never again used by any subsequent official throughout the history of the Roman Empire as an official government symbol.[94]

The Roman date of the sixteenth year of the reign of Tiberius Caesar was found on the back of one of the surviving Pilot lepton coins. Arabic numbers did not yet exist at that time, so the coin bore Greek letters to indicate the date. There was an "L" (which signified that the following letters represented numbers), followed by "I" (used to denote a value of ten), followed by a Stigma letter (which looks likes a rounded five and represents the number six). In summation, the surviving Pilate lepton coin was dating the coin as the *sixteenth year of the reign of Tiberius Caesar*,[95] which would have been approximately 28-30 (A.D./C.E.).[g] Unfortunately, the Shroud's image does not

---

[g] Tiberius became the ruling Caesar on August 19, year 14 (A.D./C.E.). However, there is a slight possibility that the counting the 16th year of Tiberius may have been counted from the time when Tiberius began an earlier co-regency with emperor Augustus Caesar—about two years prior. (*The International Standard Bible*

display that particular side of the coin. However, it is generally accepted that all Pontius Pilate coins bearing the lituus symbol were minted between 29-32 A.D./C.E.[96]

This aspect of the Shroud (where coins appear over the eyelids) renders another instance of circumstantial evidence pointing toward identification of the Shroud victim. From this attribute, it would indicate that the Shroud victim was crucified sometime approximating 29-32 A.D./C.E. This was the same time frame when *Yeshua* was crucified. Furthermore, because the coins on the Shroud bore the unique official Roman lituus emblem of Pontius Pilate, this adds affirmation that the Shroud victim was crucified within the vicinity of the regional jurisdiction of the Roman Judean Prefect (governor) Pontius Pilate—who *personally* authorized the Roman crucifixion of *Yeshua*.

Some have suggested that the appearance of coins on the Shroud is only a coincidence of the weave patterns of the Shroud cloth. However, the following considerations argue against this:

(1) The coins would never have caught the attention of scientists except that they protruded over each eye when viewing the three-dimensional image from the VP-8 Image Analyzer,

(2) The letters are precisely in the correct position relative to the lituus staff (a 9:00 to 11:30 position above the staff handle when the staff is viewed vertically).[97]

(3) The letters are sequenced in the proper order.[98]

(4) The letters are all aligned and facing in the proper direction (not up side down, sideways, at differing angles, or inverted, etc).[99]

Encyclopaedia, (Grand Rapids: Wm. B. Eermans Publishing Co.,1974), s.v. "Tiberias" (by S. Angus); Kenneth F. Doig, *New Testament Chronology*, (Lewiston, NY: Edwin Mellen Press, 1990), chapter 12.

(5) The shape and the facing direction of the curved hook on the lituus staff symbol matched the surviving Pilate coins.[100]

(6) The ratio size of each characteristic relative to the size of the other characteristics, the size of the coin compared to the body, the size of the letters compared to the lituus staff, and the shape of the coin (being clipped at the 1:30 to 3:30 clock position) matched the surviving Pilate lepton coins.[101]

(7) The odds that the coin images should appear at this precise location on the Shroud (not just once, but twice— once over *each* eye) rather than at some other part of the 14'3" x 3'7" (or 4.34 m x 1.10 m) cloth are a factor.

(8) The mathematical probabilities of these various characteristics occurring by accident were calculated and found to be astronomical (one chance in eight million). This is a formidable mathematical argument against this aspect being a coincidental weave pattern of the Shroud cloth.[102]

(9) Studies utilizing a polarized image-overlay technique identified some *74 points of congruence* between the Shroud coin and the Pilate lepton coins.[103] It only requires 14 points of congruence to certify the identity of a fingerprint in a U.S. court of law. However, the Shroud had 74 points of congruence on the coin over the right eye and 73 over the left eye.[104]

The ancient Jewish burial tradition of placing coins over the eyelids was not discovered until the final decades of the 20th century. Since then, many such archeological findings have been disinterred. Evidence indicates that this use of coins was a Jewish burial tradition practiced within the vicinity of Jerusalem during the first century B.C./B.C.E and the first century A.D./C.E.[105] Considering that this Jewish burial tradition with coins was not discovered until the late 20th century, how would a medieval forger think to include these features on the Shroud? How would the forger happen to obtain possession of a rare Roman Pontius Pilate coin (which during his medieval time was already 1,300 years old) to compare with and copy onto the Shroud? (For more information about the Shroud coins, see end notes.[106])

Your appraisement regarding the apparent three-dimensional Pontius Pilate coin images over the Shroud eyelids: Is this most likely a concoction by a medieval counterfeiter? Or, could this be collateral evidence synchronized to the date, history, and location of *Yeshua* of Nazareth? (I.e. the *date*: coins dating *circa* 29-32 A.D./C.E.; the *history*: the historic Roman governor Pontius Pilate's official Roman lituus emblem on the coins, and the *location*: Pilate's regional jurisdiction of Judea).

From these coin features we find that there are more than just *unique* crucifixion wounds that point toward *Yeshua* as the Shroud's potential crucifixion victim (i.e. the unique crown of thorns, the unique postmortem pierced side wound, and the scourge marks). Here, in this case, the Pontius Pilate coins now further point in the direction of *Yeshua* as the potential Shroud victim (i.e. via the date of such coins, the historical figure of Pilate, and the geographic region of Pilate's jurisdiction). Was the hand of God orchestrating these clues?

Chapter 13

EVIDENCE FROM THE SCIENCE OF
FORENSIC PALYNOLOGY

alynology is the scientific study of pollen and spores from flowering plants and trees. Forensic palynology includes the plant's identification, as well as where and when any given object came in contact with the pollen. It can be used to argue with evidence whether an object was at a certain place at a certain period of time. Pollen has been used in U.S. courts of law and in other nations to provide evidence for criminal trials.[107] Pollen is the irritant that makes us sneeze in the spring season when flowers bloom. It is microscopic in size and invisible to the unaided eye. It typically ranges from 10 to 70 micrometers. Each type of flowering plant produces its own unique type of pollen. Pollen is resistant to decay and can remain remarkably well preserved for thousands of years.[108]

Tests were performed by the scientists to assess samples of pollen from the Shroud. Dr. Max Frei (an internationally renowned criminologist and botanist from Switzerland with expertise in Mediterranean flora) led the STURP scientists in this investigation of the Shroud's pollen.[109] The objective was to identify what species or types of plants were identified from the pollen found on the Shroud. From that they could track the regions of the world where such plants exist. Consequently, from that, the scientists could ascertain the geographical history of the Shroud (what places around the world the Shroud had been to). Dr. Frei identified 58 different pollen species from his Shroud samples. As expected, there was pollen from France and Italy where the Shroud has resided during the most recent centuries. However, a surprising result from this test was that the vast majority (78%) of the pollen species (45 of 58) found on the Shroud do *not* grow in Europe. Pollens were found that grow in Urfa, Turkey

(Edessa) and Istanbul, Turkey (Constantinople) where we also have the historical record of the Shroud. But the preeminent discovery was that 72% (42 of 58) of Dr. Frei's pollen species grow in the *vicinity of Jerusalem.*[110] This was a compelling indicator that the Shroud originated from that region of the world.

One particular, and very rare pollen specie (*Gundelia Tournefortii*), drew special attention. The pollen *Gundelia Tournefortii* comes from a flowering plant bearing long, fearsome-looking thorns with the sharpest of spines.[111] Could this be the plant that was weaved into the crown cap of thorns placed over *Yeshua's* head? Dr. Uri Baruch, a palynologist with the Israel Antiquities Authority in Jerusalem, Israel (having earned his Ph.D. from dissertations on the flora of Israel) said that the pollen from this *Gundelia Tournefortii* thorn plant is *scarce and rare to find*. For example, when searching for pollen in Judea, Dr. Baruch never found more than one or two grains of this specie at any site.[112] Yet, surprisingly, some grains from this very rare pollen were found on the Shroud within the area of the head. Most significantly, the pollen from this plant is *not* wind borne, but *only insect borne.*[113] It seems unlikely that insects bearing this very uncommon pollen would have been crawling over the Shroud. But if this is the burial Shroud that covered the body of *Yeshua*, then a logical explanation would be that *Gundelia Tournefortii* pollen from the crown cap of thorns must have fallen directly off the thorn plant onto the head of *Yeshua*, and then from the head onto the Shroud.[114]

Upon further analysis, Dr Uri Baruch found that among the 165 pollen grains he examined from the Shroud, 27% were from this one particular *rare* specie (*Gundelia Tournefortii*).[115] This was a stunning discovery. Why would 27% of the grains be from a plant whose pollen is so rare to find and is only insect borne (not wind borne)? Another discovery was that the majority the *Gundelia Tournefortii* pollen were found on different areas of the Shroud (not just the area of the head). Eventually, Shroud researchers discovered that very faint images of a variety of flowering plants (including *Gundelia Tournefortii*) could be seen on the Shroud. These flower images are extremely faint, requiring special processing enhancement of the photos and life-size enlargement to be recognized. Nonetheless, early century art depictions of the Shroud (such as from coins bearing the Shroud's face from the 7th century) display floral facsimiles next to the head "that accurately match floral images seen on the Shroud today." Researchers suggest that the floral depictions on the Shroud may have been clearer to see during the early centuries.[116] Flowers of various plants had been placed inside the Shroud (that wrapped the body). The flowers were present near the sides of the head, shoulder, and lower abdomen of the body.[117] A flower of *Gundelia Tournefortii* was distinctly identified among the flower images and authenticated by Dr. Avinoam Danin, Professor Emeritus of Botany from the Department of Evolution, Systematics and Ecology of the Hebrew University of Jerusalem, Israel. This would appear to explain why there was an abundance of *Gundelia Tournefortii* pollen on the Shroud. Professor Danin was also able to identify twenty-seven plant images on the Shroud that grow within the area of Jerusalem and between Jerusalem and Jericho.[118] The variety of flowers had likely been deposited as an expression of respect for the victim, but they also could have served as a form of burial aromatics to mask the expected future odors of a decomposing body (John 19:40, Grk *ar-o-ma*).[119] German physicist Oswald Scheuermann was able to demonstrate from experimental tests that high-energy electrical ionizing induced corona discharge could produce images of flowers onto a linen cloth very similar to that found on the Shroud.[120]

However, there is something else which provides independent evidence that *Gundelia Tournefortii* was very likely the plant used to weave the crown cap of thorns. The Bible documents that a head cloth was placed over *Yeshua's* head after his death. This cloth removed from *Yeshua's* head to a separate part of the tomb when he was placed in the tomb. After the resurrection, *Shimon Kefa* (Simon Peter) entered the tomb and noticed the head cloth rolled up in a separate place by itself (John 20:7). There exists such a head cloth today called the *Sudarium of Oviedo*—a linen cloth 84 x 54 centimeters (34" x 21 ¼" inches) that would have covered the front, back and top of the head along with the neck.[121] Naturally, that cloth does not have any image because it was removed from *Yeshua's* head when he was placed in the tomb. It does, however, have blood stains, as well as fluid from pleural oedema which was release through the nostrils. The history of the Sudarium of Oviedo is well documented. The cloth (revered as the head cloth placed over *Yeshua's* head) was kept in the land of Israel until the early seventh century when Persians began to attack Jerusalem. It was then transported through North Africa until it arrived in Spain together with refuges that were fleeing the Persians. Today, this head cloth resides in Oviedo, Spain.[122]

The following factors furnish impressive evidence that the Sudarium of Oviedo is the head cloth that was placed over the crucified victim of the Turin Shroud after his death. If this was *Yeshua*, then these factors also provide evidence that *Gundelia Tournefortii* was the thorn plant used to weave the crown cap of thorns.

(1) The blood on the Shroud (as well as on the Oviedo cloth) both bear the same rare blood type: AB. Only 3.2 percent of the world's population has this type of blood. The mathematical chance that this specific AB blood type would be found by accident on two separate cloths is 1/1000.[123]

(2) Dr. Alan Whanger performed Polarized Image Overlay Technology which revealed seventy points of congruence between the blood stains on the Shroud as compared to the Oviedo head cloth on the front of the head, and fifty points of congruence between the blood marks on the back of the head.[124]

(3) Recent tests performed by researchers from the University of Oviedo and the Spanish Center of Sindonology using X-ray fluorescence analysis on the Oviedo cloth discovered a surprising deposit of dirt on

the nose area bearing a large excess of calcium and low concentrations of strontium. This new discovery matched the previous discovery of dirt on the nose of the Turin Shroud. Both dirt discoveries equated to the same rare type of limestone (with corresponding levels of calcium and strontium) that exists in the vicinity of the crucifixion site and nearby tombs in Jerusalem. Not only is the chemical composition of this dirt unique, but it would also be unexpected to find *any* concentration of dirt on *any* nose—much less on *both* cloths. It is thought that if this victim was *Yeshua*, then the dirt on the nose of the Shroud was acquired by *Yeshua* from a fall on his face while attempting to bear the cross beam on the way to his execution. We know that *Shimon* of Cyrene was conscripted by the Romans to take over the bearing of *Yeshua's* cross to the crucifixion site of *Gulgolta* (Jewish Aramaic for Golgotha), John 19:17, Luke 23:26).[125]

(4) Like the Shroud, a variety of species of pollen found on the Oviedo cloth are limited to the land of Israel—indicating that the Oviedo Sudarium had once resided there.

(5) The pollen from the thorn plant *Gundelia Tournefortii* (which is rare to find, not wind borne, and only insect borne) was not only found on the Shroud of Turin, *it was also discovered on the Sudarium of Oviedo*. It is understandable that flowers of sympathy might be placed inside the Shroud next to the corpse of *Yeshua* (bearing this pollen), but it is illogical that flowers would be stuffed inside an empty, bloody head cloth. Thus, if it wasn't a bouquet of flowers that provided the *Gundelia Tournefortii* pollen inside the Oviedo head cloth, then certainly a crown of *Gundelia Tournefortii* thorns (bearing long, fearsome-looking thorns with the sharpest of spines) could readily provide this rare thorn pollen inside the Oviedo head cloth.

One of the floral species identified on the Shroud by Drs. Wanger, Danin, and Baruch is *Capparis aegyptia*. This specie grows at Jerusalem and blooms in the season of spring. An unusual trait of the flower is that its buds begin to gradually open at midday and become fully opened about a half hour before sunset. The *Capparis aegyptia* flowers found on the enhanced photos of the Shroud revealed (by the stage of budding) that the flowers had been picked about 3 p.m. to 4 p.m. (modern time). The process of opening of the buds of *Capparis aegyptia* ceases once the flower is picked unless water is added. Thus, the flower images indicate a time of 3-4 p.m. when they were picked. As we shall see in chapter 20, this was the very hour when *Yeshua* died on the cross, and when such flowers would be picked to prepare for his burial. In addition, the wilted condition of the flower images on the Shroud indicates that the flowers had been in a state of wilting for a couple days when their image was formed on the Shroud. Altogether, this evidence corresponds to *the time of day at death when preparations would have begun for the burial of Yeshua* (3 p.m. to 4 p.m. when the *Capparis aegyptia* flowers were picked). And the state of wilting of the flowers displayed on the Shroud *provides a general indication as to how much time had elapsed between the burial until the time when the image was formed on the Shroud* (i.e. about two to three days).[126]

It was all these various flowers placed in direct contact with the Shroud that provided the additional abundance of pollen (including additional *Gundelia Tournefortii*) found on the Shroud—but this led to another important discovery.

The pollen from all these flowers effectively provided a geographical map and time chronology. Dr. Avinoam Danin (eminent Israeli botanist, acknowledged world leading expert on the flora of Israel)[127] states that the presence of *Gundelia Tournefortii* pollen grains on the shroud proves that the Shroud came into some sort of contact with the plant *during the time of its blooming (February to May)*.[128] Dr. Danin adds (referencing his database of over 90,000 sites of plant distribution) that the assemblage of certain plant pollens and their corresponding images on the Shroud best fits *one specific* geographical place in the *entire world*: namely, the narrow geographical region embracing 10-20 km (16 to 32 miles) from east to west of Jerusalem.[129] Dr Danin also pointed out that the season when these variety of plants are in bloom (releasing their pollen) is *March through April*[130] — precisely the months of the Jewish Passover.

In summation, the totality of pollen found on the Shroud provides physical evidence of:

(1) A *specific geographical location of the world* (the narrow geographical region 10-20 km [16 to 32 miles] east to west of Jerusalem where such variety of Israeli flowers are uniquely found together).

(2) A *limited time of the year* (March - April, the only months when the Passover occurs and the only months when the combined variety of Israeli flowers are in bloom releasing their pollen).

(3) The *Specific hour of the day when the death occurred and when preparations would begin for the burial* (3 p.m. to 4 p.m. modern time — the time indicated by the state of the opening of the buds of the flower *Capparis aegyptia* when it was picked to prepare for the burial).

(4) The *duration of elapsed time between the burial until the formation of the Shroud image* (i.e. a couple days) indicated by the degree of wilting of the flower images, and

(5) *Evidence of what could be the thorn plant used for the crown cap of thorns* (i.e. *Gundelia Tournefortii*). (Among historical records, *only one person* was ever reported to be punished with a crown of thorns: namely, the mocking of *Yeshua* of Nazareth as the King of the Jews.[131])

Concerning the identification of the crucified victim of the Shroud, one might think it would have been ideal if the Roman governor Pontius Pilate had left some official Roman seal attached to the

Shroud to authenticate that this was the shroud that wrapped the body of *Yeshua*. Of course, everyone would then question whether the Roman seal was authentic. As it turns out, these unexpected ancillary scientific discoveries (not just the pollen, but also the Pontius Pilate lepton coin images and many other findings) have provided far more credible forms of identification. It also points to the potential sovereign hand of God, engineering all these intricate facets to be finally disclosed by scientists some 2,000 years later.

The pollen likewise provided corroboration supporting the recorded geographical history of the Shroud *prior* to 1350. In this regard, it revealed that the majority of the Shroud's pollen did *not* come from Europe but rather from plants uniquely found within the vicinity of Jerusalem, as well as pollen from Edessa (corresponding to the first century and sixth century recorded history of the Shroud), pollen from the Constantinople region of the Middle East (which corresponds to the 10th through 13th centuries of recorded history of the Shroud), and those places in Europe where the Shroud has resided ever since the 1300s.

How would a medieval forger think to account for this geographic pollen map of the history of the Shroud when the pollen was invisible to the unaided eye? The existence of pollen was unknown during medieval times. Pollen would not be discovered until 1640 by English botanist Nehemiah Grew (300 years after the 1350's).[132] The first millennium of recorded geographical history of the Shroud had not been well researched until 1979 by Ian Wilson.[133] Yet, the pollen discoveries on the Shroud bear confirmation of this geographical recorded history of the Shroud: namely, from Jerusalem to Edessa, to Constantinople, to France, and then to Italy. How could a medieval forger guess what types of pollen would be necessary to confirm the pre-1350's historical locations of the Shroud? How would the medieval forger think to apply pollen (which was unknown in his time and invisible to the natural eye until it was discovered from microscopes 300 years after 1350's)?

Your determination: Is it more credible that a medieval artisan discovered pollen 300 years earlier than the rest of the world, and then selected specific microscopic pollen unique to the region of Jerusalem to place on the Shroud? Or, is this more convincing of an authentic relic, such that the pollen/floral discoveries further served to pinpoint the location, the time of year, the time of day, and various time durations between key events of *Yeshua*: namely, (1) the floral *geographic region* 10-20 km (16 to 32 miles) east and west of Jerusalem, (2) the *time of the year* (March – April/the months of Passover), (3) the *specific hour of death* (3-4 p.m./modern time provided by the burial flower *Capparis aegyptia*), and (4) the *elapsed time frame between the burial event until the image formation/resurrection* (two to three days, indicated by the state of wilting of the burial flowers and the stage of rigor mortis of the body).

This confluence of evidence resolves into a surprising **progressive narrative** of the Shroud victim (including events and time frames)— matching the chronicle of the Nazarene. Add to this the significance of the Pontius Pilate coins over the eyes (providing historical dates, identification of the specific named historical Roman governor who sentenced *Yeshua*, and his location of regional jurisdiction/Judea), and then add also some unique crucifixion wounds (such as the crown of thorns with its thorn pollen found on the head, and the unique lance pierce wound to the side). All these factors coalesce into a surprising narrative pointing toward identification of the Shroud victim. Who would ever expect to find such an array of specific details of evidence for an event that transpired so far back in time—some 2,000 years ago!—according to the dating of the coins over the eyes?

Coincidence? Divine engineering? Your call.

Chapter 14

EVIDENCE FROM LIMESTONE

A nother finding from the scientists was that the Shroud contains microscopic traces of limestone upon the area of the feet. The discovery was encountered via microscopic examination. Several tombs in the Israeli/Trans-Jordan area were carved out of limestone. The limestone tends to remain wet, pliable, and easily rubs off when contacted. The researchers determined that the limestone on the feet of the Shroud was *travertine aragonite*—a rare type—and also included small traces of strontium and iron. (In contrast, the common type of limestone in Israel is *travertine calcite*). Researchers then investigated samples from nine different limestone tombs throughout the land of Israel. Yet, none of these tombs corresponded to the type of limestone found on the Shroud. It is thought that the tomb that *Yeshua* was buried in was either the Holy Sepulcher or the Garden Tomb in Jerusalem. In order to obtain samples from this specific bed of limestone, the researchers were granted permission to take specimens from the Ecole Biblique tomb in Jerusalem, which is part of the same rock shelf as the Holy Sepulcher and the Garden Tomb. This sample did match the rare travertine aragonite limestone found on the Shroud. It was the only tomb out of ten limestone tombs examined throughout Israel that matched. Furthermore, the limestone from this site also contained small traces of strontium and iron, corresponding to the limestone found on the Shroud. The limestone match was confirmed and graphed by Dr. Ricardo Levi-Setti at the University of Chicago's Enrico Fermi Institute utilizing a high-resolution scanning ion microprobe.[134]

Your appraisal concerning the limestone discovery: Does the rare *travertine aragonite* limestone found on the feet area of the image best indicate the ingenuity of a medieval forger? Or, does this finding point to an authentic relic, wherein a rare molecular element of limestone unique to Jerusalem was identified by high-resolution technology from the feet area of the image?

In summation, the foregoing analysis of the Shroud of Turin does not nearly recount all the discoveries relevant to the Shroud, but at least it delineates several of its significant highlights. (There will be more information about the Shroud in subsequent chapters.)

Chapter 15

DATING THE AGE OF THE SHROUD CLOTH

arbon-14 (C-14) radiocarbon dating is a scientific method whereby measurements are taken of the ratio of C-14 to C-12 isotopes of carbon from a specimen. The purpose is to gauge the approximate age of a sample. How does it work? All living things have a similar ratio of C-14 to C-12. However, once death occurs, the C-14 gradually dissipates away. The hypothesis of C-14 dating is that by measuring the C-14 to C-12 ratio, scientists can gauge an approximate measurement of years that have elapsed since death occurred. This renders a general approximation of the age of the material tested.[135]

In 1988, a sample was cut out of the Shroud and then carbon-14 (C-14) dated by three laboratories. These tests resulted in C-14 dates ranging from 1260-1390 A.D./C.E.[136] As far as the news media was concerned, this test settled the matter once and for all. With this announcement, the news media dismissed the Shroud as a medieval forgery. The public was told that this "proved" that the Shroud cloth was dated from approximately 1260-1390 A.D./C.E (rather than from the first century when *Yeshua* was crucified). However, the news media was biased with this report. They neglected to inform the public concerning various significant issues which would call into question the accuracy of the Carbon-14 date.

As for the radiocarbon dating result of 1260-1390, it is noteworthy that there exists a painting called the Hungarian Pray Manuscript which illustrates the Nazarene's burial *with the Shroud*. This art depiction was made no later than the year 1195. It predates the Carbon-14 dates by 70 to 200 years. Yet, the painting portrays several features found uniquely on the Turin Shroud: namely, (1) the painting shows the body to be naked, (2) the hands are crossed over the crotch area, (3) only four fingers of each hand show with missing thumbs on each hand, (4) the lower part of the painting illustrates the rare and complex herringbone twill pattern of the cloth's weave pattern, and (5) the painting clearly reveals a one-of-a-kind array of burnt poker holes found on the Turin Shroud. The sets of burnt poker holes on the Shroud are either three holes in a row, or three holes with a fourth side hole forming a configuration like a number 7 or letter L. Most likely the shroud was folded in layers when someone rammed a hot poker with four prongs (shaped like a three-pronged fork but with a fourth additional side prong) into the Shroud. The side prong of the poker apparently did not go deep enough to penetrate all the layers of the folded Shroud. Thus only the top folded layer clearly presents the full pattern of holes like a 7 or L (which may be viewed on the dorsal [back side] of the Shroud's body image).[137] How could it be happenstance that all these unique depictions from the Hungarian Pray Manuscript should precisely match the Shroud of Turin? Yet this art predates the Carbon-14 dates by 70 to 200 years.

Pertaining to the radiocarbon dating news coverage, there was important information that was glossed over by the news media. First of all, it is important to understand that C-14 dating is incorrectly perceived by the public as being something that is impeccable and infallible. Archaeologist William Meacham (who has undertaken extensive research of the Shroud) wrote the following prior to the radiocarbon tests of the Shroud:

> There appears to be an unhealthy consensus approaching the level of dogma . . . that C-14 dating will "settle the issue once and for all time." This attitude sharply contradicts the general perspective of field archaeologists and geologists, who view possible contamination as a very serious problem.[138]

The general public is not aware that Carbon-14 dating has yielded a perpetual history of providing *erroneous dates*. For example, *living* snail shells have been dated as 26,000 years old; a freshly killed seal dated 1300 years old; a Viking horn (probably 900 to 1300 years old) was C-14 tested with a date that was 18 years into the future, and a caribou rib was dated back 27,000 years (while the innermost part of the same rib dated back only 1350 years).[139]

What causes such erroneous radiocarbon results? The reasons vary, but the most common source is contamination of the sample.[140] William Meacham stated: "The possibility of contamination is not of course in any way reflected in the margin of error given with each result."[141] (The stated *"margin of error"* pertains to the accuracy of the measurement of C-14 alone; *it has nothing to do with whether the sample itself might have been contaminated*.) Meacham further noted (prior to the 1988 Carbon-14 test): "There is no doubt that the Shroud has had an enormous exposure to a host of contaminants during its history."[142] As a professional archeologist, Meacham pointed out that archeologists do not normally have the slightest hesitation for rejecting dubious C-14 dates.[143] The section that was cut out of the Shroud for radiocarbon testing came from its top left-hand corner. This corner was undoubtedly one of the most contaminated parts of the Shroud—a corner that was often hand-held throughout the centuries while displaying the Shroud.[144]

When reporting the radiocarbon dating results, some glaring and prominent issues were ignored by the news media. For example, in 1982, an unauthorized test was conducted on a thread extracted from the Shroud called the *Raes-sample*. This specimen was taken from the Shroud on a different occasion. The sample was C-14 tested during 1982 at the University of California nuclear accelerator facility. One end of the thread dated to 200 A.D./C.E., while the other end (contaminated with starch) dated to 1000 A.D./C.E.[145]

Another important matter was omitted by the news media. The British Museum provided three test samples involving six laboratories in order to inter-compare two new carbon dating technologies in preparation for dating the Turin Shroud. The result was that 41% of the test results (7 of 17 tests) were in error by more than half their historical age. In some cases, the errors were off by 1,000 years. The official concluding report concerning these tests fairly much glossed over these errors. The 1,000-year dating errors were even omitted from the report's final statistical analysis.[146]

Another concern was raised when the custodian of the Shroud made a last-minute change to restrict the Shroud test to only three labs (in stead of the seven labs originally assigned to carbon test the Shroud). All the labs (including the final three that actually performed the Shroud tests) signed a protest letter stating: ". . . we would be *irresponsible* if we were not to advise you that this fundamental modification in the proposed procedures may lead to *failure*" (italics added).[147] Thus, the very labs that performed the C-14 test on the Shroud warned of the possibility of erroneous dates. A report was also published in *Science News* (after consulting prominent experts in the field of radiocarbon dating) expressing "a grave concern" about the new *accelerator technology* (which was used to test the Shroud samples) "largely because of the *frequency of spurious readings* from small samples" (italics added).[148] Meanwhile, the news media in 1988 simply disregarded these matters and instead reported the Carbon-14 dates (1260-1390 A.D./C.E.) as the final, authoritative, and definitive conclusion regarding the date of the Shroud.

Three New Tests for Dating the Age of the Shroud Cloth

In June, 2015, a scientific conference was convened at Padua University in Italy titled: "Workshop of Paduan Scientific Analysis on the Shroud." It announced the results obtained from Padua University in collaboration with five other European universities:

Bologna, Modena, Parma, Udine, and Polytechnic of Bari[149] pertaining to their latest scientific tests and findings of the Turin Shroud.

Summarizing their assessment of the original 1988 Carbon-14 tests, they reported:

> Regarding the TS [Turin Shroud] dating, **after the demonstration that the 1988 radiocarbon result is not statistically reliable, probably because of environmental pollution,** alternative dating methods based on chemical and mechanical tests showed that **its age is compatible with the period in which Jesus Christ lived in Palestine.** (Emphasis added)[150]

Among the peer reviewed scientific papers presented by the scientists were three new dating tests of the Shroud which employed modern dating methodologies more innovative than the thirty-year-old 1988 radiocarbon tests. The following abstract was written by professor Giulio Fanti (who has headed the Shroud Science Group consisting of about 140 scientists[151]), Pierandrea Malfi, and Fabio Crosilla. The abstract below summarized their findings as follows:

> The present paper discusses the results obtained using innovative dating methods based on the analysis of mechanical parameters . . . and of opto-chemical ones (FT-IR and Raman) . . . . [T]wo opto-chemical methods have been applied to test the linen fabric, obtaining a date of 250 BC by a FT-IR ATR analysis and a date of 30 AD by a Raman analysis. These two dates combined with the mechanical result, weighted through their estimated square uncertainty inverses, **give a final date of the Turin Shroud of 90 AD +/-200 years at 95% confidence level.** While this date is both compatible with the time in which Jesus Christ lived in Palestine and with very recent results based on numismatic dating, it is not compatible with the 1988 radiocarbon measurements . . .(Emphasis added)[152]

In your opinion, what weighs more plausible regarding the dating of the Shroud material? Does the 1988 radiocarbon test convince you that the Shroud is the product of medieval craftsmanship from the 1300s? Or, do the three tests from year 2015 of the Shroud (performed three decades more recent than the 1988 carbon-14 tests and utilizing more recent state-of-the-art technology) better indicate an authentic relic approximating the first century?

(For those interested in the Raymond Rogers' hypothesis of repair threads from the original radiocarbon material, see reference notes.[153])

Chapter 16

HOW WAS THE SHROUD
IMAGE FORMED?

I
s there a scientific explanation which can account for the formation of the Shroud's image? **It is *mandatory* that any hypothesis offered regarding the formation of the Shroud's image must be consistent with a comprehensive explanation which is compatible with *every* characteristic discovered about the Shroud. A hypothesis that succeeds for one characteristic but which would then contradict against other verified aspects about the Shroud *must* be ruled out.**[154] To date, a proposition called the *Historically Consistent Hypothesis* is a premise which passes this criterion.[155] It is currently the *only* hypothesis which addresses and is compatible with every known attribute thus far discovered about the Shroud.[156] The hypothesis was formulated by Shroud science historian Mark Antonacci (President of Test the Shroud Foundation)[157] and Ph D physicist Arthur Lind, combined with contributions from the Protonic Model of Image Formation developed by biophysicist Dr. Jean-Baptiste Rinaudo (of the Center of Nuclear Medical Research in Montpellier, France, and the Grenoble Nuclear Studies Center in France), the Cloth Collapse Hypothesis of John Jackson (Ph D Physics), and radiation experiments from Dr. Kitty Little (retired nuclear physicist from Britain's Atomic Energy Research Establishment in Harwell), as well as various other postulations.[158]

The following is a very brief summation of the *Historically Consistent Hypothesis*. According to this supposition, the Shroud and everything in its physical environment *adhered to the natural laws of physics—except for the body*.[159] Evidence shows that the Shroud image fibers were not burned or scorched, but rather denatured by low-energy, low temperature particle radiation.[160] It has been demonstrated that nuclear radiation emits certain particles which can induce the distinct attributes found on the Shroud. In fact, only radiation thus far can account for all the explicit primary and secondary effects identified with the Shroud image. Radiation accounts for over 30 extraordinary features of the Shroud image.[161] If the body suddenly disappeared into an alternate dimensionality, leaving behind residual particle radiation, then (as various tests confirm) such particle radiation could induce all these outcomes. Various types of radiation could be emitted, especially protons and neutrons—and possibly electrons and gamma rays.[162] The denaturing of the Shroud image fibers would result primarily from proton particles, which are weak.[163]

In accordance with the *Historically Consistent Hypothesis*, where the Shroud coheres within the laws of physics, the image formation begins upon the cloth's interaction with radiation. Corresponding to the configuration of how the Shroud was draped over and under the supine body, the entire Shroud bearing that draped formation fell by gravity and was drawn into the vacuum of the disappearing body downward through the ventral (front) and suctioned upward through the dorsal (back) of the body's residual radiation. (The immediate suction was more powerful than the force of gravity.) The image indicates that the radiation impacted the Shroud as the cloth passed through it in a straight-line vertical path between the Shroud and the body. As the cloth passed through the residual particle radiation of the body, both the dorsal (back) and the ventral (front) of the body would have received an approximate equal dose of the radiation (as evident from the Shroud cloth).[164]

Protons and alpha particle radiation are weak and rapidly attenuate. For example, they travel only about 3 centimeters (1.18 inches) in air.[165] Only the body disappeared, but the air between the body and the Shroud would have remained within the Shroud. Since proton and alpha particle radiation rapidly attenuate and die out in air, those parts of the cloth that were closer in proximity to the body would have received a greater quantity of radiation strikes, and those parts of the body that were farther distant from the collapsing cloth would have received a fewer number of radiation strikes. Referencing the attenuation of proton radiation in air, physicist Arthur Lind cites that there is no body image wherever the body was more than four inches away from the originally draped position of the Shroud cloth. For example, there is no image underneath the area surrounding the crossed hands because that was more than four inches away from the original position of the draped Shroud. Apparently, the radiation had fully died out before the Shroud reached that point.[166] The attenuation of the radiation would also explain why there is a gap devoid of body image at the *mid-horizontal sides surrounding* the supine body that were initially more than four inches away from the draped cloth. This is most apparent when observing the three-dimensional view of the body.

The straw yellow color of the Shroud image is microscopically superficial. One single linen thread may consist of two hundred or more fibers.[167] Yet the radiation only penetrated no deeper than the outermost surface of exposed fibers (not covered over by other fibers) and not deeper than 0.2 microns (0.000008 of an inch, or one hundredth of the diameter of an approximate 20 micron diameter fiber). Radiation explains how such microscopic superficiality of coloring of the fibers would be possible. This microscopic, thin, outermost, superficial coloring is consistent with all fibers that are colored.[168]

At the Grenoble Nuclear Studies Center in France, Dr. Jean-Baptiste Rinaudo radiated proton beams onto white linens with a particle accelerator. This, combined with artificially induced aging experiments, produced the same straw-yellow color found with the external Shroud image fibers. Also, the interior part of such colored fibers remained white—just as the Shroud image fibers do.[169] Retired nuclear physicist Dr. Kitty Little, who had previously performed similar experiments with similar results of radiation at Britain's Atomic Energy Research Establishment in Harwell, stated: "Now it seemed almost certain that the image must have been caused by some sort of radiation."[170]

All image fibers have the same approximate color and intensity. So how is it that the Shroud has lighter and darker areas to reveal its image? It was the quantity/density of *how many* fibers were irradiated at each point of the image which produced the lightness or darkness to display the Shroud's image.[171] The quantity/number of colorized fibers would have been determined by the initial distance between the body and the Shroud cloth (because proton radiation rapidly attenuates in air.)

Experiments by physicist Arthur Lind in 2017 using a cyclotron at the University of Missouri demonstrated that the radiation had to be *extremely fine tuned within a very narrow range of parameters* in order to produce the image of the Shroud—otherwise the Shroud could have been burnt through, or if too many of the fibers had been colored it would have left only a dark area instead of an image, or if the radiation source was too week or too far away from the cloth it would not have left any radiation effect (as exhibited from the circumference of the mid-horizontal area of the supine body which was too distant from the cloth to leave any image). So how finely tuned did the radiation have to be in order to produce the Shroud's image? Dr. Lind's experimentation indicated that the proton energy had to be confined within an extremely narrow spectrum of 0.2 to 0.4 MeV level. Likewise, it also required a perfection of proton density quantity to produce the image. Would not this evidence (of a narrow, constrict range of parameters essential in order to produce the image) seem most indicative of design—rather than an accident of nature? Scientists typically require numerous trial and error runs to perfect a process; yet this Shroud (dating from centuries long ago) would seem to have had only one shot at the process. It nailed it, with meticulous precision, on the first try. (See the video presentation by physicist Arthur Lind identified in the end notes.[172])

How was the three-dimensional aspect of the image produced? It would be the quantity/density number of radiation strikes that would encode the three-dimensional distance information between the body and the cloth. Since proton radiation rapidly attenuates and dies out (especially in air), more radiation strikes would impact the cloth where the Shroud was originally closer to the body and fewer radiation particles would strike where the body was originally further away from the cloth—thus encoding distance (three-dimensional) information based on the quantity/density of colorized fibers.[173] As the Shroud continued to pass through, it would also reach and encode parts of the body that were not originally touching the draped cloth.[174] Altogether, this indicates that every pin point part of the body (including the hair) had to emit its own particle radiation upon the Shroud and do so in proportion to its distance from the Shroud, impacting the cloth in a straight-line vertical manner between the body and the Shroud.[175] Physicist Thomas Phillips (of the High Energy Physics Laboratory at Harvard University), biophysicist Jean-Baptiste Rinaudo (of the Center for Nuclear Medical Research in Montpellier, France, and the Grenoble Nuclear Studies Center in France), and Dr. Kitty Little (retired nuclear physicist from Britain's Atomic Energy Research Establishment in Harwell) **have each hypothesized that particle radiation irradiated the Shroud and** that the *source* **of the particle radiation was the body itself.**[176] Dr. Little stated "that the source of the illumination that had formed the image came from within—that is, from the body . . . as a whole."[177] In other words, the radiation did not come from some external source; rather, **the radiation's origin was** *directly from* **the body—from every pinpoint location of the body.**[178] This facet (wherein each micro part of the body—the source of the radiation—radiates directly and exclusively from its specific point on the body to that corresponding exclusive point on the Shroud, thus irradiating an image) is something that no one has yet been able to reproduce.[179] (*How could a medieval artisan accomplish this? In fact there is no technology yet in existence which can reproduce this.*[180]) STURP chemist Dr. John Heller remarked: "It is as if every pore and every hair of the body contained a microminiature laser."[181]

The quantity number (density) of radiation strikes would also create the photonegativity effect of the image.[182] Gamma rays and neutron radiation would pass through the cloth without encoding any body image. However, neutron radiation would be able to excite the copper elements of coins, causing the coins to emit their own proton, alpha particle, deuterium, or low-energy gamma rays, and this could cause the coins to discharge an image onto the cloth.[183] Scientific tests have also demonstrated how a corona discharge from a coin would induce sparks or ions to fire off as streamers from the elevated points and rough spots of a coin (but not from the smooth/flat areas of a coin) producing an image of a coin onto a cloth. German physicist Oswald Scheuermann was given an actual Pontius Pilate lituus lepton coin and he promptly produced a corona discharge off the coin onto a piece of linen which was remarkably similar to the Shroud's coin mages.[184]

Experiments at Isotrace Radiocarbon Laboratory have demonstrated that neutron flux emission would cause the formation of new Carbon-14 isotopes in the Shroud material. This would explain the surprising renewing and strengthening of the Shroud material. It could also make the Shroud's carbon dating results appear to be far younger (or more recent).[185]

Why does the Shroud blood remain red instead of turning to the normal dark brown or black? Experiments by Dr. Carlo Goldoni confirmed that when blood is exposed to neutron radiation followed by ultraviolet light (such as sunlight) it causes the blood to retain its red color. Furthermore, tests utilizing ultraviolet-visible spectrophotometry and tests by Fourier Transform Infrared (FTIR) micro spectrophotometry have confirmed the presence of bilirubin in the Shroud blood which would also cause the blood to retain its red color.[186] (Bilirubin in blood occurs when a person suffers tremendous violence and undergoes a state of traumatic shock.)[187]

There is one other facet that has not yet been mentioned. The image on the Shroud also reveals various *internal skeletal features* such as bones *within* the hands, underlying teeth on the right side of the mouth, the backbone, and various other skeletal features.[188] This is further confirmation of the Historically Consistent Hypothesis. It accounts for this as the Shroud would fall by gravity and be sucked into the residual radiation of the body extending *beyond* the outer surface radiation of the skin and going *deeper* into some of the skeletal features of the body. How do you get a cloth to pass through a corpse to capture skeletal imagery? Such attributes were not visible on the Shroud until many centuries after the 1300s, when photography was invented.[189]

For a medieval artisan to create the Shroud, it would have required him to have extensive knowledge in numerous fields of science *centuries before the world made such discoveries.* The medieval architect would have needed specialized knowledge in archeology, endocrinology, forensics, hematology, human physiology, light spectrometry, microscopy, palynology, pathology, and radiology to name a few.[190]

After decades of investigation by scientists throughout the world, various researchers have brought forth impressive credible and scientific explanations pertaining to the physical properties of the Shroud, such as the chemistry of its image, and evidence of radiation being the agent that denatured the image fibers. One of the implications provided by physicists is how the radiation source was from the body itself (which was wrapped within the Shroud). But, apparently, this is the limit to which science can take us. What science cannot explain is how the body would simply disappear from *inside its wrapped Shroud*—thus inducing the collapse of the cloth passing through the body's residual radiation, thus irradiating the three-dimensional image of the full body (head to toe, front and back) within the *interior* side of the wrapped burial cloth that was facing the body.

At the June 9th, 2015 scientific conference hosted at the University of Padua, Italy, (which was convened to present the latest news and the continuing scientific research of the Turin Shroud) they documented that the Shroud body image **"is *not explainable by Science nor reproducible up to now"* (italics and emphasis added).[191] The Shroud has now withstood over forty years of international scientific scrutiny; and this is where we're at. If the sum of all scientific knowledge that exists in the world today, combined with all the modern-day technology available in the world today, and if after more than four decades of exhaustive scientific research it is *still impossible* for scientists to reproduce an image with all the characteristics found on the Shroud—how then could a medieval artist from the 1300s accomplish this?

Mark Antonacci affirmed:

> [S]omething unique happened to the man in the Shroud that distributed *all* the unfakable evidence . . . . The extensive evidence on this cloth is not only consistent with, but also comprises *unforgeable* evidence of every aspect of the passion, crucifixion, death, burial and resurrection of the historical Jesus Christ.
>
> This evidence will especially stand out at the atomic and molecular levels . . . . [See chapter 24].[192]

Many have wondered what sort of findings might have resulted had modern scientists been given an opportunity to scrutinize one of the many reported miracles of the Christ. Results documented here may offer just such an evaluation.

In summation, by the exercise and application of *inductive logic*, the Shroud may be found herein to offer convincing and multifaceted scientific support in favor of: *life after death*.

(For those interested in the ultraviolet hypothesis of the image formation, see end notes.[193])

The following is the official summary ("Final Report") by the Shroud of Turin Research Project (STURP) scientists and specialists at the conclusion of their years of study and evaluation of their research data. This report was distributed at their final press conference in 1981:

Official STURP Conclusions

No pigments, paints, dyes or stains have been found on the fibrils. X-ray, fluorescence and microchemistry on the fibrils preclude the possibility of paint being used as a method for creating the image. Ultra Violet and infrared evaluation confirm these studies. Computer image enhancement and analysis by a device known as a VP-8 image analyzer show that the image has unique, three-dimensional information encoded in it. Microchemical evaluation has indicated no evidence of any spices, oils, or any biochemicals known to be produced by the body in life or in death. It is clear that there has been a direct contact of the Shroud with a body, which explains certain features such as scourge marks, as well as the blood. However, while this type of contact might explain some of the features of the torso, it is totally incapable of explaining the image of the face with the high resolution that has been amply demonstrated by photography.

The basic problem from a scientific point of view is that some explanations which might be tenable from a chemical point of view, are precluded by physics. Contrariwise, certain physical explanations which may be attractive are completely precluded by the chemistry. For an adequate explanation for the image of the Shroud, one must have an explanation which is scientifically sound, from a physical, chemical, biological and medical viewpoint. At the present, this type of solution does not appear to be obtainable by the best efforts of the members of the Shroud Team. Furthermore, experiments in physics and chemistry with old linen have failed to reproduce adequately the phenomenon presented by the Shroud of Turin. The scientific consensus is that the image was produced by something which resulted in oxidation, dehydration and conjugation of the polysaccharide structure of the microfibrils of the linen itself. Such changes can be duplicated in the laboratory by certain chemical and physical processes. A similar type of change in linen can be obtained by sulfuric acid or heat. However, there are no chemical or physical methods known which can account for the totality of the image, nor can any combination of physical, chemical, biological or medical circumstances explain the image adequately.

Thus, the answer to the question of how the image was produced or what produced the image remains, now, as it has in the past, a mystery.

We can conclude for now that the Shroud image is that of a real human form of a scourged, crucified man. It is not the product of an artist. The blood stains are composed of hemoglobin and also give a positive test for serum albumin. The image is an ongoing mystery and until further chemical studies are made, perhaps by this group of scientists, or perhaps by some scientists in the future, the problem remains unsolved.[194]

Chapter 17

THE SHROUD ADDRESSES SOME OF LIFE'S MOST FUNDAMENTAL QUESTIONS

There are many more facets about the Shroud than this book addresses. Only since the late 20th century has the world acquired the scientific knowledge and technology that has made it possible to discover these insights about the Shroud. If the Shroud is an authentic historical relic from *Yeshua*, then it would appear to be a miracle passed down from *Yeshua*—especially targeted for our generation. The fact that it was the world's esteemed scientists (*not* religious leaders) who took the initiative, performed the research, made the discoveries, verified the test results, published the research in numerous scientific papers and journals—all out of their own personal voluntary time, expense, and labor is noteworthy. The Shroud opens an opportunity to explore some of life's most fundamental questions. Death is a certainty. Is there life after death? Is there a purpose to life? Is there something we must do during this life which determines our eternal future? Many of us have postponed coming to terms with these issues. Yet not facing such matters is, in itself, a decision. All of us (at one time or another) have postponed dealing with a matter. And then we eventually found ourselves reaping the consequences of our procrastination. Or, perhaps we neglected to be diligent enough. Although consoled by our good intentions, it did not spare us from the consequences of our lack of diligence. Having read about the Shroud, this may be an ideal time to give some special consideration to matters that could bring special meaning and purpose to your life—and perhaps even a joyful outlook for life after death.

What is the significance of the Shroud? How does the Shroud address some of life's most fundamental questions? First of all, if the man on the Shroud is the Biblical *Yeshua* of Nazareth, then the Shroud would comport to capture that moment of the resurrection which radiated the image onto the Shroud burial cloth. *The more you grow convinced that the Shroud is authentic, at that point the Shroud's message becomes . . .* **there is life after death!** *In fact, it becomes tantamount to* **PHYSICAL EVIDENCE** *of life after death:* left behind and irradiated upon the **physical fibers** *of* the Shroud by the power of the resurrection. You can see it with your own eyes; you can touch it with your hands; scientists worldwide could lavish meticulous scrutiny on its physical properties . . . for decades. And this witness was furnished by the very person whose mission and message was his promise of *everlasting life.* For the average person, *the Shroud (combined with the discoveries of the scientists) is probably the closest one will come to witnessing proof of life after death.* It still requires faith. But *not* blind faith. You have been invited to exercise your own inductive logic and offer your own conclusions for many aspects about the Shroud and its scientific research.

If the man on the Shroud is the Biblical *Yeshua* of Nazareth, then we must ask what is the purpose and meaningfulness of this *suffering and death* found on the Shroud? For that we must refer to the Hebrew Scriptures. (Please! Read the following brief summary carefully. It will ultimately resolve into an unexpected insight related to the suffering found on the Shroud.) The significance of the suffering on the Shroud begins with the book of Genesis when God created Adam and Eve and placed them in paradise—Eden's garden. This was God's ideal for humanity. There was no sickness, no pain, no suffering, no death and food was provided without laborious work. Some people reject God because of all the suffering experienced in the world. How could God allow that? However, the Hebrew Scriptures record that there was no such suffering when God created Adam and Eve. God gave them a free will to choose to follow Him or to rebel and sin against the Creator. God did not want people to be like robots that would automatically love and obey Him. God was looking for a people who would *voluntarily* choose Him. But God, being perfect in holiness, also warned that if they did sin by eating the forbidden fruit of only one, single, specific tree—the *tree of the knowledge of good and evil*---then that disobedience would eventuate in the *experience of death*. Thus, with the arrival of sin, suffering and evil entered the world. According to the Bible, they eventually did eat the forbidden fruit of **the tree of knowledge of good and evil**. This was the first ever sin. As a result, humanity became subject to *death*, and all of life's sufferings and malicious evils. *It was not until this first sin that Adam and Eve became aware of **their shame of sin and nakedness** before God* (Gen. 3:7). God told them that as a result of sin, they would experience the curse of sin. Henceforth, they would now have to toil by the *sweat* **of the brow** to provide for their needs. In their effort to provide food, they would be afflicted by *thorns* and thistles (Gen. 3:18-19). According to the Bible, Satan had enticed this sin, so God announced to Satan that *a special child born from the seed of a woman* would defeat Satan (Gen. 3:15; Hebrews 2:14-15). (What an odd statement. Children are born from the "seed of a man"—not the seed of a woman.) But the Creator also declared to Satan that he *(i.e. Satan) would bruise the heel/foot of this child* (Gen. 3:15). God then *shed the blood* of an animal to provide its skin *as a covering* for Adam and Eve to hide their shame of guilt and nakedness (Gen. 3:21). They were then **banished from the Garden of Eden where they had enjoyed that special intimate presence with God** (Gen. 3:23-24).

With this original sin, the Bible records how the Creator immediately reached out to provide a way for humanity to be reconciled back into fellowship with God. Beginning with the "shed blood" of the animal whose skin God gave to "cover" Adam's "shame of nakedness" (Gen. 3:21), and then on to the animal sacrifice of Abel (the son of Adam, Gen. 4:1-5) and on throughout the various Jewish sacrifices, the people could make "atonement" to "cover" their sins by shedding the blood of certain unblemished animals (Lev. 16:34; 17:11). That was a lesson for sinful humanity. The Hebrew Scriptures continued on through the Law of Moses. There we find how atonement for sin was made by placing of hands upon the head of an unblemished lamb (or certain specific animals) while making confession of sins to God (Lev. 4:3-4,27-35; 5:1-6;16:21;17:11). This practice symbolically represented the transferring of the people's sin onto the head of the innocent unblemished lamb as a *substitute* sacrifice for their sin.[h] The blood of the sacrifices was offered to provide atonement for the people's sin (Lev. 17:11). The Hebrew word for "atonement" is *chapeir*—which means "to cover." Just as God had *"covered"* the first sin of Adam by shedding the blood of an animal to *"cover"* Adam's guilt of nakedness with its skin, likewise, the Jewish sacrifices could make atonement (Heb. *chapeir*, "covering") for sin. But such sacrifices could not "take away" sin. They could only *"cover"* (Heb. *chapeir*) sin in the sight of God.

All this dovetailed into a prophetic model ultimately pointing to the crucifixion of *Yeshua*. When *Yochanan* (aka: John the Baptist) immersed *Yeshua*, *Yochanan* proclaimed: "Behold, the **Lamb of God** who **takes away** the **sin of the world!**" (John 1:30 TLV, emphasis added). The various animal sacrifices of Judaism could only "cover" (Heb. *chapeir*) sin, but *Yeshua* became the ultimate, unblemished (i.e. sinless) "Lamb of God" whose shed blood would actually "take away sin" (not merely "cover" sin). This was the atonement that actually "takes away" sin. From this we can now appreciate the meaning of the suffering and death found on the Shroud. The purpose for *Yeshua's* "suffering and death" was to provide that atoning sacrifice that *"takes away* (not merely covers) *the sin of the world"* (John 1:30).

---

[h] Instead of wasting the sacrifices, such sacrifices were often eaten afterward as a sacrificial meal.

From the Foregoing Review,
The Panoramic Scene of the Crucifixion Now Reveals Profound Symbolic Imagery

When *Yeshua* was crucified, although he was "sinless" (like an "unblemished" lamb), he became sin on our behalf—bearing the judgment of sin for the entire world, throughout all the ages. With this background, now when we reflect upon the scene of the crucifixion, we can more fully grasp the significance of its panoramic spectacle. **God *manipulated the setting* of the crucifixion to be *filled with symbolism*.** Its symbolisms were like signposts pointing far back in time (even back to the very first sin and its resulting curses in the Garden of Eden). Concomitant, it then displayed God's atonement for all humanity's sin. How so? Was the curse of sin upon Adam the pain of "**thorns**" (Gen. 3:18)? So *Yeshua* was crowned with thorns. Was the curse of sin "**sweat**" (Gen3:19)? So *Yeshua* began sweating drops that were mixed with blood (hematidrosis: the rare excretion of blood within sweat when under extreme stress) while praying before his arrest and execution: ("in His anguish, He was praying fervently; and **His sweat was like drops of blood** falling on the ground"—Lk. 22:44 TLV, emphasis added). Was the curse of sin "**death**" (Gen. 3:19)? *Yeshua*, (though undeserving of death), tasted death on behalf of *all humanity* (Hebrews 2:9). Did sin come into the world by means of a **tree**—the "**tree** of knowledge of good and evil" (Gen. 2:17 KJV; cf: Gen. 3:1-6)? So *Yeshua* was **nailed to the beams of the tree**. Was the shame of Adam's sin **nakedness** before God (Gen. 3:6-7)? So *Yeshua* hung (as it were) *naked* upon the cross while soldiers cast lots for his garments (Matt. 27:35; Ps. 22:17-18). (The Shroud of Turin itself displays this very image of nakedness.) Was the curse of sin that **Satan would "strike the heel"** of the **seed of the woman**? (Gen. 3:15 NIV). (Note: seed of a woman? Not the seed of a man?). So *Yeshua* (son of a woman, but not the son of the seed of a man) bore the *strike* of the spike through his feet. (See note below how the Hebrew word for "heel" can embrace the entire dimension of a footprint or footstep).[i] Did the curse of sin result in **banishment from the special intimate presence of God** in the Garden of Eden (Gen. 3:22-24)? Likewise, *Yeshua* cried out from the cross: "'*Eli, Eli, lama azavtani?*' That is, 'My God, my God, why have you forsaken me?'" (Matt. 27:46 MW).

The sublime backdrop of the scene of the crucifixion was thoroughly a symbolic panorama (composed by the sovereign hand of God). It harkened all the way back through the ages of time to the very first origin of sin and its list of curses in the Garden of Eden; it then answered back with God's solution of redemption **upon the cross for humanity.** All this went right over the heads of those who watched the crucifixion. Nobody at the cross realized the significance (symbolism) of what they were witnessing!

This symbolic setting transpired *independent of contriving initiative on the part of Yeshua.* Rather, God employed the very *enemies* of *Yeshua* to effectuate this striking array of figuration! Did *Yeshua* place the *thorns* on his own head to mimic the curse of sin? Did *Yeshua* execute himself to *death* (to reflect sin's curse of death)? Did *Yeshua ask to be nailed specifically to a tree*? (The source of original sin.) Did *Yeshua* offer to *strip off his clothes* (in order to bear *the shameful nakedness of sin*) so the soldiers could cast lots for his robe? Did *Yeshua* request a *spike to bruise his feet*? **Every detail of this crucifixion panorama reflected far back through time, pointing to the very original inception of sin with its curses—while at the same time—***juxtaposing* **(side by side with this symbolism) God's ultimate provision of redemption for all humanity! The whole scene at the cross (carried out by the very enemies of *Yeshua*) was engineered by God to frame a majestic, poetic, metaphor.**

---

[i] The Hebrew word for "heel" (in Gen. 3:15) is *aqeiv*—it can embrace not only the "heel," but also the full dimensions of a "footprint" (Psalm 77:19-20) or "footstep" (Ps. 89:51). The Shroud also displays this pierce wound to the feet (from the crucifixion spike).

Chapter 18

CONSIDERATIONS FROM THE BOOK OF ISAIAH, AND THE DEAD SEA SCROLLS

The significance of the suffering visible on the Shroud is aptly summarized by a prophecy from the Hebrew Scriptures found in the book of the Jewish prophet *Yesha'Yahu* (Isaiah) chapter 53. As you review this text below, please bear in mind that this prophecy from the prophet Isaiah was written *700 years before* the birth of *Yeshua*. (Note: copies of this book of Isaiah were recovered from among the Dead Sea Scrolls in Israel—with Hebrew texts inscribed and copied as far back as 125 years *before* the birth of *Yeshua*.[195])

(The text of Isaiah 53 below is highlighted and is quoted from the New International Version (NIV). This author's annotations have been interjected within brackets and indented throughout this quotation. Emphasis has also been added with bold font.)

(1) [**LORD**, j] [196]

Who has believed our message and to whom has the arm of the LORD [*YHVH*]k been revealed? . . .

(3) He was despised and rejected by mankind, a man of suffering, and familiar with pain. Like one from whom people hide their faces he was despised, and we held him in low esteem.

(4) Surely he took up our pain and bore our suffering, yet **we considered him punished by God, stricken by him,** and afflicted.

---

j The opening word "LORD" is not found in surviving Hebrew texts of Isaiah 53. However, the fact that this word "LORD" does exist at this point in the Greek translation of the Jewish Septuagint of Isaiah 53 provides evidence that the word "LORD" [or Heb. *YHVH*] did originally exist in the ancient Hebrew texts when the Jews of Alexandria, Egypt translated Isaiah from Hebrew into Greek during the 2nd or 3rd century B.C./B.C.E. Dead Sea Scroll scholars have found impressive evidence from their research of the Dead Sea Scrolls that the Jewish translation of the Hebrew Scriptures into Greek was translated from what at that time was considered *best and oldest* of the ancient Hebrew manuscripts. Thus, the opening word "LORD" in Isaiah 53:1 from the Jewish Septuagint would indicate that Isaiah chapter 53 was a prayer from the prophet *Yesha'Yahu* (Isaiah) directed to the "LORD" God on behalf of himself and Isaiah's people Israel—rather than some alleged report being articulated by gentiles of something they had "never heard of before," "nor understood" (Isa. 52:15). The superiority of the Septuagint's Hebrew base text as compared to the Masoretic Text is substantiated by Emanuel Tov in *The Earliest Text of the Hebrew Bible: The Relationship between the Masoretic Text and the Hebrew Base of the Septuagint Reconsidered,* Ed. Adrian Schenker (Atlanta: Society of Biblical Literature, 2003). Septuagint and Cognate Studies. See Emanuel Tov's contribution pp. 137-144. Emanuel Tov is considered one of the world's foremost and eminent scholars of the Dead Sea Scrolls. He was appointed by The Israel Antiquities Authority as Editor-in-Chief of the Dead Sea Scrolls Publication Project where he was in charge of a team of sixty scholars worldwide. Also, it is highly significant that every citation of Isaiah 53:1 by Yeshua's personal first century *talmidim* (disciples) do include the word "Lord" in their quotations of Isa. 53:1 (John 12:38, Rom. 10:11). It is quite likely the word "Lord" (Heb. YHVH) did still exist in Hebrew manuscripts during the 1st century.

k Throughout this book, *YHVH* represents the English transliteration from the Hebrew letters of the actual name of God wherever it appears within the Hebrew text.

(5) **But he was pierced for our transgressions,**

> [I.e. Pierced wounds to suffer God's judgment for our sins.]

he was crushed

> [Hebrew *dacha*: bruised, smitten.]

for our iniquities;

> [I.e. for our sins.]

the punishment that brought us peace was on him, and by his wounds

> ["Wounds" here is the Hebrew word *chaburah*: meaning **scourge marks**, stripes, stroke marks on the skin.]

we are healed.

(6) **We all, like sheep, have gone astray, each of us has turned to our own way; and the LORD [*YHVH*] has laid on him the iniquity of us all.**

> [I.e. God laying our iniquity, our sin, upon him.]

(7) **He was oppressed** and **afflicted, yet he did not open his mouth; he was led like a lamb to the slaughter,**

> [I.e. like a sacrificial lamb.]

and as a sheep before its shearers is silent, so he did not open his mouth.

> [*Yeshua* was silent before his accusations at his trial— Matt.26:62-63; 27:12-14.]

(8) By oppression and judgment he was taken away. Yet who of his generation protested?

> [Some translations use the words "his descendants" here instead of "his generation." However, the Hebrew word is *dor*, meaning "generation" (such as used in Gen. 15:16), or "age." Also, the Jewish Greek Septuagint has *genean autou* translated "his generation" (not "his descendants.")]

For **he was cut off from the land of the living;**
> [I.e. Killed.]

for the transgression of my people he was punished.
> [I.e. Punished as a substitute sacrifice for the transgression/sin of the people.]

(9) He was **assigned a grave with the wicked,**
> [I.e. His executioners assumed he would be buried with other wicked criminals.]

and **with the rich** in his death,
> [I.e. There would be a deviation from the original plan for burial among wicked criminals. Here, the Dead Sea Scroll, namely, the *Great Isaiah Scroll* from Cave 1(QIsa-a) Masoretic Text of the Dead Sea Scrolls states that his grave would be via *"a rich man his tomb."*[197] Instead of a community grave among wicked Roman criminals, *Yeshua* was hastily buried in the nearby tomb of a rich man named *Yosef* of *Ramatayim* (Joseph of Arimathea) who just happened to have his own newly hewn tomb nearby. Even still, there was barely enough time to place *Yeshua* in the tomb before the approaching evening which initiated the festival Sabbath of the Pharisees. Matt. 27:57-60).]

though he had done no violence, nor was any deceit in his mouth.

(10) Yet it was the LORD'S [*YHVH*] will to **crush**
> [Heb. *dacha*, bruise, smite.]

him and cause him to suffer, and **though the LORD [*YHVH*] makes his life an offering for sin,**
> [The word "offering" is the Hebrew word *asham* – the very same word used in Lev. 5:6 for the "guilt offering" atonement for sin sacrificed at the Temple.]

he will see his offspring

> [I.e. "will see posterity, future generations," not "his offspring." The word "his" is **not** in the Hebrew text **nor** in the Jewish Greek Septuagint. See note below.[1]]

and prolong his days,

and the will of the LORD [*YHVH*] will prosper in his hand.

(11) **After he has suffered, he will see the light of life** and be satisfied;

> [Here we have a Hebrew triplet. This is a Hebraism where the same concept is rephrased three times in three different ways. It provides clarity, reinforcement of the message, and emphasis. In preparation for this triplet, notice in the prior verses 8-10 that the suffering servant (represented as "an offering for sin"—literally the Hebrew "*asham*"—the Temple's "guilt sacrifice" of Lev. 5:6), then dies being "cut off from the land of the living," and his grave is reassigned to a rich man's tomb. Then, immediately following these references to his death, the three Hebrew triplet statements begin in succession starting in verse 10: namely, (a) he "sees posterity, future generations," (b) "his days are prolonged," and (c) "*after* he has suffered, *he will see the light of life.*" This Hebrew triplet points to *life after death*: namely, resurrection. (Read this end note to learn how the discovery of the Dead Sea Scrolls brought new information about this verse and "the light of life").[198]]

---

[1] "*His* offspring" in verse 10: The word "his" is **not** in the Hebrew text. If the Hebrew word used here was *zaro* it would have meant "his offspring." Instead, the Hebrew word used here is *zera*, which means "offspring" (not "his offspring"). This word *zera* can also be translated as "posterity" or "future generations" and it is clearly used with that meaning in Psalm 22:30 where it speaks of "posterity" and "future generations" that will serve the Messiah. Note how the word "his" is also omitted in the Jewish JPS English translation of both Isa. 53:10 and Ps. 22:30-31. The Hebrew word *zera* used here means that the suffering servant will see "posterity, future generations"—not "his" personal offspring.

by his knowledge my **righteous servant** will **justify many, and he will bear their iniquities.**

> [This sentence (verse 11) establishes that the suffering servant of Isaiah 53 is specifically God's **"righteous servant."** Nowhere in Isaiah, nor within the entire Bible, is the nation Israel *ever* identified as "God's *righteous* servant." In fact, just the opposite! Throughout the prior chapters of Isaiah, it is important to note that Isaiah is building a sharp contrast between two different servants: namely, the servant nation of Israel who is lamented as God's "wayward and disobedient servant"--Isa. 42:17-25; 43:22-44:1; 21-22; 48:1, 4-5, 8-10, 12, 18) contraposed to God's "righteous Messiah servant" (42:1-4; 52:13-15; 53:1-12) who does no violence (53:9), nor has any deceit in his mouth (53:9), who intercedes for his transgressors (53:12), and whose vivid details throughout Isaiah 53 match the sacrificial mission of *Yeshua*). It is specifically this "righteous servant" who "bears the iniquities" of many as a "guilt offering" in order to effectuate their "justification" from the guilt of sin before God.]

(12) Therefore **I will give him a portion** among the great, and **he will divide the spoils** with the strong, **because he poured out his life unto death,**

> [Once again, this is another reference to resurrection of life after death for the suffering servant: namely, *because* he poured out his life *unto death,* therefore *after* his death he will ultimately be given "a portion among the great," and "will divide the spoils."]

and **was numbered with the transgressors.**

> [Corresponding to this servant, *Yeshua* was numbered with (or crucified between) two Roman criminals (John 19:18).]

For **he bore the sin of many**, and made **intercession for the transgressors.**

> [While *Yeshua* "bore humanity's sin" on the cross, he prayed, making "intercession" to God for his transgressors and executioners: "Father, forgive them; for they know not what they do" (Luke 23:34 KJV).]

It is impressive that the above prophecy was **written by Isaiah 700 years before the birth of Yeshua.** This prophecy from *Yesha'Yahu* (Isaiah) was revealing that the Jewish sacrificial offerings were prophetic: that they ultimately pointed beyond the sacrificial animals to a *person* (Messiah) who would become "the Lamb of God who takes away the sin of the world" (John 1:29 NASB): namely, the (Heb.) *asham*—i.e.: the "guilt offering" for sin (Lev. 5:6).

Chapter 19

HOW TO APPROPRIATE
GOD'S REDEMPTION

Pertaining to the eternal Kingdom of God, the Bible reports that "nothing impure will ever enter it . . . but only those whose names are written in the **Lamb's book of life"** (Rev. 21:27 NIV, emphasis added). How can we have our name "written in the Lamb's book of life"?

According to the Bible, God must judge sin to enforce righteousness. Since all of us have sinned, then according to the Bible everyone is in need of atonement for sin—no matter how good a person we may be. Consequently, we must either appropriate the atonement provided by *Yeshua* for our sin, or else we will have to bear our own judgment for our sin from God. The Bible strongly affirms this. We need salvation and atonement. (The name *Yeshua*—assigned prophetically prior to his birth—means *"salvation"*). If we did not need salvation and redemption from judgment, then there is no reason why *Yeshua* would have to die for our sins. **This explains the purpose and significance of the suffering found on the Shroud.** It is part of the Shroud's message.

The Bible teaches that God is the sovereign LORD: the Almighty Creator of the universe and all existence—anyone who seeks to come to God *must do so on His terms . . . (not ours)!* But how can we appropriate *Yeshua's* redemptive sacrifice for us personally? The best example for that is illustrated like a model from the event of the Passover in Egypt. **How did the Jews "become redeemed" so as to become "God's own people"? The Jews became God's own people/nation through the *redemptive* event of the Passover in Egypt:**

Say, therefore, to the sons of Israel, I am the LORD [*YHVH*], and **I will bring you out from under the burdens of the Egyptians**, and I will deliver you from their bondage. **I will also REDEEM you** with an outstretched arm and with great judgments. **Then I will take you for My PEOPLE, and I will be your God** . . . . (Exod. 6:6-7 NASB, emphasis added).

And **who** *is* **like Your PEOPLE Israel**—the one nation on the earth whom God went out **to REDEEM** as a **PEOPLE** for Himself . . . Your **PEOPLE, whom You REDEEMED, from Egypt? You have made Your PEOPLE Israel Your own PEOPLE forever**; and You, *ADONAI* [LORD, *YHVH*], became their God (1 Chron. 17:21-22 TLV, emphasis added).

(The word "people" has been capitalized in the above verses to indicate where it is translating the Hebrew word *'am* [which means "people/nation/community."] This is an important clarification. The redemption in Egypt was *not for individuals*—rather it was a corporate redemption making Israel God's nation/people.)

At the Passover event in Egypt, God's *judgment* against sin (i.e. the tenth plague) was about to bring death to all the firstborn sons in Egypt—especially for their idolatry:

For I [God] will go through the land of Egypt on that night and strike down every firstborn, both men and animals [i.e. many animals in Egypt were venerated as symbols of Egyptian idolatry]: and **I will execute judgments against all the gods [idolatry] of Egypt. I am** *ADONAI* [LORD, *YHVH*] (Exod. 12:12 TLV, emphasis added).

But God also made provision for a *redemptive* sacrifice—the unblemished Passover lamb—which could provide the people salvation from divine judgment:

> Your **lamb shall be without blemish** . . . Now you shall keep it until the fourteenth day of the same month. Then the whole assembly of the congregation of Israel shall kill it at twilight. And they shall take *some* of the blood and put *it* on the two doorposts and on the lintel of the houses . . . **Now the blood shall be a sign for you** . . . . And **when I see the blood, I will pass over you; and the plague shall not be on you to destroy** *you* **when I strike the land of Egypt.** . . . **You shall remove leaven** from your houses. For whoever eats leavened bread . . . that person shall be cut off from Israel (Ex. 12:5-7, 13, 15 NKJV, emphasis added).

Again, how were the Jewish people instructed to find *redemption* from God to become *"God's own people"*? At the Passover in Egypt the Israelites were directed to procure *salvation from God's judgment* (the tenth plague of death) *by exercising faith*. God's redemption did not apply to agnostics. The redemption only applied to those who exercised faith by personally taking refuge under the blood of the Passover lamb. In so doing, such people could obtain salvation from divine judgment (the 10th plague), and become "redeemed" so as to "belong to God"—to become a part of God's own people/nation. They were also to remove all leaven from their homes. (Note: among the variety of sacrifices in the Law of Moses, the Passover was identified as the **only redemption sacrifice** in the entire Law of Moses.)

This historic event of the Egyptian Passover is a Hebrew *tavniyt* (a "model/pattern") which instructs us how we likewise can appropriate God's provision of *redemption* for ourselves *personally*. The historic model illustrates precisely how God invites us to appropriate His redemption and salvation from judgment that we too might become God's people. Just like the Israelites, we also are to *exercise faith* (i.e.

by **taking refuge from divine judgment under the shed blood of** *Yeshua*—namely, **placing our trust in the unblemished, sinless Lamb of God who was sacrificed for our redemption**). We likewise are to trust in the blood of *Yeshua* for our salvation from divine judgment:

> In him we have redemption through his blood, the forgiveness of sins . . . . (Eph. 1:7 NIV)

> God presented Christ as a sacrifice of atonement, through the shedding of his blood—to be received by faith (Rom. 3:25 NIV).

> **YOU** know that **YOU** were redeemed . . . not with perishable things . . . but with the precious blood like that of a lamb without defect or spot, the blood of Messiah (1 Peter 1:18 NIV, emphasis added).

(The above citations—which refer to Yeshua's redemption—provide another important clarification pertaining to the concept of "redemption." The Passover redemption in Egypt was a "corporate redemption" making the people of Israel God's "nation/people." In contrast, the redemption accomplished by Yeshua was a "personal redemption for individuals" providing personal forgiveness and atonement of sins for individuals—salvation from personal divine judgment.)

What about the leaven? How does getting rid of leaven at Passover fit in with this? Leaven is yeast (a *corrupting* agent) which causes bread to rise. *Sha'ul* (*Paulos*) wrote concerning how leaven applies to us:

> Don't you know that a little *hametz* [i.e. leaven] leavens the whole batch of dough? **Get rid of the old *hametz*** [leaven], so you may be

a new batch, just as you are unleavened—**for Messiah, our Passover Lamb, has been sacrificed**. Therefore let us celebrate the feast not with old *hametz*, **the *hametz* [leaven] of malice and wickedness**, but the unleavened bread—the *matzah* of sincerity and truth (1 Cor. 5:6-9 TLV, emphasis added).

In this manner *Sha'ul* (*Paulos*) instructed that the leaven of Passover symbolically represented the ***corruption*** of wickedness, or sin (just as leaven is a *corrupting agent* causing bread to rise). The riddance of leaven associated with Passover instructs that we also must make a sincere commitment to avoid the leaven (corruption) of sin in our lives. The Hebrew word for "repentance" is *shuv*, which means *to turn (i.e. "from sin" and "to God")*. You are going in one direction (your own way), now you make the *decision "to turn* to God" (redirecting your life to follow Him). God knows that we will still sin during life's sojourn. That is why the Bible teaches that "if we confess our sins, He is faithful and just to forgive us our sins" (1 John 1:9 NKJV). By "turning toward God" (Heb. *shuv*) **our new life's dedication must henceforth be aimed toward seeking to please God, and endeavoring to avoid the "leaven of sin" in our lives.**

He [*Yeshua*] said to them, "So it is written, that the Messiah is to suffer and to rise from the dead on the third day, and that **repentance for the removal of sins** is to be proclaimed in His name to all nations, beginning from Jerusalem (Luke 24:45-47 TLV, emphasis added).

The Lord is . . . not willing that any should perish but that all should come to **repentance** (2 Pet. 3:9 NKJV).

Those who are sincere about *"shuv"* (*turning* from sin to God) may confirm their sincerity by studying the Bible to learn what pleases God and what is sinful to God. *Yeshua* taught that the Bible is *bread for the soul* which encourages and nurtures us in our relationship with God:

> He [*Yeshua*] answered and said, "It is written, *'Man shall not live by bread alone, but by every word that proceeds from the mouth of God'"* (Matt. 4:4 NKJV).
>
> Yeshua then said to those sectarian Jews who had believed him, "If you remain in my word, then you are truly my disciples. You will know the truth, and the truth will make you free" (Yoḥanan/John 8:31 MW).

(It is also expedient to attend a congregation where the Bible is studied.)

And so it is that the historic Passover was prearranged by God to depict a Hebrew *tavniyt* ("model/pattern") instructing us how to find *redemption* and *how to become God's people*. In the same fashion (just as the Israelites did in Egypt), we too can appropriate God's provision of individual redemption to become God's people by (1) deliberately placing our faith in the redemptive sacrifice provided by *Yeshua* on the cross, by taking refuge under the blood of the Lamb of God for salvation from the judgment that our personal sin deserves, and (2) by redirecting our life to turn away from the leaven of sin—henceforth to "turn to God" to live endeavoring to please God. If this is your decision for God, then you can rest assured that your individual name is in the "Lamb's Book of Life" (Rev. 21:27).

Many people like to express this commitment directly to God. In fact, when *Yeshua* was crucified, two criminals were also crucified next to him. One of them mocked and reviled Yeshua. But the other rebuked the mocker—turning to *Yeshua*, he implored: **"Remember me when You come into Your Kingdom"!** (Luke 23:42 TLV). *Yeshua* acknowledged and confirmed his request of faith right there on the cross.

It is highly significant that this gospel redemption narrative from the Passover resides within the very core foundation of Judaism; namely, within *Torah Moshe* (the Law and instruction of Moses—the first five books of the Bible). *Yeshua* affirmed that "he [Moses] wrote about me" (Yoḥanan/John 5:46 MW).

Chapter 20

PROPHECY WITHIN THE PASSOVER? (AND HOW THE SHROUD RELATES TO PASSOVER)

To the complete surprise of Judaism, the *talmidim* (disciples) of *Yeshua* discovered (*after the resurrection* of *Yeshua*) that the great Egyptian Passover was not just the foundational birth of Judaism, but that underlying the Passover narrative resided a hidden prophetic paradigm. It forecast precisely the role that God's Messiah would undertake (namely, as the "lamb of God"). Furthermore, the disciples also learned that *Yeshua's* sacrifice had accomplished a redemption which was not limited to Jews, but in this case, embracing the *entire world*—on a global scale—far exceeding the Egyptian Passover! The monumental foundation of Judaism (the Egyptian Passover) had turned out to be but a mere microcosm of something on a far grander scale: namely, redemption for the world—not solely for the people of Israel!

(Does God *only* care for Jews? Does God not also care for the world? Wouldn't it make sense then that God would offer to reach out, providing the opportunity of redemption to the world? This was the mission of *Yeshua*.)

Shim'on Kefa (Simon Peter) wrote:

> For you know that **you were redeemed . . . by precious blood, as of a lamb without spot** [unblemished by sin], **the blood of Messiah** (Shimon Kefa 1:18/1 Peter 1:18 MW, emphasis added).

Sha'ul (*Paulos*) wrote:

> **Messiah, our Passover Lamb, has been sacrificed** (1 Cor. 5:7 TLV, emphasis added).

Yochanan (John) wrote:

> . . . *Yeshua* **the Messiah,** the just one. **He is the atoning sacrifice for our sins,** and not for ours only, **but also for the whole world.** (1 Yoḥanan/1 John 2:1-2 MW, emphasis added).

There is yet another momentous aspect to this. It is stunning to discover that **the historic Passover in Egypt prophetically forecast the *precise date on the Jewish calendar* when the Messiah would be executed—namely the 14ᵗʰ day of the Jewish month** *Aviv*! How did the Passover predict this? We find it recorded in twelfth chapter of the book of Exodus:

> "'This month *shall be* your beginning of months: it *shall be* the **first month of the year** to you. . . . 'Your lamb shall be without blemish . . . . 'Now you shall keep it until the **fourteenth day of the same month**. Then the whole assembly of the congregation of Israel shall **kill it at twilight.** 'And they shall take *some* of the blood and put it on the two doorposts and on the lintel of the houses where they eat it (Exod. 12:2,5-7 NKJV, emphasis added).

The Hebrew Scriptures designate the first month of the year by the name *Aviv* (Exod. 13:4). The word *aviv* means "green ear."[199] It refers to the *aviv* stage of ripeness of the barley crop which occurs during March or April.[200] The Biblical Jewish months were to begin with the visual sighting of the *waxing crescent* new moon.[201] Therefore the first

Jewish month of the year in Biblical times occurred when the new moon was sighted *and* the barley crop was simultaneously found to be in this stage of *aviv* ripeness (March or April). Thus, the Passover was to be sacrificed on the *fourteenth day of this first month* of the year (called the month *Aviv*) according to the Biblical Jewish calendar.

The term "Passover" (in its most literal sense) expressly refers to the sacrificial lamb itself and its slaying:

> Draw out and take you a lamb according to your families, and **kill the passover** (Exod. 12:21 KJV, emphasis added).

The commandment furthermore specified the *specific time of day* when the Passover was to be sacrificed. *And that, as it turned out, resolved into an impressive, prophetic forecast. It presaged the precise time of day when the Messiah would be executed*:

> Then the whole assembly of the congregation of Israel is to **kill it** [i.e. the Passover lamb] **at twilight** (Exod. 12:6 NASB, emphasis added).

The Hebrew expression here translated as "twilight" is *beiyn haarbayim*. This is an extremely unique phrase within the Hebrew Scriptures. It literally means "between two evenings." According to *Torah Moshe* (the Law and instruction of Moses—the first five books of the Bible), the Jewish day begins after sunset at evening and extends until after the close of the next sunset at evening. The Hebrew expression *beiyn haarbayim* ("between two evenings") was interpreted by the Pharisees in a manner where when the sun initially begins to descend was called the "first evening," and the actual sunset was called the "second evening." The *beiyn haarbayim* would be the time "between the two evenings." [202] First century Jewish historian *Yosef ben Matityahu* (more famously known by the name Flavius Josephus) was born 37 A.D./C.E.—just a few years after the crucifixion of *Yeshua*. He chronicled that the Jewish priests during the first century understood this expression *beiyn haarbayim* ("between the evenings") to be the time from the "ninth" to the "eleventh hour" of the day according to the Jewish first century reckoning of time (which would be 3:00 p.m. to 5:00 p.m. according to our modern time in the northern hemisphere, approximating the early spring season).[203]

Jewish historian Flavius Josephus recorded the following during the first century, identifying the time of day when the Passover was to be sacrificed:

> So these high priests, upon the coming of their feast which is called the **Passover, when they slay their sacrifices**, from the **NINTH HOUR** to the **ELEVENTH**, but so that a company not less than ten belong to every sacrifice . . . . (emphasis added)[204]

At this point we can begin to trace how all this played out when *Yeshua* was crucified. The book of Luke reported the time of the day when *Yeshua* actually died:

> It was now about the sixth hour, and darkness came over the whole land until **THE NINTH HOUR**.[205] The sun was darkened, and the veil of the Temple was torn in two. Crying with a loud voice, *Yeshua* said, "Father, into Your hands I commit my spirit!" Having said this, he breathed his last (Luke 23:44-46 MW, emphasis added).

This text clearly identifies that it was the "**ninth hour**" (3:00 p.m. by our modern time reckoning) when *Yeshua* died. This was the *beiyn haarbayim*, the **ninth hour** of the day that first century Jewish historian Flavius Josephus reported that they would begin to slay the Passover sacrifice at the Temple. **It confirms that *Yeshua* died at the very hour**

(the ninth hour) prophetically foreshadowed by the Passover.
Significantly, this was the same hour that matched when the flower
Capparis aegyptia (found on the Shroud) was picked to prepare for the
burial. The buds of this flower begin to gradually bloom open about
midday and becomes fully opened about a half hour before sunset.
Once the flower is picked, the buds remain at that stage of opening
(unless water is added). The degree of opening of this flower's buds
(as found on the Shroud) indicates that it was picked to gather floral
preparations for burial upon death at about 3:00 p.m. modern time
(which would be the "ninth hour" according to first century Jewish
reckoning).

However, what was the date? Is there any evidence available
confirming which *date* it was on the Jewish calendar when *Yeshua* was
executed? Did the crucifixion occur on the 14th day of the first month
Aviv—the date when the Passover was to be sacrificed?

The ancient Jewish b. Talmud has a tractate titled *"Sanhedrin."* This
tractate recorded information from the Jewish ruling body of the first
century called the Sanhedrin. It was the Sanhedrin that presided over
the Jewish trial of *Yeshua*. The oldest surviving complete b. Talmud
manuscript (the Munich Talmud[206]) reports in tractate Sanhedrin 43a
that *Yeshua* of Nazareth was executed on the **"eve of the Passover."**
That would be the 14th day of the month *Aviv* when the Passover was
to be sacrificed.

(Note: Galilean Jews with their unique dialect pronounced the name
"Yeshua" as *"Yeshu."*[207] Likewise, other Jews sometimes pronounced
the name as *"Yeshu"* as a shortened form of the name *Yeshua*. See
notes for more detailed information about the name *Yeshu*[208]).

The ancient Jewish b. Talmud records the following in tractate
Sanhedrin 43a:

> **On the eve of the Passover they hung** [i.e. by crucifixion, Acts 5:30, 10:39] ***Yeshu* the *Notzri*** [i.e. *Yeshu* the Nazarene]. [Cf. b. Talmud Sanhedrin 43a, manuscript Munich. See also end notes for valuable additional information.[209]].

> (The above Hebrew word *Notzri* is a variant of the Hebrew word *Natzrati* meaning "Nazarene." However, in modern times the Hebrew word *notzri* is most commonly used to mean "Christian.")

With this record from ancient times, we have historic Jewish documentation passed down from the Sanhedrin itself (*the very ruling body that presided over the Jewish trial of Yeshua*).[210] It clearly states that: ***"Yeshu* the Nazarene"** was executed **"on the *eve of the Passover."*** Thus, both the date on the Jewish calendar (the **"14th day of month *Aviv"***) and the hour of day (the **"ninth hour"** according to first century Jewish reckoning) of *Yeshua's* crucifixion death are both authenticated from two of the most highly esteemed Jewish sources of antiquity: namely, the writings of first century Jewish historian Flavius Josephus, and the Sanhedrin tractate of the Jewish b. Talmud.

However, the gospels reported that the Last Supper *prior* to *Yeshua's* crucifixion was a Passover supper. If *Yeshua's* Last Supper was a Passover supper, wouldn't that indicate that the Passover lambs would have been sacrificed *before Yeshua* ate the Last Supper (a Passover meal)? Wouldn't that signify that *Yeshua* was crucified on the next day *after* the Passover was sacrificed? Is this a contradiction? It is not a contradiction. Although most every item of the Passover ritual is mentioned in the various gospel accounts of the Last Supper, the most important and symbolic item of the Passover meal is missing: namely, there is not one mention of the Passover *lamb* in *any* of the various gospel narratives of the Last Supper!

It is well documented that during the first century various Jewish sects held differing views and interpretations regarding the Jewish calendar and what day the Passover should be observed.[211] Likewise, the Jewish Jerusalem Talmud documents that there were differences of opinions between Jewish sects about when the new moon was visually observed. That too could alter which day was to be the first day of a new month according to the Jewish calendar. The Dead Sea Scrolls also reveal that the first century Qumran community used a different 364-day calendar.[212] In summation, it is a fact that various Jewish sects during the first century followed various *calendrical differences*, including which day was to be the day of Passover. However, the Law of Moses (*Torah Moshe*) did command that the "whole assembly of the congregation" must kill the Passover **together at the same time**:

> And you shall keep it [i.e. the Passover lamb] until the fourteenth day of the same month, then the **whole assembly of the congregation of Israel** is to kill it at twilight (Exod. 12: 6 NASB, emphasis added).

During the first century, the *Bet Din* court in Jerusalem held the sole authority to "sanctify the new moon" declaring which day was the official day of the new moon (i.e. the first day of a new month) pertaining to all activities performed at the Temple where the sacrifices were offered.[213] The *Bet Din* court held this authority which was authorized by the Law of Moses.[214] It was their pronouncement which established which day would be the official day for the Passover sacrifice at the Temple for the entire nation. *All* the various Jewish sects—even with their differing calendrical interpretations— had to adhere to this specific day declared by *Bet Din* court as to what day would be the official day for the Passover sacrifice at the Temple.

Torah Moshe (the Law of Moses) commanded that Jews may only sacrifice and eat the Passover at the place that God had chosen (Deut. 16:2,5-7)—namely, the Passover could *only* be sacrificed at the Temple in Jerusalem. As a result, those Jews who lived too far away from the

Temple (such as Jews of the Diaspora who resided in various foreign nations) had for centuries prior to *Yeshua* developed a tradition of eating a Passover supper *without* the Passover lamb.[215] *In fact, the expression "eat the Passover" eventually came to be used loosely to refer to all suppers eaten during the entire week of the Feast of Unleavened Bread.*[216] Accordingly, since first century Jewish sects held conflicting calendrical interpretations or differences as to which day was to be the Passover, there was available for them this ancient Jewish tradition of observing a Passover supper *without* a Passover lamb. (All the various Jewish sects could observe a lambless Passover supper on whatever day suited them.)

The sanctifying of the new moon by the *Bet Din* court in Jerusalem officially determined the first day of a new month, which in turn determined the day/date for all offerings at the Temple. Sometimes the new moon sighting was difficult to determine. Cloud cover was a factor. (It was a requirement that the new moon sighting must be observed without *any* cloud covering it.[217]) The Jewish Talmud Yerushalmi in tractate Rosh Hashanah 2:1 (57d – 58a) reports that Jewish sects during the first century would sometimes have different opinions regarding when the new moon was sighted causing there to be differences of opinion about when the Passover was to be observed. This tractate also reports that witnesses would sometimes give false reports of sighting the new moon to distort the calendar in favor of their sect. In one case, the Pharisees caught the Jewish sect of the Boethusians bribing witnesses to give a false report as to which day the new moon was sighted.[218] This is an example of some of the calendrical differences between Jewish sects. Why would a witness seek to distort which day the new moon was sighted? Typically, it would be to manipulate the calendar for the Passover sacrifice in favor of a particular sect—especially between Pharisees, Sadducees, and Boethusians. The Talmud Yerushalmi tractate Rosh Hashanah reports that the officially sanctified day of the new moon determined by the *Bet Din* court for the Temple offerings *could not be changed once*

his Father's kingdom. (Hence, the association of the fourth cup with the theme of *kingship.*) *Yeshua* thus affirmed: "But I say to you, **I will never drink of this fruit of the vine from now on** [i.e. beginning from the omission of the 4th cup of the Passover], **until that day when I drink it anew with you in My Father's kingdom**" (Matt. 26:29 TLV, emphasis added). *Yeshua* never drank the fourth cup of wine of the Passover. He would wait until the momentous arrival of the *"Messianic Kingdom of God"*!

Originally, the Jewish *Afikoman* tradition existed for the purpose of symbolically representing the *missing* Passover lamb (the last bite to be eaten at the Passover meal) for those Jews of the Diaspora who lived too far away to come to Jerusalem to eat the Passover lambs sacrificed at the Temple. In the same manner, the *Afikoman* is still observed by Sephardic Jews in Israel to this day (because the Temple no longer exists, and therefore the *Korban Pesach* [Passover offering] cannot be sacrificed).[233] The fact that *Yeshua* followed this Jewish *Afikoman* tradition *confirms* that *Yeshua's* Last Supper was indeed a *lambless* Passover. The ancient Jewish Talmud Yerushalmi (Pesahim 10:8A) reports that when a Passover sacrificial offering lamb was eaten, the *Afikoman* tradition was *omitted*! If the Passover lambs had been sacrificed prior to *Yeshua's* Last Supper, and *Yeshua* failed to eat the Passover lamb, but instead substituted the lamb with the *Afikoman* (the symbolic representation of the *missing* Passover lamb) then *Yeshua* would have *sinned* by violating the Law of Moses because he was not residing in some far distant land but rather right in Jerusalem itself where the Passover lambs were to be sacrificed at the Temple.

In summation, the fact that *Yeshua* utilized the *Afikoman* tradition clearly *confirms* that the Passover lambs had not yet been sacrificed at the time of the Last Supper. The Last Supper, therefore, was one of those *lambless* Passover meals which utilized the Jewish *Afikoman* tradition to represent the *missing* Passover lamb (the last bite to be eaten at the Passover).

But as for the formal day for the Passover sacrifice at the Temple, the *Bet Din* court in Jerusalem held the sole jurisdiction for determining which day was to be the official 14th day of the month with regard to when the Passover was to be sacrificed at the Temple and eaten that night.[234] The *Bet Din* court in those days exercised the authority authorized by Moses (Deut 17:8-13). Their decision was in compliance with the Law of Moses which said that *"the whole assembly of the congregation* of Israel is to kill it [i.e. the Passover lamb] at twilight [between the evenings]"* (Exod. 12:6 NASB). All Jewish sects, *"the whole assembly of the congregation,"* regardless of their various calendrical interpretations, were to sacrifice the Passover lambs *together* at the Temple on the same day (identified by the *Bet Din* court in Jerusalem).

Yochanan (John) was one of *Yeshua's* very closest disciples. *Yochanan* (John) lived many years after the synoptic gospels (Matthew, Mark, and Luke) were written. He was very familiar with these gospels. He wrote the fourth and final gospel many decades after the synoptic gospels were written. His apparent mission for writing the fourth gospel was to record information that was not included in the three synoptic gospels (and in so doing he deliberately omitted redundant stories of the synoptic gospels. Also, another apparent reason for John's fourth gospel was to clarify misunderstandings from the synoptic gospels. John, a unique *first hand witness* of all these events, having thorough familiarity with the synoptic gospels, and having lived many decades after the three synoptic gospels were written, his clarifications (about the misunderstandings of the synoptic gospels) hold the ultimate cogent and authoritative weight wherever he makes a clarification. One of the misunderstandings that John's gospel clarifies was that *Yeshua* was indeed crucified on the very day when the Passover was sacrificed at the Temple. For example, on the morning when *Yeshua* was brought to the Roman governor Pontius Pilate, the Jewish authorities would not enter Pilate's Praetorium lest they be *ritually defiled* and thus forbidden to sacrifice or eat the Passover offering (which was to be sacrificed later that day and then eaten at evening after sunset). Below is how *Yochanan*/John reported this:

> Then they led *Yeshua* from Caiaphas [i.e. the high priest] to the Praetorium. It was early. They themselves did not enter the Praetorium, **so they would not become unclean** but **might eat the Passover**. Therefore Pilate came out to them and said, "What charge do you bring against this man? (John 18:28-29 TLV, emphasis added).

The above phrase "so they would not become *unclean* but might *eat the Passover*" is a Jewish expression that pertains to being ritually unclean/defiled (Hebrew: *tamei*) and thus disqualified by the Law of Moses from killing (or eating) the *Korban Pesach* (Passover sacrifice). (This expression did not apply to eating a lambless Passover supper. It applied *only* to sacrificing and eating the actual Passover sacrifice lambs offered at the Temple.) The reference for this commandment is found in Numbers 9:4-12:

> So Moses told the Israelites to celebrate the Passover, and they did so in the Desert of Sinai at twilight on the fourteenth day of the first month. The Israelites did everything just as the LORD [YHVH] commanded Moses. But **some of them could not celebrate the Passover on that day because they were ceremonially unclean** [Heb. *tamei*, unclean] on account of [touching] a dead body. So they came to Moses and Aaron that same day and said to Moses, **"We have become unclean** [Heb. *tamei*, unclean] **because of** [touching] **a dead body**, but **why should we be kept from presenting the LORD'S** [YHVH] [Passover] **offering** with other Israelites at the appointed time? (Num. 9:4-7 NIV, emphasis added).

John documents that the Jews would "not enter the Praetorium so they would not become **unclean** but might eat the Passover" (John

18:28-29 TLV). This makes it *unmistakable* that the day of *Yeshua's* trial was the very day when the Passover was to be sacrificed at the Temple later that same day. It was the *only* day of the year when the entire congregation of Israel was permitted (and commanded) to kill the Passover together (regardless of calendrical differences between various Jewish sects). But anyone "unclean" or "defiled" was forbidden to sacrifice (or eat) the Passover lamb that day.

Yochanan (John) also provided two additional references in his gospel confirming that the trial of *Yeshua* occurred on the day when they were preparing to kill the Passover.

> So when Pilate heard these words, he brought *Yeshua* out and sat down on the judge's seat at a place called the Stone Pavement (but in Aramaic, Gabbatha). It was the **Day of Preparation for Passover** . . . . (John 19:13-14 TLV, emphasis added. I.e. It was the day of *preparation* for the Passover sacrifice).

> He [Pilate] went out again to the Judean leaders. He said to them, "I find no case against Him [*Yeshua*]. But it's your custom that I release someone for you **at Passover**. So do you want me to release to you the King of the Jews? (John 18:39 TLV, emphasis added).

These citations from John, transpiring on the day when *Yeshua* was to be crucified, confirm that *Yeshua* was indeed executed on the day when the Passover was to be sacrificed at the Temple.

Like pieces of a puzzle now assembled in place, we can begin to witness the omnipotent hand of God. His sovereign and majestic engineering begins to come into focus. Centuries earlier, the original historic event of the Egyptian Passover in Egypt prophetically prefigured the *very date on the Jewish calendar* and the *very hour of the day* when the redemption sacrifice of God's Messiah (the Lamb of God) would take place. After *Yeshua* resurrected *El'azar* (Lazarus), the

Jewish authorities feared for the loss of their political power, influence, and control over the Jewish community. *Yeshua* was becoming too popular amongst the Jewish people:

> And so the multitude who were with Him [*Yeshua*] when He called Lazarus out of the tomb, and raised him from the dead, were bearing Him witness. For this cause also **the multitude** went and met Him, because they heard that He had performed this sign. The Pharisees therefore said to one another, "**You see that you are not doing any good; look, the world has gone after Him**" (John 12:17-19 NASB, emphasis added).

The Jewish political authorities then became urgent to kill *Yeshua*—fearing his influence over the Jewish community:

> Then the ruling *kohanim* [priests] and elders of the people were gathered together in the court of the *kohen gadol* [high priest] named Caiaphas. They plotted together in order that they might seize *Yeshua* by stealth and kill Him. "**But not during the festival** [Passover]," **they were saying, "so there won't be a riot among people.**" (Matt. 26:3-5 TLV, emphasis added).

The Jewish political authorities carefully plotted to kill *Yeshua*: secretly. However, *they deliberately planned to avoid doing this during the Passover* for fear that it would cause a riot—due to the adulation of *Yeshua* among the Jewish community. Notwithstanding, the betrayal by Judas during the Last Supper forced the hand of the Jewish authorities to seize *Yeshua* ahead of their plan—at the very time they wanted to avoid—namely, on the morning when the Passover was to be sacrificed later that same day (John 13:21-30).[n] Contrary to their scheme, the omnipotent hand of God was at work.

Previously, the *Bet Din* court at Jerusalem had already officially proclaimed that this day was the *fourteenth day* of the first month (*Aviv*)—the day for the Passover sacrifice at the Temple. And it was forbidden to change this date.[235] At the sixth hour (noon by our time), when the sun should have been at its brightest, the sky grew eerily dark—while *Yeshua* hung on the cross. In obedience to the Law of Moses, upon the **ninth hour** (according to first century Jewish reckoning—3:00 p.m. by modern time), the Jews were commanded to begin slaying the Passover lambs at the Temple. The *date on the Jewish calendar*, and *the hour of day* prophetically prefigured by the original historic Passover in Egypt had now arrived:

> It was now about the sixth hour, and darkness fell over the whole land until the **NINTH HOUR** [i.e. *the ninth hour* when it became time to begin sacrificing the Passover lambs], for the sun died out. And the curtain of the Temple was torn in two. And *Yeshua*, crying out with a loud voice, said, "Father, 'into Your hands I entrust My spirit.'" When He had said this, **He breathed His last.** Now when the centurion saw what had happened, he began glorifying God, saying, "Truly this was a righteous Man." And all the crowds assembled for this spectacle, when they saw what had happened, began to turn back, beating their breasts (Luke 23:44-48 TLV, emphasis added).

Sha'ul (*Paulos*) wrote to the Corinthians: "Messiah, our Passover Lamb, has been sacrificed" (1 Cor. 5:7 TLV). However, the Law of Moses mandated a unique stipulation regarding the Passover offering which did not apply to *any* of the *other* Jewish sacrifices. This

---

[n] John's gospel adds clarification about the Last Supper. The disciples thought Judas had left the Last Supper to "buy the things we have need of for the feast" (John 13:29 NASB). This infers that they expected to eat the actual Passover sacrifice the next day.

stipulation *only* applied to the Passover: namely, *no bone of the Passover lamb was to be broken*. The Law of Moses states:

> It [i.e. the Passover lamb] is to be eaten in a single house; you are not to bring forth any of the flesh outside of the house, **nor are you to break any bone of it** (Exod. 12:46 NASB, emphasis added).

> They shall leave none of it until morning, **nor break a bone of it**; according to all the statute of the Passover they shall observe it (Num. 9:12 NASB, emphasis added).

Per statute of *Torah Moshe* (the Law of Moses), the evening after the Passover sacrifice initiated the start of the next Jewish day (the 15th of the month *Aviv*), which was to be a day forbidden to work (Lev. 23:7). The Pharisees interpreted that this was to be treated as a *festival Sabbath* (i.e. not the normal 7th day Sabbath, but rather a "festival Sabbath": the first day of the Feast of Unleavened Bread — Lev 23:6-7). As they began preparing for this *festival Sabbath*, bear in mind that the Law of Moses had commanded that *not one bone of the Passover lamb was to be broken!* Although *Yeshua* had died, the hand of God was still at work:

> It was the Day of Preparation, and the next day [i.e. that evening after sunset, the 15th of *Aviv*] was a **festival *Shabbat*.** So that the bodies should not remain on the execution stake during *Shabbat*, **the Judean leaders asked Pilate to have the legs broken** and to have the bodies taken away. So **the soldiers came and broke the legs of the first and then the other** who had been executed with *Yeshua* [i.e. to hasten their death]. Now when they came to *Yeshua* and saw that He was already dead, **they did not break His legs**. But one of the soldiers pierced His side with a spear, and immediately blood and water came out . . . These things happened so that the Scriptures would be fulfilled, "**Not a bone of His shall be broken**. And again another Scripture says, "They shall look on

119

Him whom they have pierced." (John 19:31-34 TLV, emphasis added, cf. Exod. 12:46; Zech. 12:10).

With this report, we again confront God's intervention (independent of any initiative on the part of *Yeshua*). God was framing His Messiah as the Passover Lamb. In doing so, God thwarted the schemes of *Yeshua's* enemies:

(1) The Jewish political authorities had requested the Romans to break the legs of *Yeshua* and the two others who were crucified with him. Once the legs are broken, a crucified victim would be unable to push and pull off the spikes to breath and would soon die. Subsequently, the two criminals on either side of *Yeshua* have their legs broken—but not *Yeshua*. He was the Lamb whose bones the commandment of the Passover had forbidden to be broken (Exod. 12:46). He was already dead. So instead the Roman soldiers pierced his side to confirm he was dead. (Like the crown cap of thorns, this post mortem pierce wound to the side was another one of those atypical crucifixion wounds—unique to *Yeshua*).

(2) Previously, *Yeshua's* disciple Judas had betrayed *Yeshua* at the Last Supper in order to inform the Jewish political authorities where they could find and arrest *Yeshua*. This discomfited the scheme of the Sanhedrin who would then be forced to seize and kill *Yeshua* ahead of their plan: namely, on the very day they wanted to avoid (the Passover) lest the people riot (Matt. 26:3-5). But this was the date that God had foreordained for the Messiah's Passover death.

(3) Ultimately, *Yeshua* died at the precise hour (the "ninth hour" by first century Jewish reckoning) when the Jews would begin to slay the Passover lambs at the Temple

(Luke 23:44-46). The Pharisees would then eventually document within the Talmud tractate Sanhedrin (from the Sanhedrin's report) the date of *Yeshua's* crucifixion as occurring on the "eve of the Passover" (i.e. the 14th day of the month *Aviv*). This documentation was something the enemies of *Yeshua* would eventually regret, as it provided corroboration from *Yeshua's* enemies confirming the prophetic Passover scenario. (Evidence exists of messy attempts to erase this from various Talmud manuscripts prior to the invention of the printing press. See PDF within note 209.)

The foregoing affords additional thematic examples where God is found overriding human affairs to demonstrate His sovereign substantiation of *Yeshua's* Messianic credentials.

It is self-evident that God exquisitely crafted His plan for world redemption; to wit, meticulously coordinating its execution, spanning its unfolding events and its typology over centuries and millenniums, conscripting *Yeshua's* enemies to accomplish key objectives, and linking together its ultimate results with prophetic themes, and precision of timing.

There is nothing like this in any other religion of the world:

(1) In what other religion is there a relic like the Shroud of Turin which baffles science, and where the modern technology of the world cannot reproduce its like?

(2) In what other religion did any other so-called god intervene into *actual* human history of an *actual* historic nation forcibly coercing the most powerful kingdom on earth at that time (ancient Egypt) and the most powerful emperor of the world (Pharaoh) to accomplish his purpose—then once finished with that nation (Egypt),

annihilated their entire military(!) without a firing a shot, drowning them in the sea. What other so-called god impacted actual human history like that?

(The Egyptian Pharaoh had previously given the decree: "Every Hebrew boy that is born you must throw into the Nile [i.e. drown], but let every girl live." Yet eventually, once Pharaoh's army pursues to attack the Israelites who were fleeing from Egypt, God ultimately intercedes. This time we find it is the *Egyptian males* who are now the ones *drowning* in the sea, which the Israelites had just passed through on dry ground—the entire Egyptian military, including specifically Pharaoh himself *drowned* in the sea [Ex. 1:22 NIV; 14:23-28.])

(3) In what other religion of the world is there a prophetic model like Passover which figuratively depicts (by means of powerful *historic* events in Egypt) how to obtain a relationship with God (i.e. *how to be redeemed* to become one of God's people).

(4) And then prophetically prefigures how God's Messiah would accomplish this redemption (by becoming God's *Passover redemption Lamb).*

(5) And then *foreshadows the specific date on the Jewish calendar,* and *forecasts the precise time of the day* (Hebrew: *beiyn haarbayim,* the 9th hour by Jewish time reckoning[236]) when *Yeshua* would die and when Jews would begin to slay the Passover at the Temple— **prophetically predicting this exact "date" and this precise "hour" ONE THOUSAND FIVE HUNDRED YEARS IN ADVANCE!**

There is nothing like this in *any* other religion in the world.

With reference to historical evidence of the "drowning annihilation of Egypt's powerful military by God without firing a shot," Egyptologist David Rohl has expounded concerning what happened next to Egypt. Egyptologist Rohl recounts from the written historic chronicles of the ancient Egyptian Priest Manetho via Rohl's quotation from first century Jewish historian Flavius Josephus the following Egyptian historical record concerning **the plagues of Egypt** and **a subsequent invasion of Egypt by foreign invaders**. Ancient Egyptian Priest Manetho documented:

> In his reign [i.e. *Tutimaos / Dudimose*: the Pharaoh who opposed Moses (according to the latest updated Egyptian chronology)] . . . **a blast of God** [not "gods" plural] smote us [cf. the Biblical plagues that befell Egypt], **and unexpectedly, from the regions of the East,** ○ **invaders of obscure race marched in confidence of victory against our land** [Egypt]. By main force **they easily seized it** [i.e. easily seized formerly powerful Egypt] **without striking a blow**. (Emphasis added.)[237]

How could the world's most powerful kingdom (Egypt) surrender to foreign invaders "without" the invaders "striking a blow"? Answer: Egypt's military had been decimated (drowned in the sea—Exod. 14).

(Readers are encouraged to obtain a DVD or digital copy of the multi award-winning movie documentary *Patterns of Evidence: Exodus*— winner of thirteen awards.[P] The old chronology of Egypt was formulated long ago during the 1800's. Since then, vast, abundant, and impressive archeological findings have been uncovered in Egypt. This correlates remarkably with the recently updated Egyptian

---

○ Rohl references medieval authors of Arabia who wrote that the Hykos invaders of Egypt were the Amalekites. This would coincide with the Biblical record where the Amalekites battled in warfare against the Israelites soon after their departure from Egypt (Ex. 17:8-13). David M. Rohl, *Pharaohs and Kings: A Biblical Quest* (New York: Crown Publishers, Inc., 1995), 286.

P https://patternsofevidence.com/

chronology. Frankly, any large population which is purported to have dwelt in a geographical location for hundreds of years *must inevitably* leave behind *vast* archeological evidence. If such archeological attestation does not exist, then that would seriously imply that the purported civilization never existed! The movie documentary encompasses all these matters, including interviews with many of the world's foremost Egyptologists. It examines archeological discoveries that support these events. It also reviews *surviving Egyptian papyrus documents, such as a list of Jewish slaves, and a detailed eyewitness Egyptian account matching the Biblical exodus narrative.* These Egyptian papyrus museum documents date to their Biblical periods of Egyptian history. They bear the unique hieroglyphic style, grammar, and literary figures dating from such times.)

We refer once more to recall the record from the Jewish Sanhedrin preserved in b. Talmud tractate Sanhedrin 43a from the oldest existing complete document of the b. Talmud (the Munich Talmud). It states:

> **On the eve of the Passover they hung** [i.e. by crucifixion] *Yeshu* **the** *Notzri* [i.e. *Yeshu* the Nazarene].(b Talmud Sanhedrin 43a, emphasis added.)[238]

This was the record from the Sanhedrin court which presided over the Jewish trial that condemned *Yeshua*.[239]

Among the many various types of sacrifices prescribed throughout the Hebrew Scriptures, the Passover was the *ONLY* **sacrifice** defined as a *redemption* **sacrifice**.[240] It forecast that climatic *date* and *hour* specifically appointed by God—from amid the entire span of human history—wherein God determined to accomplish His redemption for humanity.[241]

For those who are persuaded that the Turin Shroud is authentic, the Shroud exhibits this crowning event—such that future generations (some two thousand years later) could personally view this event (by looking back through the corridors of time) to behold with our own eyes this actual affair with the crucified Lamb of God *three-dimensionally displayed* from the two-dimensional Shroud cloth. It presents as though it was proffered a gift from God, so that we might see God's redemption Lamb for ourselves, and also personally witness the moment of his resurrection. Likewise, it is ponderous to reflect that the Shroud should thus represent **physical evidence** of life after death (radiated upon the *physical* Shroud by the event of the resurrection). We can see it with our eyes; we can touch it with our hands; we can visit it in Turin, Italy—a physical by-product of resurrection—left behind from the very One who repeatedly promised life after death.

The *Pesach* offering in Egypt was also unique from among all the other various sacrificial offerings in the Law of Moses by one other surprising respect: namely, the original Passover in Egypt was the *only* sacrifice specifically recognized in the Hebrew Scriptures as producing an effect which transcended beyond its moment in history—so that its redemption effect reached throughout to future generations. (Imagine this: an historic sacrifice accomplishing an ongoing perpetual effect throughout future generations.) In this regard, the Creator instructed the Jews that once they eventually entered the Promised Land, they were to continue to teach subsequent generations to annually honor the historic Passover in Egypt as the sacrifice that redeemed them (future generations) to become God's own people/nation throughout their *forthcoming generations*. The commandment specified that future Israelites were to annually celebrate the Egyptian Passover as though they were *personally present* at the event in Egypt—for this was the occasion in Egypt wherein God redeemed future Israeli generations—as well as the historic generation that lived back in Egypt (Exodus 13:1-8).

> And Moses said to the people, "Remember this day in which you went out from Egypt. . . . And it shall be **when the LORD [YHVH] brings you to the land** . . . which He swore to your fathers to give you . . . that you shall observe this rite in this month. . . . **And you shall tell your son on that day, saying, 'It is because of what the LORD [YHVH] did for ME when I CAME OUT OF EGYPT.'** . . . Therefore, you shall keep this ordinance at its appointed time from year to year." (Exod. 13:3, 5, 8, 10 NASB, emphasis added).

Even to this day, the tradition (wherein Jews consider themselves as being personally present during the historic Egyptian Passover) remains in modern times a prominent feature within the Jewish Passover liturgy.[242]

Five centuries after the event in Egypt we read how *melech David* (King David) gave glory to God for the ongoing redemption of his people/nation throughout their generations who were redeemed specifically by that *original* historic Passover in Egypt (1 Chron. 17:16,21-22).

The historic Egyptian Passover (which procured redemption for ongoing Jewish generations) in like manner prophetically foreshadowed the ultimate Passover offering of *Yeshua*. Like the Egyptian Passover (but this time on a far grander scale) the Pesach offering of *Yeshua* likewise provided a redemption which transcended *all* generations—not just for *future generations* but now also for *past generations* who embraced God by faith (Hebrews chapter 11), and not just for *Israelites*, but now for *all the world!* The great Passover event in Egypt, which had brought about the birth of Israel as God's nation/people, had turned out to be but a mere microcosm of God's consummate redemption on a far grander scale—redemption provided for *all humanity!*—not just for Israelites. **It is manifest that the Passover was God's blueprint plan for the redemption of the world. The Passover had met its ultimate fulfillment in Messiah.**

> But this Man [*Yeshua*] after He had offered **one sacrifice for sins forever**, sat down at the right hand of God . . . **For by one offering He has perfected forever** those who are being **sanctified** (Heb 10:12, 14 NKJV, emphasis added).

Sha'ul (*Paulos*) wrote:

> **Messiah, our Passover Lamb, has been sacrificed** (1 Cor. 5:7 TLV, emphasis added).

Yochanan (John) wrote:

> . . . *Yeshua* the Messiah, the just one. **He is the atoning sacrifice for our sins**, and **not for ours only, but also for the whole world** (Yoḥanan/John 2:2 MW, emphasis added).

People tend to assume that the "crucifixion" was a fortuitous choice made by God as to how to provide redemption for humanity. But this choice was not random, at all. We have seen how the Passover was a prophetic blueprint for our redemption. Furthermore, back in **chapter 17** we discovered that **the panoramic scene at the crucifixion sight was filled with numerous visible symbolisms, fashioning a profound symbolic metaphor**. The visual symbolisms at the crucifixion scene pointed all the way back, specifically spanning the entire breath of human history, precisely extending back to the Garden of Eden, reminiscing of the origin of sin, and recollective of the curses resulting from sin. It then juxtaposed this symbolic display of the curses of sin side-by-side with God's provision of redemption for humanity upon the cross—all of this visually depicted at the scene of the cross. The crucifixion scene was not some random, haphazard event. It was engineered!

Also associated with the Passover was the *Omer Reishiyt* offering—the *sheaf of first fruits* of the barley harvest. This "first fruits" offering was always scheduled on the Jewish Biblical calendar to be presented at the Temple during Passover week (Lev. 23:5-11) on the day **after** the weekly Sabbath day (i.e. Sunday, Lev. 23:5-11) during the Feast of Unleavened Bread.q [243] This was another major milestone of the mission of the Messiah! And here we find, once again, that this event of the *"first fruits"* barley offering prophetically forecast *one thousand five hundred years in advance* the EXACT DAY ON THE JEWISH CALENDAR for the RESURRECTION: namely, "Messiah, the *FIRST FRUITS* from the *DEAD*." All this transpired precisely on its scheduled *day* of the Jewish Biblical calendar during the month of *Aviv*. **Sha'ul/Paulos cited this "First Fruits" fulfillment to the Corinthians:**

> But now **Messiah has been raised from the dead**. He became the **FIRST FRUITS** of those who are asleep . . . For as in Adam all die, so also in the Messiah all will be made alive, but each in his own order—**Messiah**, the **FIRST FRUITS**, then those who are the Messiah's at his coming (1 Cor. 15:20, 22-23 MW, emphasis added).

Could the prophetic timing of the *Passover date* of the crucifixion, and now, here again, this *first fruits day* of the resurrection both be a coincidence of timing? These were both epic events. And yet each had been foreshadowed from the Law of Moses some fifteen centuries in advance—now fulfilled on their exact days.

---

q The *Tz'dukim* (Sadducees) controlled the Temple with its rituals and affairs. This was their scriptural interpretation (Lev. 23:5-11) and edict as to when the barley first fruits were to be offered at the Temple: namely, on the first day of the week (Sunday) during the Feast of Unleavened Bread. End reference note 221 has very important information about this.

How the Shroud Intersected with the Passover Theme

As to how the Shroud of Turin relates to Passover, we have seen in Chapter 13 that there exists a combined variety of species of pollen identified on the Shroud which reside together only in one geographical location in the entire world: the region embracing 10-20 km (16 to 32 miles) from east to west of Jerusalem. Furthermore, these flower species bloom releasing their pollen during the season of the Passover when *Yeshua* was crucified. In addition, the floral images of the flower *Capparis aegyptia* (identified on the Shroud) indicated (from the degree of opening of their buds) that the flowers were picked at the same hour when *Yeshua* died (when preparations would begin for his burial). This was also the same time of day (the 9th hour by first century Jewish reckoning, 3:00-4:00 p.m. by modern time) when the Passover was being sacrificed at the Temple. (See chapter 13 for details.)

People today admire God's creation, the beauty of nature, the constellation of stars at night, and life (both of plants and creatures) with all their exquisite elaborateness, variety, and design. In the same manner God has also orchestrated humanity's redemption with that same magnificence.

Chapter 21

OBSERVING THE HAND OF GOD
AT WORK

The common experience of human life is that it is typically haphazard, and often frustrating. For example, you may have faced the dilemma of being late for something important . . . and not finding an available place to park your car! You drive up and down stressed to find a parking spot. At last you find one, and then someone else pulls into it just before you get there. This is the typical frustrating human experience.

In contrast, when it comes to fulfilling God's plan of redemption through His Messiah, the sovereign hand of God's engineering comes into view. It is truly impressive to see this in action. Again, this is unlike anything found in any other religion.

Notice, from the following citations, the vicious brutality and distain wherewith the guards lavished their arrogant power over *Yeshua*:

> Now the men who were guarding *Yeshua* began mocking and beating Him. They blindfolded Him and kept asking Him, saying, "Prophesy! Who is the one who hit You?" And reviling Him, they were saying many other things against Him (Luke 22:63-65 TLV).

> And after he [Pilate] had *Yeshua* scourged, he handed Him over to be crucified. Then the governor's soldiers took *Yeshua* into the Praetorium and gathered the whole cohort around Him. They stripped Him and put a scarlet robe around Him. And **after braiding a crown of thorns, they placed it on His head** and put a staff in His right hand. And falling on their knees before Him, they mocked Him, saying, "Hail, King of the Jews!" They spat on Him,

and they took the staff and beat Him over and over on the head
[while he wore the crown cap of thorns]. When they finished
mocking Him . . . they led Him away to crucify Him (Matt. 27:26-
31 TLV, emphasis added).

The seventy-sixth Psalm declares: **"Surely the wrath of man shall
praise You** [i.e. praise God]" (Ps. 76:10 NKJV, emphasis added). Little
did the Roman soldiers realize while heaping their abuse upon *Yeshua*
that two thousand years later the pierce thorn wounds on the head
from the crown cap of thorns, and the pollen grains from that thorn
plant (*Gundelia Tournefortii*) would provide a unique marker toward
confirming the identity of the victim on the Shroud. The pollen also
identified: (1) the season of the year of the crucifixion (March-April,
the time of the Passover when this flower blooms), and (2) the
geographical location (16 to 32 miles east and west of Jerusalem)
where this plant resides. No other man in *recorded history* ever wore a
crown of thorns—other than *Yeshua*—because he was specifically
mocked as the King of the Jews.[244] In spite of their intended abuse, the
wrath of the Roman soldiers had ended up serving God's purpose. It
provided evidence pointing toward identification of the victim on the
Shroud: namely, the blood trails from the thorns on the head and its
unique thorn pollen (*Gundelia Tournefortii*) found on the Shroud.
"Surely the wrath of man shall praise You" (Ps. 76:10 NKJV,
emphasis added).

There was a rush to get *Yeshua* buried before the evening. Fortunately,
one of *Yeshua's* disciples was a very rich man: *Yosef ha Ramatayim*
(Joseph of Arimathea). Joseph had coincidently already paid a hefty
price to have his personal tomb hewn out of the limestone rock
nearby, and so he offered to have *Yeshua* buried in his nearby tomb. It
was a privilege to be buried in the limited vicinity of the Temple
Mount. Only a rich man like Joseph could afford that. *Little did Joseph
of Arimathea know that this would fulfill the prophesy found in the Dead Sea
Scroll of Isaiah 53, the Great Isaiah Scroll* (1QIsa-a) MT which specific
scroll is dated by scholars as copied by scribes about 125 B.C.E where

it says that his grave was "with a rich man *his* tomb" (Isa. 53:9).[245] This prophecy (as originally written by Isaiah seven centuries prior to *Yeshua*) was thus fulfilled.

Apparently *Yeshua's* feet were dragged across the floor as they drew him into the tomb. His feet collected limestone from the floor of the tomb. That limestone then became deposited on the feet area of the Shroud. *Whoever dragged Yeshua with his feet along the floor of the tomb had no idea that 2,000 years later scientists would discover this limestone on the feet area of Shroud image.* The scientists tested the limestone of *ten different limestone tombs* throughout the land of Israel. Yet *only* the rock shelf hosting both the Holy Sepulcher and the Garden Tomb (where *Yeshua* is thought to have been buried) contained this rare *travertine aragonite* form of limestone found on the Shroud. None of the other nine limestone tombs tested throughout the land of Israel matched the type of limestone found on the Shroud.[246]

Before securing the Shroud over the ventral (front) of the body, *Yeshua's* followers arranged flowers next to the body. *They could not have imagined that 2,000 years later the significance* of how the flowers placed within the Shroud would include the floral specie *Capparis aegyptia* (which flower buds begin to bloom open at midday and become fully opened about a half-hour before sunset). This would provide evidence (2,000 years later) pointing to the time of death when preparations for the burial would begin. Its floral images on the Shroud correspond to the degree of opening of the buds at around 3:00 p.m. to 4:00 p.m.[247] (the time of day by modern time reckoning when *Yeshua* died and when they would begin gathering flowers for the burial). Such budding ceases its process of opening once the flower is picked (unless water is added).[248] Also the "wilted state" of flowers viewed on the Shroud indicate that a couple days had elapsed since the flowers had been picked until the time when the image was radiated onto the Shroud.

Yeshua's disciples undoubtedly had no idea that the Pontius Pilate coins placed over the eyes would be noticed 2,000 years later when scientists would be viewing the three dimensional image of the Shroud and discover what appeared to be buttons over the eyes—drawing their attention to discover the apparent extremely significant Pontius Pilate coins over the eyes.

Little did the artisan who crafted the Lirey Pilgrim Medallions as souvenirs for the visitors from surrounding nations (who came to view the Shroud expositions in Lirey, France during the 1300's) realize that the medallion would one day provide visual confirmation centuries later that the Shroud which today resides in Turin, Italy is the same Shroud that existed during the 1300's in Lirey, France.

Only now, with 2,000 years hindsight, can we begin to see how significant these haphazard, unwitting human interactions of *Yeshua's* followers were (as well as those of his enemies). They have dovetailed together millenniums later with seemingly exquisite design. This was not merely one coincidence—this was a series of important incidents from a variety of players (including enemies of *Yeshua*) who were oblivious to the profound significance that their actions would bear millenniums later. This is not how normal, frustrating, random, human experiences work. Yet this exemplifies how God interacts within human affairs when He intervenes with sovereignty and precision on behalf of His Messiah.

(On a personal level, sometimes we too—like the first century disciples—are unaware of ways in which God's hand is personally guiding and directing our lives for His purpose and glory.)

Chapter 22

OBJECTIVES OF THE SHROUD

E ven if the Shroud was proven to be a medieval forgery, it would not alter the truth of the Messiah known from traditional sources. However, if the Shroud is authentic, then God has left behind this one crowning miracle of *Yeshua* which future generations could personally witness for themselves—a miracle which could be subjected to modern scientific scrutiny. And it is not solely a miracle. For those who consider the Shroud to be authentic, the Shroud also appears designed to indicate an additional underlying purpose. **For it is not insignificant that the story of the Shroud** *cannot possibly be told without also reciting the account of Yeshua's crucifixion death, burial, and resurrection.* (Is that by chance?) This may represent an implied directive from the Shroud expressed without words. The inferred directive would ostensibly imply that the Shroud is intended to be used as a fulcrum for communicating *the story of the gospel — the good news* (Heb. *hab'sora*).[r]

Sha'ul/Paulos wrote the following summation defining distinctly what constitutes the "good news" (the gospel):

> Moreover, brethren, I declare to you **THE GOSPEL** which I preached to you, which also you received and in which you stand, by which also you are saved . . . For I delivered to you first of all that which I also received: that **Christ DIED for our sins** according to the Scriptures, and that **He was BURIED,** and that He **ROSE AGAIN** the third day[s]. . . . (1 Cor. 15:1-4 NKJV, emphasis added).

---

[r] Naturally, skeptics of the Shroud would not be expected to do this.
[s] Even the detail of being raised within three days is indicated from the Shroud in that the body still exhibits the effects of rigor mortis (which wear off after three days).

How can it be happenstance that the story of the Shroud *cannot possibly be told* without also explaining the report of the Messiah's (1) crucifixion death, (2) burial, and (3) resurrection—precisely the definition of the gospel (Heb. *hab'sora*) as defined by *Sha'ul/Paulos*?

If the Shroud is authentic, then would it not make sense that *Yeshua* would want the story of the Shroud to be told, and used as a platform to share the gospel (the good news)? The Shroud is also able to reach people who ordinarily would have no belief or respect for the Bible, and do so on terms (science) which they can relate to. Atheists, agnostics, Buddhists, Hindus, Muslims, and people from all walks of life and various religions have indeed found faith in *Yeshua* through the Shroud.

Remember, *Yeshua* affirmed that his works and miracles were meant to bear witness to His credentials:

> Now when John [a.k.a. John the Baptist] heard in prison about the **works** of the Messiah, he sent word through his disciples and said to *Yeshua*, **"Are You the Coming One** [i.e. the Messiah]**, or do we look for another?"** *Yeshua* replied, **"Go report to John what you hear and see: the blind see and the lame walk, those with** *tza'arat* [i.e. leprosy] **are cleansed and the deaf hear, and the dead are raised** and the poor have **good news** proclaimed to them. Blessed is the one who is not led to stumble because of Me (Matt. 11:2-6 TLV, emphasis added).

> I [*Yeshua*] have a greater witness than *that* of John [a.k.a. the Baptist]: for the **works** which the Father hath given me to finish, the same **works** that I do, **bear witness of me**, that the Father hath sent me (John 5:36 KJV).

Believe me that I *am* in the Father, and the Father in me; **or else believe me for the very works' sake** (John 14:11 KJV, emphasis added).

Whenever sharing matters with others, we must always be careful to conduct our selves with *graciousness* and *respect*—not engaging in contentious debates, but respectful of people to draw their own conclusions. *Sha'ul/Paulos* wrote to the Colossians:

Conduct yourselves with wisdom . . . . Let your speech always be with grace, seasoned with salt, to know how you ought to answer everyone (Col 4:5-6 TLV).

During the days following *Yeshua's* crucifixion, his disciples cowered in fear. They fled into hiding. *Shim'on Kefa* (Simon Peter) also denied *Yeshua* three times. But later these same disciples are found boldly and respectfully proclaiming *Yeshua*—even before the very face of the Jewish rulers who threatened them with execution. What can account for this transformation of resolute boldness? It was the proof of *Yeshua's* resurrection and the outpouring of the **Ruach HaKodesh** (the Holy Spirit). Like these disciples, we also, at some point might be called upon to die for our faith. May the story and science of the Shroud give you comfort and courage in that hour of trial.

It is human nature to let the *significance* of these things gradually fade away from memory. Many Jews might have forgotten the Passover if God hadn't made it an annual feast to recall. Let your family make it *an annual tradition* to re-read this publication during the yearly anniversary of the crucifixion and resurrection of *Yeshua*. If you continue to reflect upon the Shroud, you may begin to experience a profound effect in your own life. When you do so, please consider those you know who might benefit from a copy of this book. If you appreciate that God has guided your life to discover the Shroud, then keep in mind family members, extended family relatives, friends, neighbors, associates, and other acquaintances which God has sovereignly brought into your life--deliberately, *for a purpose.* They are a unique sphere of people which God has directed into your life. They know you. They trust you. They know you care about them. Naturally, it is not your job to tell them what to think or believe. But just give them a chance to see this and draw their own conclusions. Have compassion to reach out to others. Give them a copy of this book so they may educe their own opinion. You may be surprised to find many enthusiastic reactions as they learn about the Shroud. Most people still have not heard about the Shroud and are clearly fascinated to learn about it. Even amongst those who are aware of the Shroud, few are informed about the rich details and latest discoveries recorded in this book. Purchase them a copy and invite them to "thumb through the book" to see if it interests them. After all, scientists throughout the world have thought it worth looking into. Such scientists have continued for decades investigating the Shroud. Their labor, expense, time, and exhaustive research were voluntary-- not part of their paid occupations. Yet, their efforts have ultimately resulted in making the Shroud the single, most scientifically studied artifact in human history.

When we help others, God will not fail to recognize *any* caring act of benevolence in our life. You can direct your life to be *filled* with meaning and purpose: *a legacy that will last for all eternity!* (Matt. 6:2-4) Perhaps you may find someone who will be forever and eternally grateful that you cared to reach out to them. How significant is that!

Finally, set aside and forget all this science for a moment. Take some time to ponder what God is expressing through the Shroud to you personally. If the Shroud is authentic, then consider that tormented body . . . what you see is a display of God's UTTERMOST LOVE!—*for you*. *Yeshua* was willing to bear such horrendous brutality and torment . . . for *you!* How else could he possibly endeavor to express more profoundly his depth of love for you? God is not *reluctant* to give you everlasting life: rather, God is dying for the opportunity to give you everlasting life if you will but *only* respond. Reach out to Him! The crucified body reveals that painful message.

> For God **so LOVED** the world **that He gave His only begotten Son**, that whosoever believes in Him should **not perish but have everlasting life. For God did not send His Son into the world to condemn the world, but that the world through Him might be saved** (John 3:16-17 NKJV, emphasis added).

> This is the will of the Father who sent Me [*Yeshua*], that of all He has given Me I should lose nothing, but should **raise it up at the last day. And this is the will of Him who sent Me, that everyone who sees the Son and believes in Him may have everlasting life; and I will raise him up at the last day** (John 6:39-40 NKJV, emphasis added).

> I know that my Redeemer lives, and at the last He will take His stand on the earth. Even after my skin is destroyed, Yet from my flesh I shall see God (Job 19:25 NASB).

> It is through his Son that we have redemption—that is, our sins have been forgiven. He is the visible image of the invisible God. He is supreme over all creation, because in connection with him were created all things—in heaven and on earth, visible and invisible, . . . For it pleased God to have his full being live in his Son (Col. 1:14-16, 19 CJB).

> And God said: 'Let **US** make man in **OUR image** . . . .' (Gen. 1:26 JPS 1917, emphasis added).

> Who hath ascended up into heaven, and descended? Who hath gathered the wind in his fists? Who hath bound the waters in his garment? Who hath established all the ends of the earth? What is his name, and what is his **SON'S** name, if thou knowest? (Proverbs 30:4 JPS 1917, emphasis added)

Chapter 23

CONSIDERATIONS REGARDING VARIOUS RELIGIOUS SKEPTICISMS ABOUT THE SHROUD

1. *After the resurrection, why didn't the Bible mention anything about the disciples discovering an image on the Shroud?*

Based on scientific research of the Turin Shroud, it would be expected that no image would have been visible on the Shroud for many years. The image was not burnt or scorched on the Shroud, nor is there any substance on the Shroud (such as paint or pigmentation) that makes its image. If it had been, then the image would have immediately appeared. Rather, evidence from the Shroud is conclusive that, where its image exists, it is due exclusively to *molecular changes to its image fibers* which gradually caused the image fibers to *yellow and darken faster over time* than the overall Shroud cloth (like an old newspaper under the sun). According to the Historically Consistent Hypothesis, the likely source inducing the molecular change was proton and alpha particle radiation acquired when the Shroud collapsed by gravity and was sucked into the vacuum and residual radiation of the disappearing body when the body transferred into an alternate dimensionality. The radiation would break apart many of the molecular bonds of the image fibers causing carbon and oxygen atoms to double-bond with each other. This molecular change resulted in *conjugated carbonyl (double-bonded) groups* within the molecular structure of the cellulose fibers of the Shroud image. Subsequent air and sunlight exposure would gradually induce oxidized, dehydrated cellulose, causing the image fibers to *yellow and darken faster than the non image fibers of the cloth over time—slowly revealing its image as the cloth aged*. This enlightens as to why there was no mention in the Bible of an image found on the Shroud at the time of *Yeshua's* resurrection. Even today, the image cannot be seen unless standing at least six to ten feet away from the Shroud—any closer than that the image fades away into the straw-yellow background color of the cloth.[249]

Biophysicist Dr. Jean-Baptiste Rinaudo (of the Center of Nuclear Medical Research in Montpellier, France, and of the Grenoble Nuclear Studies Center in France) developed the Protonic Model of Image Formation which demonstrates this. At the Grenoble Nuclear Studies Center, Dr. Rinaudo radiated proton beams onto white linens with a particle accelerator. The linens remained white until Dr. Rinaudo performed artificially induced aging on the linens. This gradually resulted in the same straw-yellow color found on the Shroud. In addition, only the outer surface of the fibers were radiated and colored, the inner part of the fibers remained white—just as the Shroud's fibers do. Another effect of the proton radiation was how it matched the Shroud's response to fluorescence. Linen fluoresces under ultraviolet light. The Shroud also fluoresces under ultraviolet light—except where the image exists. The radiation experiments produced this same corresponding effect. Namely, wherever radiation was applied to a linen cloth the fluorescent response also disappeared. Another result of the radiation experiments is that it also replicated the identical chemical/molecular changes to the linen molecules, resulting in conjugated carbonyl (double bonded) molecular groups, and after artificial aging, oxidized, dehydrated cellulose—precisely what is found with the image fibers of the Shroud.[250] Dr. Rinaudo deduced that this evidence provides indication that a radiated image would begin to appear only gradually after a period of years.[251] Dr. Kitty Little, retired nuclear physicist from Britain's Atomic Energy Research Establishment in Harwell, performed similar experiments with the same results.[252]

From this understanding, **we may now more precisely comprehend what a medieval forger from the 1300's must do in order to craft *this* specific Turin Shroud image. The *medieval* artisan must produce the**

image (not by applying paint or pigment to the Shroud but) **by discharging proton particle radiation(!) in a manner that (1) specifically modifies the *molecular structure* of the cloth's image area fibers (forming conjugated carbonyl, double-bonded groups), (2) do so in a manner that configures the molecules to form a photographic-like image (when revealed five centuries later after the invention of photography), and (3) embeds the image molecules with three-dimensional encodement—the grey scale. (During the late 20th century, scientists would develop technology to interpret this encodement and discover its 3-D image.) A medieval craftsman would have to do all this without being able to see any effect of what he was trying to do to the Shroud until years later when the Shroud began to age and yellow revealing (at that time) *only* the blurry image seen by the natural eye.** *These three facts are universally undisputed features of the Shroud.* The only question is whether you think a medieval craftsman from the 1300's could have accomplished this.

(Note: If you were to tell a medieval craftsman that he must make the image *ONLY* by modifying the molecules of the linen fibers, his first question would be: "What's a molecule?" Have you ever seen a molecule with your naked, unaided eye? Neither could any medieval artist. And yet the artist must create the photographic-like image and the 3-D image *EXCLUSIVELY* by modifying the molecules of the Shroud linen fibers. The existence of molecules was not proven until 1926 when French chemist Jean Baptiste Perrin won the Nobel Prize in Physics for proving mathematically the existence of molecules. Even at that time molecules still could not be visually seen.[253] Molecules were finally seen for the first time in year 2009, when IBM created the first Atomic Force Microscope with a carbon monoxide tip.[254] Scientists were not able to generate particle radiation until the 20th century.[255] Three-dimensional holography was not invented until Dennis Gabor originated its concept in 1947 and won the 1971 Nobel Prize in Physics for the invention of the holographic method.[256])

2.   Isn't the Shroud a violation of the commandment that forbids making a graven image?

This is one of the most common objections that some Christians have raised regarding the Shroud. The prohibition comes from one of the Ten Commandments:

> Thou shalt not make unto thee any graven image, or any likeness *of any thing* that *is* in heaven above, or that is in the earth beneath, or that is in the water under the earth (Exod. 20:4 KJV).

But of course, if the Shroud is authentic, then man did not make the image—God did.

Nonetheless, sincere intentions motivate this question. It is helpful to understand this commandment from the Jewish perspective. The Hebrew Scriptures sometimes articulate a style of Hebraism known as a *Hebrew doublet*. It is a Hebrew manner of expression wherein a statement is made, but then immediately following that statement a subsequent restatement of the matter is provided that is designed to provide further clarification or understanding as to the meaning of the prior statement. This is what is found with this prohibition against graven images (Exodus 20:5-6). The subsequent restatement following this prohibition provides the Hebrew doublet which clarifies the meaning of the prior statement. Below is the subsequent Hebrew doublet statement:

> **Thou shalt not bow down thyself to them**, nor serve them: for I the LORD [*YHVH*] thy God am a jealous God . . . (Exod. 20:5-6 KJV, emphasis added).

The above Hebrew doublet (Exodus 20:5-6) explains that the prohibition against graven images applied to making images *for the purpose of idolatrous worship*. If it were not for this Hebrew doublet clarification, then all images would be prohibited (including all photographs, paintings, statues, etc. of anything in heaven above, the earth beneath, or in the ocean).

Variations of this commandment are also found in other passages. And those verses are likewise conjoined with corresponding subsequent Hebrew doublets—which likewise serve the purpose to clarify that the commandment applies to images created *for the intention of idolatrous worship*:

> You shall not make for yourselves **idols**, nor shall you set up for yourselves an image or a *sacred* pillar, nor shall you place a figured stone in your land **to bow down to it**. . . . (Lev. 26:1 NASB, emphasis added).

> You shall not make for yourself a carved image—any likeness *of anything* that *is* in heaven above, or that *is* in the earth beneath, or that *is* in the water under the earth; **you shall not bow down to them nor serve them** (Deut. 5:8-9 NKJV).

The foregoing Hebrew doublets are also reinforced by additional details from other Hebrew Scriptures. For example, the Temple of Solomon—which God sanctified with the cloud of His presence such that the priests could not stand (1 Kings 8:10-11)—this same Temple was decorated with *images* of twelve oxen (2 Chron. 4:3), four hundred pomegranates (2 Chron. 4:13), and figures of lions and palm trees (1Kings 7:36).

In another passage, God Himself commanded the Israelites to forge a graven image of a snake. During a plague of snakes, God instructed

Moses to mold this image as a bronze metal serpent and set it up on a pole so that anyone who was bit by a snake could look upon the bronze serpent and then be saved from death (Num. 21:8-9). Certainly, this bronze serpent was not made for the purpose of worshiping it as an idol. God would never contradict His commandment prohibiting graven images made for idol worship. However, centuries later some Jews did begin to worship this very serpent as an idol, therefore King Hezekiah had it destroyed (2 Kings 18:4). Centuries later *Yeshua* referenced this bronze serpent *in a positive* light. *Yeshua* did not view the snake image as a violation of the commandment against making graven images—even though it eventually was worshiped as an idol. Why? *Yeshua* explained that the purpose of the serpent image was to provide salvation from death. (It was not made *for the purpose of idolatry.*) *Yeshua* declared:

> As Moses lifted up the serpent in the wilderness, even so must the Son of man be lifted up; that whosoever believeth in him should not perish, but have eternal life [just as the Israelites found salvation from death when they looked upon the snake image] (John 3:14-15 KJV).

Another example is cited where God Himself commanded to make a *graven image of two golden cherubim* to cover the mercy seat upon the ark of God inside the Holy of Holies. (This was the most holy place on earth. Imagine placing graven images there!) Then God said that He would commune with Moses from between the graven images of the two cherubim (Exod. 25:18-22).

3.   *What about relics? Many religions such as Buddhism, Christianity, Islam, Hinduism, Shamanism, and others, have venerated relics. The Catholic Church in particular has numerous relics which many consider to be dubious*

or fake. It seems as though there are a lot of dubious relics. Wouldn't God be against relics?

For the record, the Roman Catholic Church did not come into possession of the Shroud until very recently in 1983 when the last king of Italy, Umberto II, died bequeathing ownership of the Shroud to the Pope of the Roman Catholic Church.[257] Also, the Vatican takes no official position regarding the authenticity of the Shroud.[258]

Relics would naturally fall under the same Biblical rule as graven images. It would be idolatry to worship a relic. However, preserving a relic is not equivalent to worshiping a relic. In the Bible, God Himself commanded to set aside various relics, not for the purpose of worship, but rather for a testimony to future generations. In Exodus 16:32-34, God commanded to place some of the manna that the Israelites ate in the wilderness to be kept in a vessel specifically for future generations "that they may see the bread wherewith I have fed you in the wilderness, when I brought you forth from the land of Egypt" (Exod. 16:32-34 KJV). In Numbers 17:10, God also commanded to preserve Aaron's rod that budded as a relic and a token for future generations. And where do we find that these relics were stored? They were laid within the most sacred place of all: namely, inside the ark of the covenant within the Holy of Holies of God's sacred presence.

The book of Hebrews references these relics:

> And after the second veil, the tabernacle which is called the Holiest of all: which had the golden censer, and the ark of the covenant overlaid round about with gold, wherein *was* **the golden pot that had manna**, and **Aaron's rod that budded** (Heb. 9:3-4 KJV, emphasis added).

145

4. *The book of John chronicles that the body of Yeshua was bound with strips of linen during the burial (John 19:40; 20:5). Wouldn't that indicate that the body was wrapped all around with strips of linen like a mummy?*

> They took, therefore, the body of Jesus, and **bound it with linen clothes** with the spices, according as it was the custom of the Jews to prepare for burial (John 19:40 YLT).

Three gospels make it perfectly clear that *Yeshua* was wrapped in one shroud cloth large enough to wrap his entire body (Matt. 27:59; Mark 15:46; Luke 23:53). It was also customary to tie the jaw shut with a cloth strip wrapped over the head and under the jaw. Evidence of this can be seen on the Shroud of Turin. The strip under the jaw caught the middle bottom of the beard under the cloth such that this part of the beard directly under the chin cannot be seen on the Shroud. (Or, it is also possible that this part of the beard was plucked out when soldiers beat *Yeshua* before the crucifixion.) The frontal view shows the beard appearing like an up-side-down letter "V" under the chin—with missing hair directly under the chin. Other evidence of this chin band is evident on the Shroud where there is no image formed on the sides of the head (between the face and the hair on the head). This also left a gap on the image of the beard from the side views where the cloth strip covered that part of the beard such that no image could be formed on that area of the beard on the Shroud.[259]

Pathologists who have studied the Shroud have theorized that the body underwent a "cadaveric spasm." This is where the body undergoes a rapid state of rigor mortis very soon after death. The arms of the victim would then have been frozen stiff in the position how they were outstretched when hung on the cross. Accordingly, Dr. Alan Whanger (who spent thousands of hours examining the Shroud from specially enhanced and life-sized photos produced by Gamma Photographic Laboratories of Chicago) indicates that the

Shroud exhibits a chin band, probably a wrist band (so the arms would not extend outside the Shroud), and possibly a band around the ankles.[260]

The book of John documents that when *El'azar* (Lazarus) died and was placed in the tomb that his hands and feet were likewise bound together with strips of cloth—similar to the Shroud victim:

> Jesus said to her, "Your brother will rise again." Martha said to him, "I know that he will rise again in the resurrection at the last day." Jesus said to her, "I am the resurrection and the life. The one who believes in me, even if he dies, will live. . . ."
>
> And *when he* [*Yeshua*] had said these *things*, he cried out with a loud voice, "Lazarus, come out!" The one who had died came out, **his feet and his hands bound with strips of cloth**. . . . Jesus said to them, "**Untie him and let him go**." (John 11:23-25; 43-44 LEB).

5. *John 20:7 states that Yeshua's head was wrapped in a head cloth? Wouldn't that prevent his head from making an image on the Shroud?*

This matter has already been extensively addressed concerning the Sudarium of Oviedo within chapter 13.

6. *John 19:40 clarifies that Yeshua was buried "in accordance with Jewish burial customs" (NIV). If that was so, then what about the Jewish custom of washing the body before burial? What about anointing the body at burial? Wouldn't such customs cause the removal the blood trails found on the Shroud?*

The answer to these questions involves some technical matters which must be addressed, but ultimately everything falls into place in a manner that is not only fascinating but inspiring.

During the times of antiquity, it was indeed the norm of Jewish customs to wash the body as part of the burial process. At times, the body was also anointed. However, the Jewish burial custom also included an exception to this tradition which would clearly apply in the case of *Yeshua*. Concerning this matter, Shroud historian Ian Wilson wrote:

> As has been explained by Jewish-born Victor Tunkel of the Faculty of Laws, Queen Mary College, University of London,[261] in these circumstances, and only in these circumstances, traditional Jewish burial rites positively and unequivocally insisted upon absolutely no *taharah*, or washing of the body. The belief among the Pharisees of Jesus's time, shared by Jesus's own followers, was that the body would be *physically* resurrected at the end of time, thereby requiring that anything and everything that formed an essential part of it, such as an amputated limb, or its life-blood, should be buried together with it in anticipation. This has been expressed in an abridged version of the *Shulhan Aruch*, the great sixteenth-century *Code of Jewish Law* which modern-day Jewish scholars recognize as codifying laws and practices that go back to ancient times: 'One who fell [i.e. in battle] and died instantly, if his body was bruised and blood flowed from the wound, and there is apprehension that the blood of the soul was absorbed in his clothes, *he should not be cleansed.*'[262]

> Likewise, as both the *shulhan Aruch* and the great Jewish authority Nahmanides (1194-1270), go on to prescribe, over any clothes, however bloodstained, that the deceased may have been wearing when he died, those preparing him for burial were expected to wrap a white shroud—in the words of the *Shulhan Aruch*: 'a sheet which is called *sovev*'. A further requirement from the *Shulhan* was that whatever garments the deceased may have worn when he died were all that he should be buried in, clearly implying that if

he had died naked, then he should be left that way, except for the
sovev [i.e. the burial shroud].

Of particular importance here is the exact form that this *sovev* took.
As explained by Victor Tunkel, in the case of a heavily
bloodstained corpse the ritual required as much avoidance as
possible of any disturbing of the blood (and as we have seen, one
of the Shroud's marvels is the lack of disturbance to its
bloodstains). The *sovev* therefore had to be an all-enveloping cloth,
that is, a 'single sheet . . . used to go right round' the entire body.
The Hebrew verb from which *sovev* derives specifically means 'to
surround' or 'to go around', thus perfectly corresponding to the
'over the head' type of cloth that we see in the case of the Shroud,
and also, incidentally, to the *soudarion* which the John gospel
describes as having been 'over his [Jesus's] head' and 'rolled up in
a place by itself' as observed by Peter and John during their
discovery of Jesus's empty tomb.[263]

Wilson is referencing *Shulchan Aruch*, the *Code of Jewish Law*—a Jewish
text published in year 1565. It is the standard, and most widely
consulted and accepted compilation of halakhic rulings and Jewish
legal codes in Rabbinic Judaism.[264] Some examples of texts from
which *Shulchan Aruch* is interpreting this matter are drawn from the
Jewish Mishnah Nazir 49b, Oholot 1.6, and b. Talmud Baba Kama
101b. Also the book of Leviticus states: "For the life [Heb. *nephesh*,
"soul"] of the flesh *is* in the blood" (Lev 17:11 KJV). Hence, ancient
Jewish tradition often referred to blood which flowed out of a body
when death occurred as "life-blood" or "blood of the soul."[265] If the
post mortem blood was in the amount of a "quarter of a log," then all
blood on the body (including pre mortem blood) would be treated as
"unclean" blood, and was not to be touched or disturbed with the
burial (Mishnah Oholot 2.2, and also Mishnah Oholot 3.5 which
explicitly refers to a crucified victim). The Jewish b. Talmud Berachot
14a (note 8), and Mishnah Oholot 2.2 (note 9) clarify that a quarter log
of blood would be the amount of an egg and a half of blood. Merely
the lance pierce wound into the side of *Yeshua* after his death alone

would have drawn much more than a quarter log of post mortem blood. In short, this ancient Jewish burial custom forbade contacting or disturbing any blood on a corpse where such blood occurred during the death.[266] In summation, if there was death by violence and blood flowed when death occurred; *the Jewish custom was that the body was **not** to undergo the normal ritual of washing.* (Keep in mind, this was a Jewish custom—not a commandment from the Scriptures.)

Yochanan (John) recorded in his gospel that *Nakdimon* (Nicodemus) brought "a mixture of myrrh and aloes, about a hundred pounds [Grk 'litra']" to the tomb (John 19:39 KJV). The New American Standard Bible footnote indicates that some manuscripts record that this was a "package" rather than the word "mixture." Other ancient manuscripts describe it as "a roll" of myrrh.[267] The myrrh and aloes appear to be of some solid form (granulated, powdered, or solid chunks). The word translated "pounds" is the Greek word *litra*. A litra was typically a unit of "mass." A litra was 0.72 pounds, so one hundred litras would be 72 pounds. Many English Bible translations describe it as 100 pounds.[268]

John's Gospel also chronicles: "So they took Jesus' body and bound it in linen cloths with the spices (aromatics) as is the Jews' customary way to prepare for burial" (John 19:40, AMPC – Amplified Bible, Classic Edition).

Let us take this statement and dissect it: "So they took Jesus' body and bound it [Gk. *deo*, "to bind"] in linen cloths [i.e. referring to the linen shroud cloth itself as well as the linen cloth strips used to bind the wrists and ankles together, and to shut the jaw closed] with the spices (aromatics) [many translations use the word "spices" here, however, the Greek word is *aroma*, and that word does *not* mean "spices"; rather it means "aroma, aromatics"—referring to *anything* that gives off a fragrance, such as the flowers identified next to the Shroud body image] as was the Jews' customary way to prepare for burial" (John 19:40 AMPC—Amplified Bible, Classic Edition).

Concerning the flora aromatics, Dr. Whanger wrote:

> We generally think of burial spices as being in the form of
> ointments or unguents, something crushed or distilled from plants.
> But some of these plants, that is, intact whole plants, may have
> been used as burial spices. So some of them were likely there for
> that purpose, and probably also as deodorants or as mask for
> [eventual] odors."[269]

Why did Nicodemus bring 72 or 100 pounds(!) weight of myrrh and
aloes to the tomb? John reported that *Yeshua* was buried "in
accordance with Jewish burial customs" (John 19:40, NIV). This
Jewish custom forbade disturbing the blood when there was post
mortem blood on the body. Therefore, the body could not be washed,
and the myrrh and aloes could not be used in any manner that would
contact or disturb the blood on the body—such as anointing the body.
Nakdimon (Nicodemus) and *Yosef* ha *Ramatayim* (Joseph of Arimathea)
who undertook the burial of *Yeshua* were both Jewish religious
leaders who would have possessed in-depth knowledge regarding the
Jewish burial customs. They would have known the various legal
technicalities of the Jewish burial customs. Joseph was a prominent
member of the religious Counsel (Mk. 15:43), and Nicodemus was a
ruler of the Jews (John 3:1) whom *Yeshua* described as "the teacher of
Israel" (John 3:10 NASB). They would have been aware of the
exception not to disturb the post mortem blood.

So again, what was the purpose for Nicodemus to bring 72 or 100
pounds(!) of myrrh and aloes to the burial? To begin with, there was
an expectation that the body of *Yeshua* would start to decompose after
rigor mortis wore off. The myrrh, aloes, and flowers were aromatics
that could compensate for the putrid odor of a decomposing body.
Concerning the Shroud of Turin, we can see from the Shroud that
aromatics of flowers were placed inside the Shroud next to the body
in a manner that did not disturb the blood.

There is something else, however, which explains why Nicodemus would bring such a large quantity of myrrh and aloes. Throughout Jewish history there was a long-standing tradition of burning large quantities of spices as incense during the funerals and burials of Judean kings. Also, Myrrh happens to be specifically mentioned as one of the spice ingredients used in the Temple for burning incense.[270] Likewise, the spice of aloes could also be burned as incense. The following are some Biblical references to this. The prophet *Yirrmeyahu* (Jeremiah) spoke to King *Tzidkiyahu* (Zedekiah) before his death:

> "Yet hear the word of the LORD [*YHVH*], O **Zedekiah king of Judah**! Thus says the LORD [*YHVH*] concerning you, 'You will not die by the sword. You will die in peace: **and as spices were burned for your fathers, the former kings who were before you, so they will burn spices for you**; and they will lament for you, "Alas, lord! [i.e. Alas, lord Zedekiah!]" 'For I have spoken the word," declares the LORD [*YHVH*] (Jer. 34:4-5 NASB, emphasis added).

Likewise, the book of 2 Chronicles documents that a large quantity of incense were burned at the funeral/burial of King Asa:

> So Asa slept with his fathers, having **died in the forty-first year of his reign**. And they buried him in his own tomb which he had cut out for himself in the City of David, **and they laid him in the resting place which he had filled with spices of various kinds** blended by the perfumers' art; **and they made a very great fire for him** (2 Chron. 16:13-14 NASB, emphasis added).

Such funeral fires were a very expensive tradition presented to demonstrate special honor for the deceased. In contrast, King *Y'horam* (Jehoram) was an evil king. He was not given a fire, nor a special tomb at his death:

[King Jehoram's] people made no funeral fire in his honor, as they had for his predecessors . . . . He passed away, to no one's regret, and was buried . . . but not in the tombs of the kings (2 Chron. 21:19-20 NIV).

The tradition of burning spices as incense at the funerals of Jewish leaders continued to be practiced during the time of *Yeshua*. For example, we know that proselyte Onkelos burned more than 80 minas (i.e. more than 90 pounds, *an amount similar to Nicodemus*[271]) of spices at the funeral of Gamaliel the Elder/Gamaliel I (who was a contemporary during the lifetime of *Yeshua* and is cited in the Book of Acts 5:34).[272] Gamaliel was a high authority of the Jewish Sanhedrin during the first century. He is thought to have died about year 54 A.D./C.E.[273]

The cost for myrrh and aloes was *extremely* expensive. Only the wealthiest could afford to buy it. Nicodemus was a wealthy leader of the Jews, and so he was able to purchase the myrrh and aloes—even such a large quantity. (He may have previously purchased it for his own eventual funeral.) However, there was no time during the burial of *Yeshua* to burn the incense; the burning of incense would have to wait until after the Sabbath ended. For the Law of Moses forbade lighting a fire during the Sabbath (Exod. 35:3). Luke 23:54 informs that near the completion of *Yeshua's* burial "the Sabbath drew near" (Luke 23:54 NKJV). The Greek term for "drew near" in this passage is *epephosken*. The Greek word means "begin to dawn," or "begin to grow light." The Jews often employed their own Jewish-Greek definitions to Greek words because the Greek language was inadequate to fully translate all the Hebrew words and concepts. According to this Jewish-Greek usage of *epephosken*, the term referred to the twilight when some stars would begin to appear in the sky. It was beginning to "dawn" the night lights (stars) that appear as the residual light from the sun begins to fade away from the sky and transition to evening.[274] For the Jews, evening was the start of a new Jewish day. (The Jewish day begins after twilight at evening—not

153

12:00 AM midnight.) Hence, because of the impending arrival of the Sabbath, the burning of the incense purchased by Nicodemus would have to wait until after the Sabbath (i.e. until the first day of the week). But *Yeshua* would already be resurrected before they could burn the incense.

With this information, we may now begin to assemble the significance of the scenario. What comes into view is the glorious, regal hand of God at work. Whereas a casual reading of the burial of *Yeshua* might seem to convey nothing more than a record of human activities, in contrast we now begin to see another instance of God's purposeful intervention. That which befalls God's Messiah stands in contrast to the normal haphazard events of the typical human experience. The Messiah had suffered cruel brutality and humiliation from his enemies for our redemption. That redemptive suffering was now accomplished and finished. **There was no need (nor divine purpose) for any further humiliation after his death.** Therefore, at this point, God deliberately intervenes. **God sees to it that His Messiah is given the provision of a lavish, *royal* funeral—befitting of a king—even befitting Messiah King of the Jews!** The heavy volume of extremely expensive myrrh and aloes (comparable to the funerals of prior Judean kings used for burning lavish quantities of incense), the burial in a *newly* hewn *rich man's tomb* (similar to Judean kings), that tomb located on the honored and sacred grounds of the Temple mount (which only a rich man could afford)—it was nothing short of a funeral for a king. Even the burial shroud (the theme of this book) provided by the rich man *Yosef Ha Ramatayim* (Joseph of Arimathea) was of great cost—beyond the means of all but a few (Matt. 27:57-60). It bears a highly complicated woven herringbone Z twist three-to-one (3:1) twill pattern that is exceedingly rare. Such complex 3:1 twill patterns have typically only been found within tombs of Egyptian Pharaohs (Ramses III, 1200 B.C.), Kings (King Set I, 1300 B.C.), and Queens (Queen Makeri, 1100 B.C.).[275] Circumstances like this do not befall common people—much less a poor carpenter (like *Yeshua*). The Messiah was dead. Obviously, he did not contrive plans for this lavish arrangement. No one made advance plans for this royal burial—the crucifixion itself was a complete surprise. Such confluences of events do not transpire by chance. Furthermore, God also arranged that His Messiah would be *anointed for his burial* (albeit, *prior to* his death) by the *very expensive* anointing administered by *Miryam* (Mary, the sister of *El'azar*/Lazarus). When this costly anointing was pored over *Yeshua*, the immediate reaction of *Y'hudah ha K'riot* /Judas of Iscariot (John 12:4-6) and others present was indignation because of its exorbitant expense!

> But some were indignantly *remarking* to one another, "Why has this perfume been wasted? For **this perfume might have been sold for over three hundred denarii**, and *the money* given to the poor." And they were scolding her (Mark 14:4-5 NASB, emphasis added).

"*Over* three hundred denarii"! In those times, that amount was equivalent to the *entire* gross wages earned *spanning a period exceeding eleven months of labor!* (One denarius at that time was worth a day's wages—Matt. 20:2. (Jews were forbidden to work on the Sabbath. The most they could work was six days a week.).†

Mary anointed *Yeshua* to express her deep gratitude to him, as well as for the resurrection of her brother Lazarus. However, Mary did not realize, *until Yeshua* informed the people berating her, that she was actually anointing him for his *burial before his death* (*because no one would be able to anoint his body after his death*—it was the sovereign hand of God at work):

> But he [*Yeshua*] said, "Let her be. Why are you bothering her? She has done a beautiful thing for me. For you will always have the

† Denarius = a day's wage (Matt. 20:2). 300 denarii divided by six days work per week equals 50 weeks of labor.

poor with you; and whenever you want to, you can help them. But you will not always have me. What she could do, she did do—**in advance she poured perfume on my body to prepare it for burial**. Yes! I tell you that wherever in the whole world this Good News is proclaimed, what she has done will be told in her memory" (Mark 14:6-9 CJB, emphasis added).

After the Sabbath, on the morning of the first day of the week, women followers of *Yeshua* came to the tomb to *anoint his body*, but instead they discovered that *Yeshua* was resurrected! (Mk. 16:1-2) Why would these women come to *anoint his body*? The obvious answer is that they were not aware of the exception to the Jewish burial custom concerning when there was blood from death on the body. Unlike Nicodemus and Joseph of Arimathea, these women were not Jewish scholars. Since this was not a time of war, the women likely had never experienced a Jewish burial that resulted from a violent death with blood on the body. They were ignorant of the Jewish exception to the burial custom.

And so, as Isaiah 53:9 prophesied (seven centuries before *Yeshua*) regarding the initial intention of his executioners, the body of *Yeshua* was not simply discarded into a community grave with "the wicked" (i.e. with the wicked criminals of Rome). Rather, Isaiah continued on with the prophesy declaring that his grave was to be reassigned "with a rich man his tomb" [u] [276] (Isa. 53:9).

> They intended to bury him with criminals, but he ended up in a rich man's tomb . . . (Isa. 53:9 NET).

There is a glorious majesty and grandeur which subtly underlies the entire life and redemptive mission of Yeshua. We have seen this with the

---

[u] Text found from the Dead Sea Scroll of the *Great Isaiah Scroll* from Cave 1 (QIsa-a) Masoretic Text.

majestic array of symbolism displayed at the scene of the cross, also the timing of *Yeshua's* redemptive sacrifice which, in turn, linked together the historic Egyptian Passover as the background that set the stage for this redemption, also the enigma of the burial shroud which today astounds scientists thousands of years later, and here once again we discover the unexpected *royal burial* of *Yeshua*—a burial befitting a king—rather than being dumped into a community mass grave with the wicked Roman criminals. The theme of grandeur underlying God's interventions, often hidden, can easily go unnoticed. Even *Yeshua's* closest disciples confessed that they sometimes did not realize the significance of things they had witnessed until later: It went right over their heads:

> **His disciples did not understand these things at first.** But when *Yeshua* was glorified, then they remembered that these things were written about him (John 12:16 TLV).

One final observation: Throughout the centuries there has been a growing list of false Jewish messiahs who aspired to gain a following amongst the Jewish community. Judaism today acknowledges such cases as false messiahs. Like many politicians of our times, the false messiahs often concocted attestations about themselves, or conspired ploys from their own initiative to somehow impress the public with their messianic claims. Yet with *Yeshua*, we notice something in profound contrast to these manipulative political tactics. Instead, with *Yeshua*, we repeatedly find God sovereignly intervening over human affairs (deliberately eschewing any appearance of contrived scheming on the part of *Yeshua*) so as to demonstrate God's personal messianic credential upon *Yeshua*.

For example, one of the Biblical prophecies concerning the Messiah was recorded by the prophet *Mikhah* (Micah) about *seven centuries* before *Yeshua*:

And thou, **Bethleem**, house of Ephratha, art few in number to be
reckoned among the thousands of Juda; *yet* **out of thee shall one
come forth to me, to be a ruler of Israel; and his goings forth
were from the beginning,** *even* **from eternity** [Gr. *aion*, "eternal"]
(Micah 5:2, LXX).ᵛ (From the LXX ancient Greek Septuagint
translation of Micah translated from Hebrew to Greek by the Jews
of Alexandria, Egypt during the 3rd to 2ⁿᵈ century B.C./B.C.E.—
centuries prior to the controversy of *Yeshua. The Septuagint with
Apocrypha: Greek and English* with English translation by Sir
Lancelot Brenton).

Now after *Yeshua* was born in Bethlehem . . . when King Herod
heard, he was troubled, and all Jerusalem with him. And when he
had called together all the ruling *kohanim* and Torah scholars, he
began to inquire of them where the Messiah was to be born. So
they told him, "In Bethlehem, land of Judah, for so it has been
written [Micah 5:2] by the prophet: 'And you, Bethlehem, land of
Judah, are by no means least among the rulers of Judah; For out of
you shall come a ruler who will shepherd My people Israel.'"
(Matt. 2:1-6 TLV)

A false messiah might conspire to be the Messiah by making his
residence in Bethlehem for awhile—thus claiming to be the Messiah
from Bethlehem. But when it comes to *Yeshua,* here God regally
intervenes to make it perfectly clear that this is His Messiah!—apart
from any attempted maneuvering on the part of *Yeshua.* In so doing,
God conscripts none other than the most powerful ruler in the
world—Caesar Augustus, the Emperor of Rome. Like a pawn on a
chessboard, God moves the hand of the Emperor of Rome to declare
"a decree that a **census should be taken of the** *entire* **Roman world**
(Luke 2:1 NIV, emphasis added).²⁷⁷ (A divine intervention that
impacts the world!) Because Mir**yam**'s (Mary's) husband Yo**sef**

ᵛ From the LXX ancient Greek Septuagint translation of Micah translated from
Hebrew to Greek by the Jews of Alexandria, Egypt during the 3rd to 2ⁿᵈ century
B.C./B.C.E. *The Septuagint with Apocrypha: Greek and English* with English translation
by Sir Lancelot Brenton.

(Joseph) was a descendent of King David, they were **legally required** to register in the City of David, namely: Beit-Lechem (Bethlehem, Luke 2:1-5)—thus fulfilling this messianic prophesy. To further emphasize that this was not some contrivance on the part of *Yeshua*, God sees to it that *Yeshua* arrives at Bethlehem inside his mother's womb—and then was born in Bethlehem! (Luke 2:1-20).

Nothing like this happened to any of the other numerous false messiahs that Judaism proclaimed over the centuries. In fact, just the opposite: most of them met with disastrous circumstances which itself discredited them as false messiahs.[278] In contrast, the humble carpenter *Yeshua*--with only one to three and a half years of ministry—split the calendar of the entire world (B.C. to A.D. / B.C.E. to C.E.). These references certainly reflect a profound contrast between *Yeshua* versus the other false Jewish messiahs.

Chapter 24

FUTURE SCIENTIFIC RESEARCH OF
THE SHROUD

S cientific research of the Shroud continues to proceed on a global scale.[279] One item to keep an eye on pertaining to future investigation is the effects of neutron radiation. If the disappearing body within the Shroud released neutron particle radiation and neutrons were added to the nuclei of chlorine and calcium atoms, it would have created new chlorine-36 (Cl-36) and calcium-41 (Ca-41) atoms. Although these atoms are infinitesimally rare, they can be measured by instruments called *accelerator mass spectrometers* (AMS).[280] Formation of Cl-36 and Ca-41 atoms would be able to form within certain types of material, such as the Shroud's linen and blood marks, due to their existing molecular composition.[281] *If such atoms were found well-above their extremely tiny background levels, they could not have been produced by humans until the 20th century, and they could not possibly have occurred naturally. Scientists cannot make neutrons or protons radiate from a body, and unlike the 1988 carbon-14 tests, such results could not be distorted by contamination.*[282] Confirmation of a neutron effect on the Shroud could substantiate a variety of conclusions, for example:

- That the Shroud was irradiated with particle radiation.
- That neutron radiation would have distorted carbon-14 tests making the tests erroneous—so that the date of origin of the Shroud's linen would appear to be far more recent than it actually was.
- That both the Shroud cloth and its blood existed specifically from the 1st century.
- That the radiation event transpired specifically during the 1st century.

THE TURIN SHROUD   Mark Niyr

- That the source of the radiation was the body within the Shroud.
- And neutron testing of burial tombs could identify which specific tomb the event transpired within.[283]

Nuclear engineer Robert Rucker summed up the objective of neutron research in his paper *Testing the Neutron Absorption Hypothesis*:

> In general, after a hypothesis is developed that is consistent with all the characteristics of a phenomena, the hypothesis should then be used to make predictions that can be tested . . . . Efforts are being made to determine how a test can be performed to determine whether the isotopes predicted in Table 1 are present. If this test gives statistically significant positive results, it would be evidence that the neutron absorption hypothesis is true, so that the cloth has experienced some type of nuclear event in which it absorbed neutrons. This would explain why a cloth that carbon dated to an apparent date of 1260 AD could have a true date of 33 AD. If this test gives statistically significant negative results, it would be evidence that the neutron absorption hypothesis is false.[284]

(See the above endnote where you can find Robert Rucker's website to continue tracking the up-to-date developments pertaining to the neutron absorption hypothesis.)

Although scientists are currently performing experiments and research to prepare for neutron testing of the Shroud,[285] they would need to obtain permission from the Shroud owner to test the Shroud for this. The process would also require the extraction of some blood specimen from the Shroud as well as the removal of some linen samples from the Shroud cloth in order to perform the tests. The hope is that measurements could be perfected to require only very small samples.[286]

161

HOW TO FIND MORE INFORMATION
ABOUT THE SHROUD

There is much more about the Shroud than this book covers. It is by scrutinizing he details of the Shroud that its significance *leaps out*. To study more in-depth documentation, there is an excellent internationally recognized web site which maintains the largest, most extensive up-to-date research, scientific papers, and international scientific conferences related to the Shroud, as well as links to other Shroud websites and books. It is the *Shroud of Turin Website* (http://www.shroud.com) hosted by STERA, Inc. and its founder and President, Barrie Schwortz. As a professional photographer for various science projects, Barrie was one of the original STURP members which participated in the initial scientific investigation of the Shroud. Barrie (who is not a Messianic Jew, but was raised as an orthodox Jew) was very much a skeptic of the Shroud. After coming to terms with the scientific evidence, he eventually became convinced that the Shroud of Turin is both authentic and reveals the actual body of *Yeshua* of Nazareth.

Two other resources provide a virtual encyclopedia filled with detailed information and extensive documentation about the Shroud: namely, *Test the Shroud* and also *The Resurrection of the Shroud*—both excellent books by Shroud science historian Mark Antonacci, an attorney (a former agnostic who became a believer as a result of researching the Shroud, and who is now President of the Test the Shroud Foundation). We owe a great deal of gratitude to Mark Antonacci for this. Imagine if you had to research all the scientific papers about the Shroud from scratch on your own! Thankfully, Mark has meticulously devoted over 37 years of his life doing this for us. He has also personally conferred with many of the scientists throughout the world who have investigated the Shroud (investing thousands of hours of personal consultation with them).[287] You may also visit the

Test the Shroud website at https://www.testtheshroud.org/. There you will find an excellent video lecture by Mark Antonacci. Also, visit the website interview of Mark Antonacci from December, 2019: https://www.youtube.com/watch?v=hnwOkHPzUDY.

PHOTOS

National Geographic offers a wonderful gallery of specially enhanced photos of the Shroud which may be viewed from their feature article, "The Mystery of the Shroud," at:

http://home.kpn.nl/britso531/Nat.Geographic.June1980.pdf

Fig. 1.

Descent from the Cross with the Shroud of Turin painted by artist Giulio Clovio 1498-1578

This illustrates how the Shroud was wrapped around the body.

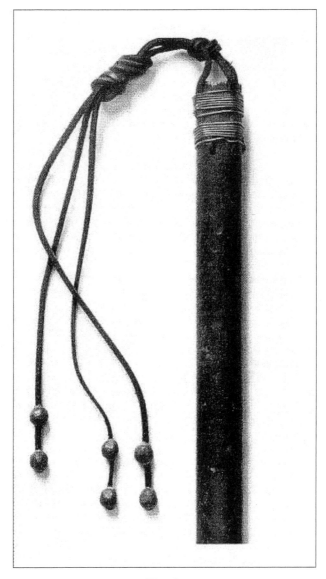

Fig. 2.

A reconstructed Roman Flagrum by French Biologist Professor Paul Vignon who died in 1943

This is a replica of a Roman Flagrum whip recovered from the Roman city of Herculaneum that was buried under the volcanic eruption of Mount Vesuvius in 79 A.D./C.E.

Fig. 3.

Hungarian Pray Manuscript 1192 – 1195 A.D./C.E. discovered by
Gyorgy Pray

(Description of Fig 3 on opposite page)

Hungarian Pray Manuscript 1192 – 1195 A.D./C.E. discovered by
Gyorgy Pray

This object of art predates the 1988 Carbon-14 dating test results of the Turin Shroud by 70 to 200 years (suggesting that the Shroud existed earlier than the 1988 Carbon dating results). The art depicts several aspects found uniquely on the Turin Shroud: (1) the upper part shows the body as naked, (2) hands crossed over the crotch area, (3) only four fingers of each hand showing with missing thumbs, (4) while the lower part emphasizes the rare herringbone twill pattern of the shroud cloth, and (5) a pattern of burnt poker holes which match the Turin Shroud (found below the right elbow of the man in the bottom middle). The burnt poker holes on the Turin Shroud are either three holes in a row or four holes arrayed like a number 7. Most likely the shroud was folded up when someone rammed the hot poker with four prongs (shaped like a 3-prong pitch fork but with one additional side prong) into the Shroud. The side prong of the poker apparently did not go deep enough to penetrate all of the layers of the folded Shroud.

Fig. 4.

***Photo of the Lirey Pilgrim Medallion by Arthor Forgeais (1822-1878)
published year 1865 in France***

This was a souvenir provided for visitors to the Shroud expositions displayed in Lirey, France during the 1350s. It is the earliest dated visual depiction of the *entire* Shroud. **It confirms that the Shroud of the 1300s was unmistakably the same shroud which today resides in Turin, Italy.** This medallion is now in possession of the Cluny Museum in Paris, France. The medallion portrays two men at the top holding the Shroud at an exposition. (Unfortunately, both of their heads have been broken off from the medallion.)

Fig. 5.

The *Lirey Pilgrim Medallion*

The three shields within a shield (lower left) was the coat of arms symbol of the Shroud owner during the 1300s: namely, Geoffrey I de Charny who eventually died on the battlefield of Poitiers on September 19, 1356. The medallion is proof that the Turin Shroud existed during the 1300s.

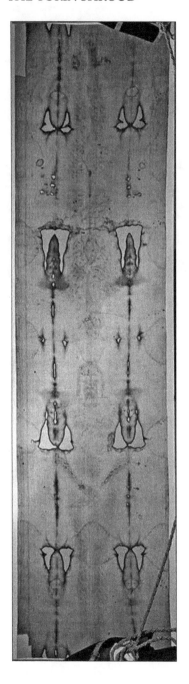

Fig. 6.

Full image of the Shroud as seen by the natural eye.

From the dorsal view (the back of the body) at the top of the photo near the waist area are found two sets of the burnt poker holes (three holes in a row with a fourth hole on the side) shaped like a letter "L" on the right side, and like an inverted letter "L" on the left side. These poker holes were also depicted on the Hungarian Pray Manuscript painting (fig.3)—a painting which conflicts with the 1988 carbon-14 dating test of the Shroud because the painting predates the range of the 1988 radiocarbon dating by 70-200 years.

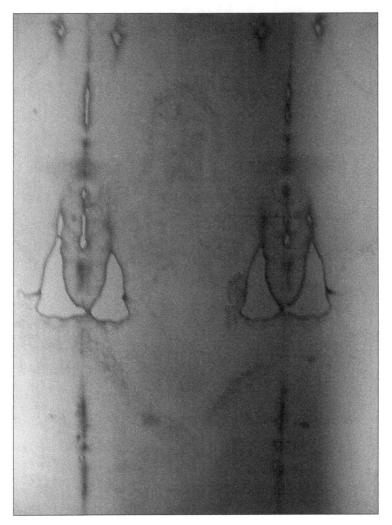

Fig. 7.

Ventral (upper front) image of the Shroud as seen in person by the
natural eye.

This is the view of the Shroud as seen by the natural eye in person. It appears
faint and blurry as though the image was made by dipping a blunt sponge to
apply some light-colored substance. Can you decipher from this natural eye
point of view that the Shroud cloth is embedded with three-dimensional
encodement? If not, then how could an alleged medieval craftsman from the
1300s create and perceive any effect of an embedded three-dimensional
code?

173

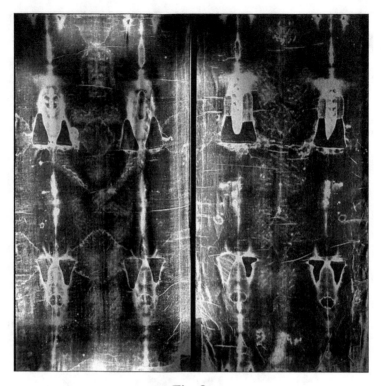

Fig. 8.

Ventral (front) and dorsal (back) photographic, life-like images from the Shroud.
(Also see back cover of the book.)

How could a medieval forger anticipate that his blurry shroud image seen by the natural eye (fig. 7) would transform into the sharply resolved focus of this life-like, photo-like image? The artist would have no cameras to see this transformation effect. Photography would not be invented until 500 years later. Compare this sharp photo image versus the blurry view from the natural eye when seen in person (fig. 7). Notice the negative image (white) blood on the wrist area from the nail wounds, and the corresponding (white) rivulets of blood trails along the forearms. Observe the (white) blood on the head (indicative of the crown of thorns). Negative image (white) blood is also evident from the nail spike through the feet. White on the right side of the chest is blood from a pierce wound to the ribs. Whipped scourge marks appear over the entire torso. All these wounds match the gospel record. Various abnormal features are from repair patches, scorch marks, and water stains that resulted centuries ago when fires broke out.

Fig. 9.

*Log E Interpretation photo of the Shroud's right eye area with a surving
Pontius Pilate coin placed to the left of it.*

Above is the apparent Pontius Pilate coin image from the Shroud's right eye
area adjacent to a surviving Pontius Pilate coin on the left. The image was
potentially produced by corona discharge that streamed off the elevated parts
of the coin. The Greek letters **UCAI** (a reference denoting "of Tiberius
Caesar") is displayed at the 11:00 position above the Pontius Pilate official
Roman lituus symbol (an astrologer's staff) which appears like a backward
question mark. Some existing Pontius Pilate coins still exist with this image
symbol and spelling. Such coins were minted for Pontius Pilate during 29-32
A.D./C.E. when he was the Roman Prefect (govenor) of Judea who
authorized the crucifixion of *Yeshua*.

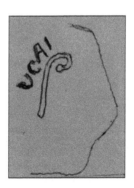

Fig. 10.

*This sketch helps to visually locate the UCAI letters above the Pilate lituus
staff symbol from the potential coin features that appear over the Shroud's
right eye area (fig 9 photo).*

There exists today surviving Pontius Pilate coins that bear the same spelling
and lituus symbol.

PHOTO CREDITS

Regarding photos from Wikimedia Commons: Wikimedia Commons only utilizes images that are *not* subject to copyright restrictions (freely licensed, public domain, etc) which would not preclude anyone from using them for any purpose or at any time if the user adheres to the terms of the license. See the following URL for full details pertaining to this: Wikimedia Commons, "Commons Licensing," https://commons.wikimedia.org/wiki/Commons:Licensing.

Book cover photo   PD-Art | PD-old-100 | PD-1923 (Public Domain). This is a faithful photographic reproduction of a two-dimensional, public domain work of art. The work of art itself is in the public domain for the following reason. This work is in the public domain in its country of origin and other countries and areas where the copyright term is the author's life plus 100 years or less.
[Wikimedia Commons contributors, "File:Shroud of Turin 001.jpg," *Wikimedia Commons, the free media repository,* https://commons.wikimedia.org/w/index.php?title=File:Shroud_of_Turin_001.jpg&oldid=142378275 (accessed January 6, 2018).
(https://commons.wikimedia.org/wiki/File:Shroud_of_Turin_001.jpg)]

Fig. 1   PD-Art | PD-old-100 | PD-1923 (Public Domain). This work is in the public domain in its country of origin and other countries and areas where the copyright term is the author's life plus 100 years or less.
[Wikimedia Commons contributors, "File:OntstaanLijkwade GiovanniBattista.png," *Wikimedia Commons, the free media repository,* https://commons.wikimedia.org/w/index.php?title=File:OntstaanLijkwade_GiovanniBattista.png&oldid=273565822 (accessed January 6, 2018).
(https://commons.wikimedia.org/wiki/File:OntstaanLijkwade_GiovanniBattista.png)]

Fig. 2   Reconstructed Roman Flagrum by French Biologist Professor Paul Vignon. Deceased 1943.

Fig. 7

Fig. 8
& back cover

Fig. 9   Photo by Fr. Francis L. Filas, S.J.
                  Professor of Theology at Loyola University, Chicago.
                  Deceased February 15, 1985.
                  http://www.shroudscience.info/index_files/THE%20SCIENTIFI
                  C%20FACTS%20Word.htm
                  and
                  https://www.shroud.com/pdfs/FilascoinsJune1982.pdf
                  and
                  https://www.shroud.com/pdfs/n10part3.pdf

Fig. 10   License: Attribution 3.0 Unported (CC-BY-3.0).
                  See license for terms of use
                  https://creativecommons.org/licenses/by/3.0/. Title: Outline
                  sketch of apparent Pilate coin over Shroud of Turin right eye.
                  Author: Mark Niyr. Source: *The Turin Shroud: Physical Evidence
                  of Life After Death? (With Insights from a Jewish Perspective).*

Note: Every effort has been made to obtain the necessary permissions with reference to copyright material, both illustrative and quoted. I apologize for any omissions in this respect and will be pleased to make the appropriate acknowledgements in any further edition.

REVIEW OF SOME OF THE
SOURCES CITED

- Yosef ben Matityahu (Flavius Josephus). (Renowned first century Jewish historian.)
- Babylonian Talmud. (Including the Munich Talmud manuscript which is the oldest surviving complete b. Talmud manuscript. The Talmudic literature contains ancient oral teachings of the Rabbis. It was written by Jews during the 3rd to 6th century.)
- Talmid Yerushalmi. (The Jerusalem Talmud. It is a collection of Jewish Rabbinic notes from the 2nd century compiled in Israel.)
- Dr. Jacob Neusner (A Jewish American academic scholar of Judaism. He is one of the most published authors in human history having authored or edited more than 950 books. His research focused on Rabbinic Judaism of the Mishnaic and Talmudic eras. His work nearly translated the entire Rabbinic cannon into English to make the writings available to scholars who were unfamiliar with Hebrew and Aramaic.)
- Dr. David Daube. (A Jewish scholar considered one of the most highly acclaimed scholars of the 20th century. His fields of scholarship were in Roman law, Biblical law, Hebraic law, Talmudic law, Jewish law, Rabbinic Judaism, and New Testament. He published something nearly every year from 1932 through 2000. He was fluent in six languages. He taught as a professor at Cambridge, Oxford, and U.C. Berkeley.)
- Emanuel Tov. (Considered one of the most eminent scholars of the Dead Sea Scrolls. He was appointed by The Israel Antiquities Authority as Editor-in-Chief of the Dead Sea Scrolls Publication Project where he was in charge of a team of sixty scholars worldwide.)
- Dr. Eugene Ulrich. (Dead Sea Scrolls scholar, Chief Editor of the biblical scrolls from Qumran, and is the John A. O'Brien Professor of Hebrew Scriptures at the University of Notre Dame.)

- David Instone-Brewer. (A senior research fellow in Rabbinics and the New Testament at the Institute for Early Christianity in the Graeco-Roman World, Tyndale House, Cambridge, and a member of the Divinity Faculty at the University of Cambridge and the British Association of Jewish Studies.)
- David Rohl. (British Egyptologist, historian, archaeologist, author, and lecturer.)
- A host of numerous scientists and specialists throughout the world from many diverse fields have been cited which have assiduously researched the Shroud of Turin and published their findings in books, articles, and peer reviewed papers.

NOTES AND REFERENCES

[1] Mark Antonacci, *The Resurrection of the Shroud* (New York: M. Evans and Company, Inc., 2000), 11; Barrie M. Schwortz, *The Post-STURP Era of Shroud Research 1981 to the Present*, https://www.upra.org/wp-content/uploads/2013/03/Lecture_1.pdf .

[2] Mark Antonacci, *The Resurrection of the Shroud* (New York: M. Evans and Company, Inc., 2000), 250; Barry Schwortz, "Welcome to our Website," *Shroud of Turin Website*, http://www.shroud.com/ (accessed March 8, 2005).

[3] Mark Antonacci, *The Resurrection of the Shroud* (New York: M. Evans and Company, Inc., 2000), 9, 12, 250-251; Mark Antonacci, *Test the Shroud* (n.p.: Forefront Publishing Co., 2015), 8.

[4] Lloyd A. Currie, "The Remarkable Metrological History of Radiocarbon Dating [II], *Journal of Research of the National Institute of Standards and Technology* 109, no. 2 (March-April 2004): 185-217, https://nvlpubs.nist.gov/nistpubs/jres/109/2/j92cur.pdf ; P. Damon, D. J. Donahue, B. H. Gore, A. L. Hatheway, A. J. T. Jull, T. W. Linick, P. J. Sercel, L. J. Toolin, C. R. Bronk, E. T. Hall, R. E. M. Hedges, R. Housley, I. A. Law, C. Perry, G. Bonani, S. Trumbore, W. Wölfli, J. C. Ambers, S. G. E. Bowman, M. N. Leese, and M. S. Tite, "Radiocarbon dating of the Shroud of Turin," *Nature* 337, (1989), 611-615.

[5] Mark Antonacci, *Test the Shroud* (n.p.: Forefront Publishing Co., 2015), 118.

[6] Why such an odd size for the Shroud (14'3 by 3'7—14 feet 3 inches by 3 feet 7 inches)? It reflects the standard of measurement that was used at the time of *Yeshua* (the 21.4-inch Assyrian cubit). Based on that ancient standard, the Shroud is an even eight by two cubits in size. Mark Antonacci, *The Resurrection of the Shroud* (New York: M. Evans and Company, Inc., 2000), 1, 115.

[7] David H. Stern, *Jewish New Testament Commentary* (Clarksville, MD: Jewish New Testament Publications, Inc., 1996), 4-5. The name *Yeshua* is also a contraction of the Hebrew name *"Y'hoshua"* (English "Joshua") which means *"YHVH* saves." Stern cites that the Galilean Jews of the first century did not pronounce the letter (*'ayin*) at the end of a word, so they pronounced the name as *"Yeshu"* instead of *"Yeshua."* The preserved Shem-Tov Hebrew Gospel of Matthew carries the spelling of the name *Yeshua* in Matt. 1:21 where the name was proclaimed by the angel, but elsewhere the Hebrew Matthew uses the shortened name *Yeshu.* George Howard, *Hebrew Gospel of Matthew* (Macon, GA: Mercer University Press, 1995), 4-5.

8 Kenneth F. Weaver, "The Mystery of the Shroud," *National Geographic Magazine*, 157, no. 6 (June 1980), 730-753, http://home.kpn.nl/britso531/Nat.Geographic.June1980.pdf .

9 "The 1978 STURP Team," *Shroud of Turin Website*, https://www.shroud.com/78team.htm; Frank Viviano, "Why Shroud of Turin's Secrets Continue to Elude Science," *National Geographic*, April 17, 2015, https://news.nationalgeographic.com/2015/04/150417-shroud-turin-relics-jesus-catholic-church-religion-science/.

10 Mark Antonacci, *The Resurrection of the Shroud* (New York: M. Evans and Company, Inc., 2000), 11.

11 Joseph Henry Thayer, *A Greek-English Lexicon of the New Testament* (Marinsville, IN: Evangel Publishing Company, 1974), s.v. "sindon" (4616).

12 Ian Wilson, *The Blood and the Shroud: New Evidence That the World's Most Sacred Relic Is Real* (New York: The Free Press, 1998),), 165-166, 263-264; Mark Antonacci, *Test the Shroud* (n.p.: Forefront Publishing Co., 2015), 203-205..

13 Eusebius, "Church History (Book 1)," chapter xiii, *New Advent*, http://www.newadvent.org/fathers/250101.htm.

14 Ian Wilson, *The Blood and the Shroud: New Evidence That the World's Most Sacred Relic Is Real* (New York: The Free Press, 1998), 162-163, 172-174, 266; Ian Wilson and Barrie Schwortz, *The Turin Shroud: The Illustrated Evidence* (New York: Barnes and Noble, 2000), 107-108; Mark Antonacci, *Test the Shroud* (n.p.: Forefront Publishing Co., 2015), 206-207.

15 Ian Wilson, *The Blood and the Shroud: New Evidence That the World's Most Sacred Relic is Real* (New York: The Free Press, 1998), 174, 263-264.

16 Ian Wilson and Barrie Schwortz, *The Turin Shroud: The Illustrated Evidence* (New York: Barnes and Noble, 2000), 107; Mark Antonacci, *Test the Shroud* (n.p.: Forefront Publishing Co., 2015), 212.

17 Mark Antonacci, *The Resurrection of the Shroud* (New York: M. Evans and Company, Inc., 2000), 123.

18 Ian Wilson and Barrie Schwortz, *The Turin Shroud: The Illustrated Evidence* (New York: Barnes and Noble, 2000), 108; Mark Antonacci, *The Resurrection of the Shroud* (New York: M. Evans and Company, Inc., 2000), 123-129; Mark Antonacci, *Test the Shroud* (n.p.: Forefront Publishing Co., 2015), 190-196.

19 Mark Antonacci, *Test the Shroud* (n.p.: Forefront Publishing Co., 2015), 190-193, 195-196; Dr. Alan and Mary Whanger, *The Shroud of Turin: An Adventure of Discovery* (Franklin, TN: Providence House Publishers, 1998), 50; William Meacham, "The Authentication of the Turn Shroud: An Issue in Archaeological Epistemology,"

Current Anthropology 24, no. 3 (June 1983) from *Shroud of Turin Website*, http://shroud.com/meacham2.htm; Ian Wilson and Barrie Schwortz, *The Turin Shroud: The Illustrated Evidence* (New York: Barnes and Noble, 2000), 108 where photo C displays a distinct transverse line across the neck of a Justinian coin.

[20] Ian Wilson and Barrie Schwortz, *The Turin Shroud: The Illustrated Evidence* (New York: Barnes and Noble, 2000), 105 citing "Story of the Image of Edessa," quoted in translation in Ian Wilson, *The Shroud of Turin*, Doubleday, 1978, 236, after the Greek text in J. P. Migne, *Patrologia Graeca*, Paris, 1857-66, vol CXIII, cols 423-54.

[21] Ian Wilson, *The Blood and the Shroud: New Evidence That the World's Most Sacred Relic Is Real* (New York: The Free Press, 1998), 148-149, 268-269, 272-273.

[22] Mark Antonacci, *The Resurrection of the Shroud* (New York: M. Evans and Company, Inc., 2000), 146.

[23] Quotation with permission from Ian Wilson, *The Blood and the Shroud: New Evidence That the World's Most Sacred Relic Is Real* (New York: The Free Press, 1998), 124, 272. Quotation from page 272.

[24] Ian Wilson, *The Blood and the Shroud: New Evidence That the World's Most Sacred Relic Is Real* (New York: The Free Press, 1998), 126, 278.

[25] Ian Wilson, *The Blood and the Shroud: New Evidence That the World's Most Sacred Relic Is Real* (New York: The Free Press, 1998), 273. This alleged letter to Pope Innocent III of Rome dated August 1, 1205 was written by Theodore in the name of his brother Michael Angelus (Despot of the Greek region Epirus which remained under Byzantine domain).

[26] Mario Latendresse, "A Souvenir from Lirey," http://www.sindonology.org/papers/clunySouvenir.shtml. Ian Wilson, *The Blood and the Shroud: New Evidence That the World's Most Sacred Relic Is Real* (New York: The Free Press, 1998), 127-128, 130, 278. To view more photos of the Lirey Medallion and read more details about how its many details match the Turin Shroud, visit Mario Latendresse, "A Souvenir from Lirey," *Sindonology (Shroud of Turin)*, June 2012, http://www.sindonology.org/papers/clunySouvenir.shtml.

[27] Ian Wilson and Barrie Schwortz, *The Turin Shroud: The Illustrated Evidence* (New York: Barnes and Noble, 2000), 29.

[28] *Encyclopaedia Britannica*, s.v. "Nicephore Niepce," (by the editors of Encyclopaedia Britannica), https://www.britannica.com/biography/Nicephore-Niepce.

[29] Mark Antonacci, *The Resurrection of the Shroud* (New York: M. Evans and Company, Inc., 2000), 34-36.

[30] John H. Heller, *Report on the Shroud of Turin* (Boston: Houghton Mifflin, 1983), 220 quoted in Kenneth E. Stevenson and Gary R. Habermas, *The Shroud and the Controversy* (Nashville: Thomas Nelson Publishers, 1990), 135, 240n4.

[31] Mark Antonacci, *The Resurrection of the Shroud* (New York: M. Evans and Company, Inc., 2000), 121.

[32] Mark Antonacci, *Test the Shroud* (*n.p.*: Forefront Publishing Co., 2015), 30; Mark Antonacci, *The Resurrection of the Shroud* (New York: M. Evans and Company, Inc., 2000), 22, 32.

[33] Petrus Soons, M.D., "Analysis of The Shroud of Turin," *Shroud of Turin 3D Holographic Research*, http://shroud3d.com/home-page/introduction-analysis-of-the-shroud-of-turin.

[34] William Meacham, "The Authentication of the Turn Shroud: An Issue in Archaeological Epistemology," *Current Anthropology* 24, no. 3 (June 1983) from *Shroud of Turin Website*, http://shroud.com/meacham2.htm; Mark Antonacci, *The Resurrection of the Shroud* (New York: M. Evans and Company, Inc., 2000), 88, 243-244, 281.

[35] Most researchers count at least 100-120 scourge marks. Giulio Ricci has counted over 220 scourge marks over virtually every part of the body. Giulio Ricci, "Historical, Medical and Physical Study of the Holy Shroud," in *Proceedings of the 1977 United States Conference of Research on the Shroud of Turin*, ed. Kenneth Stevenson (Bronx, NY: Holy Shroud Guild, 1977), 60, cited by Kenneth E. Stevenson and Gary R. Habermas, *The Shroud and the Controversy* (Nashville: Thomas Nelson Publishers, 1990), 85, 105, 232n2.

[36] Mark Antonacci, *The Resurrection of the Shroud* (New York: M. Evans and Company, Inc., 2000), 17, 102.

[37] Mark Antonacci, *The Resurrection of the Shroud* (New York: M. Evans and Company, Inc., 2000), 20.

[38] Mark Antonacci, *The Resurrection of the Shroud* (New York: M. Evans and Company, Inc., 2000), 17, 20, 32-33, 120.

[39] Various evidence, including fold marks and burnt holes on the Shroud (as well as art depictions of the Shroud) indicate that the Shroud was often folded throughout the centuries in a manner so that it only displayed the face (not the entire body). Ian Wilson and Barrie Schwortz, *The Turin Shroud: The Illustrated Evidence* (New York: Barnes and Noble, 2000), 24, 110-112.

[40] Simon J. Joseph, Ph.D., *The Shroud and the "Historical Jesus" Challenging the Disciplinary Divide*, 2012 from *Shroud of Turin Website*, http://www.shroud.com/pdfs/sjoseph.pdf; Pierre Barbet, *The Passion of Our Lord*

Jesus Christ (trans. Earl of Wicklow; Dublin: Clonmore & Reynolds, 1954); *Mark* Antonacci, *The Resurrection of the Shroud* (New York: M. Evans and Company, Inc., 2000), 22, 24.

[41] A. O'Rahilly, *The Crucified* (Dublin, Ireland: Kingdom Books, 1985), 137; Homer, *Iliad* xi 252; Hesiod, *Theog.* 150; Euripides, *Iph.* 1404; Xenophon, *Anab.* i.5,8; F.T. Zugibe, *The Cross and the Shroud* cites Zorell's *Lexicon Herbraicum et Armaicum* and Lidell-Scott's *Greek-English Lexicon*, 7th ed. (NewYork: Harper Brothers, 1883); all of the foregoing cited in Mark Antonacci, *The Resurrection of the Shroud* (New York: M. Evans and Company, Inc., 2000), 22, 284n28.

[42] William Meacham, "The Authentication of the Turin Shroud: An Issue in Archaeological Epistemology," *Current Anthropology* 24, no. 3 (June 1983), *Shroud of Turin Website*, http://shroud.com/meacham2.htm.

[43] The "thenar furrow" may be found by touching the small finger with the thumb and then tracing the resulting furrow to where it ends (nearly at the top of the wrist). The quotation is from Frederick T. Zugibe, PhD, M.D., "Pierre Barbet Revisited," *Sindon N.S.*, no. 8 (December 1995), from *Shroud of Turnin Website*, http://shroud.com/zugibe.htm.

[44] Mark Antonacci, *The Resurrection of the Shroud* (New York: M. Evans and Company, Inc., 2000), 24. The Space of Destot position gained notoriety from the research of Pierre Barbet, in which case the nail would have exited the ulnar (little finger) side of the wrist, Kenneth E. Stevenson and Gary R. Habermas, *The Shroud and the Controversy* (Nashville: Thomas Nelson Publishers, 1990), 107; Pierre Barbet, *A Doctor at Calvary*, (New York: P. J. Kennedy & Sons, 1955).

[45] Mark Antonacci, *The Resurrection of the Shroud* (New York: M. Evans and Company, Inc., 2000), 31.

[46] William Meacham, "The Authentication of the Turin Shroud: An Issue in Archaeological Epistemology," *Current Anthropology* 24, no. 3 (June 1983), *Shroud of Turin Website*, http://shroud.com/meacham2.htm.

[47] Mark Antonacci, *The Resurrection of the Shroud* (New York: M. Evans and Company, Inc., 2000), 31, 33.

[48] Mark Antonacci, *The Resurrection of the Shroud* (New York: M. Evans and Company, Inc., 2000), 17-18, 24, 31.

[49] Ian Wilson and Barry Schwortz, *The Turin Shroud: The Illustrated Evidence* (New York: Barnes and Noble, Inc., 2000), 76.

[50] Mark Antonacci, *The Resurrection of the Shroud* (New York: M. Evans and Company, Inc., 2000), 247.

[51] Mark Antonacci, *The Resurrection of the Shroud* (New York: M. Evans and Company, Inc., 2000), 18, 26-27; Miller and S. F. Pellicori, "Ultraviolet Fluorescent Photography," *Shroud Spectrum International* 9 (December 1983); Gonella, "Scientific Investigation of the Shroud of Turin: Problems, Results, and Methodological Lessons," in *Turin Shroud—Image of Christ?* (Hong Kong: Cosmos Printing Press Ltd., 1987, 29-40.

[52] Mark Antonacci, *The Resurrection of the Shroud* (New York: M. Evans and Company, Inc., 2000), 26-27, 244, 280.

[53] Murphy, Douglas B.; Davidson, Michael W, *Fundamentals of Light Microscopy and Electronic Imaging*, 2nd ed. (Oxford: Wiley-Blackwell, 2011).

[54] COSMOS – The SAO Encyclopedia of Astronomy, "Ultraviolet," The Swinburne University of Technology, http://astronomy.swin.edu.au/cosmos/U/Ultraviolet.

[55] Peter M. Schumacher, "Photogrammetric Responses From The Shroud of Turin," 1999, *Shroud of Turin Website*, http://www.shroud.com/pdfs/schumchr.pdf.

[56] Mark Antonacci, *The Resurrection of the Shroud* (New York: M. Evans and Company, Inc., 2000), 39.

[57] Ian Wilson and Barry Schwortz, *The Turin Shroud: The Illustrated Evidence* (New York: Barnes and Noble, Inc., 2000), 36.

[58] Dr. Petrus Soons, "The Grey Scale," *Shroud of Turin 3D Holographic Research*, http://shroud3d.com/conversion-process-of-2d-to-3d/introduction-the-gray-scale.

[59] Quotation with permission from Peter M. Schumacher, "Photogrammetric Responses From The Shroud of Turin," 1999, *Shroud of Turin Website*, http://www.shroud.com/pdfs/schumchr.pdf . This paper was addressed at the Shroud of Turin International Research Conference at Richmond, VA, June 18-20, 1999, *Shroud of Turin Website*, http://shroud.com/richmond.htm.

[60] Quotation with permission from Peter M. Schumacher, "Photogrammetric Responses From The Shroud of Turin,"1999, *Shroud of Turin Website*, http://www.shroud.com/pdfs/schumchr.pdf. The paper was delivered at the Shroud of Turin International Research Conference at Richmond, VA, June 18-20, 1999, *Shroud of Turin Website*, http://shroud.com/richmond.htm.

[61] In the 3-D holographic image, there is an oval area under the chin over the neck. That area is NOT three-dimensional. It indicates that something oval shaped was placed over the neck which obstructed the 3-D image from that area, *The Fabric of Time* (DVD) Grizzly Adams Productions, Inc., copyright MMVII. This movie shows several views of the Shroud with its 3-D images. Likewise, there are areas of the face which lack 3-D image. Botany professor emeritus Dr. Avinoam Danin identified flower images over those areas which had blocked the 3-D image. Dr.

Petrus Soons, "The Shroud of Turin, The Holographic Experience," August, 2008?, http://www.ohioshroudconference.com/papers/p24.pdf .

[62] Petrus Soons, M.D., "Making of the Master Hologram," *Shroud of Turin 3D Holographic Research*, http://shroud3d.com/making-holo-creation-of-the-master/making-of-the-master-hologram. The 3-D holograms on this website were not made with gimmicks or tricks such as stereo pairs and stereo windows. The 3-D holograms were derived exclusively from the "grey scale" coding of the Shroud itself; see W. Spierings, Dutch Holographic Laboratory BV, Eindhoven, the Netherlands, P.P.Q.M. Petrus Soons, "Holoprinter: 3D Image Reconstruction of Shroud of Turin data with Holography," *Shroud of Turin 3D Holographic Research*, http://shroud3d.com/making-holo-creation-of-the-master/holoprinter, and also point number 12 of Petrus Soons, M.D., "Image Qualities of the Shroud of Turin," *Shroud of Turin 3D Holographic Research*, http://shroud3d.com/home-page/introduction-image-qualities-of-the-shroud-of-turin, Dr. Petrus Soons, "The Shroud of Turin, The Holographic Experience," http://www.ohioshroudconference.com/papers/p24.pdf.

[63] "Dr. Dennis Gabor: What is Holography," *The Hungary Page, The American Hungarian Federation*, http://www.americanhungarianfederation.org/FamousHungarians/gabor.

[64] Mark Antonacci, *The Resurrection of the Shroud* (New York: M. Evans and Company, Inc., 2000), 49-55, 73.

[65] Schwalbe and Rogers, "Physics and Chemistry," 21 cited in Mark Antonacci, *The Resurrection of the Shroud* (New York: M. Evans and Company, Inc., 2000), 49, 51.

[66] Mark Antonacci, *The Resurrection of the Shroud* (New York: M. Evans and Company, Inc., 2000), 36.

[67] Petrus Soons, "Image Qualities of the Shroud of Turin," *Shroud of Turin 3D Holographic Research*, http://shroud3d.com/home-page/introduction-image-qualities-of-the-shroud-of-turin.

[68] Mark Antonacci, *The Resurrection of the Shroud* (New York: M. Evans and Company, Inc., 2000), 36.

[69] Physicist Aurthur Lind, the "International Conference on the Shroud of Turin 2017," Pasco, Washington, July19-22, https://www.youtube.com/watch?v=yANRGdYMhtA&feature=youtu.be. Mark Antonacci, *Test the Shroud* (*n.p.*: Forefront Publishing Co.: 2015), 11.

[70] Mark Antonacci, *Test the Shroud* (*n.p.*: Forefront Publishing Co.: 2015), 11.

[71] Nuclear engineer Robert A. Rucker, "Status of Research on the Shroud of Turin," *Shroud Research Network* (July 14, 2019)

http://www.shroudresearch.net/hproxy.php/Status-of-Research-on-the-Shroud-of-Turin.pdf?lbisphpreq=1.

[72] Mark Antonacci, *The Resurrection of the Shroud* (New York: M. Evans and Company, Inc., 2000), 79.

[73] Mark Antonacci, *The Resurrection of the Shroud* (New York: M. Evans and Company, Inc., 2000), 63.

[74] Ian Wilson and Barry Schwortz, *The Turin Shroud: The Illustrated Evidence* (New York: Barnes and Noble, Inc., 2000), 35.

[75] Mark Antonacci, *The Resurrection of the Shroud* (New York: M. Evans and Company, Inc., 2000), 37, 42-43.

[76] Mark Antonacci, *The Resurrection of the Shroud* (New York: M. Evans and Company, Inc., 2000), 36.

[77] Mark Antonacci, *Test the Shroud* (*n.p.*: Forefront Publishing Co., 2015), 6.

[78] Donald J. Lynn, "Use of Digital Image Processing in the Analysis of the Shroud of Turin," *Shroud of Turin Website*, http://www.shroud.com/pdfs/lynn1995.pdf.

[79] Mark Antonacci, *Test the Shroud* (*n.p.*: Forefront Publishing Co.: 2015), 6-7; Mark Antonacci, *The Resurrection of the Shroud* (New York: M. Evans and Company, Inc., 2000), 37-38. Antonacci also directly consulted with Don Lynn and Jean Lorre (NASA and STURP scientists) who performed the microdensitometer tests. G. R. Habermas and K. E. Stevenson (official spokesperson for STURP research project), *Verdict on the Shroud* (Ann Arbor, MI: Servant Books, 1981); Robert Villarreal, "The Alpha- Particle Irradation Hypothesis: Solving The Mystery Of The Shroud," October 10, 2014, *Shroud of Turin Website*, http://www.shroud.com/pdfs/stlvillarreal2abstract.pdf; Donald J. Lynn, "Use of Digital Image Processing in the Analysis of the Shroud of Turin," pp. 6,8,16,23, *Shroud of Turin Website*, http://www.shroud.com/pdfs/lynn1995.pdf ; Barrie M. Schwortz, "Some Details About the STURP Quad Mosaic Images," *Shroud of Turin Website*, http://www.shroud.com/pdfs/quad.pdf .

[80] Physicist Arthur C. Lind and Mark Antonacci, "Hypothesis that Explains the Shroud's Unique Blood Marks and Several Critical Events in the Gospels," *Shroud of Turin Website*, http://www.shroud.com/pdfs/stllindpaper.pdf; Antonacci, *Test the Shroud* (*n.p.*: Forefront Publishing Co.: 2015), 19-21, 38-39, 41, 51, 252-255.

[81] William Meacham, "The Authentication of the Turin Shroud: An Issue in Archaeological Epistemology," *Current Anthropology* 24, no. 3 (June 1983), *Shroud of Turin Website*, http://shroud.com/meacham2.htm. Also, peer response by

Giovanni Tamburelli; Mark Antonacci, *The Resurrection of the Shroud* (New York: M. Evans and Company, Inc., 2000), 17-18, 29-30, 225.

[82] Ian Wilson and Barry Schwortz, *The Turin Shroud: The Illustrated Evidence* (New York: Barnes and Noble, Inc., 2000), 75-77; Mark Antonacci, *The Resurrection of the Shroud* (New York: M. Evans and Company, Inc., 2000), 29-30.

[83] Mark Antonacci, *Test the Shroud* (*n.p.*: Forefront Publishing Co.: 2015), 22-23.

[84] John C. Iannone, *The Mystery of the Shroud of Turin: New Scientific Evidence* (New York: Alba House, 1998), 66-67.

[85] Mark Antonacci, *Test the Shroud* (*n.p.*: Forefront Publishing Co.: 2015), 22-25; 31-33, 38-39, 252-255; Mark Antonacci, *The Resurrection of the Shroud* (New York: M. Evans and Company, Inc., 2000), 26-30.

[86] Mark Antonacci, *The Resurrection of the Shroud* (New York: M. Evans and Company, Inc., 2000), 27, 77.

[87] Physicist Arthur C. Lind and Mark Antonacci, "Hypothesis that Explains the Shroud's Unique Blood Marks and Several Critical Events in the Gospels," *Shroud of Turin Website*, http://www.shroud.com/pdfs/stllindpaper.pdf; Mark Antonacci, *Test the Shroud* (*n.p.*: Forefront Publishing Co.: 2015), 41; Mark Antonacci, *The Resurrection of the Shroud* (New York: M. Evans and Company, Inc., 2000), 30,225.

[88] Mark Antonacci, *Test the Shroud* (*n.p.*: Forefront Publishing Co.: 2015), 23-24; Mark Antonacci, *The Resurrection of the Shroud* (New York: M. Evans and Company, Inc., 2000), 26-27.

[89] Dr. Alan and Mary Whanger, *The Shroud of Turin: An Adventure of Discovery* (Franklin, TN: Providence House Publishers, 1998), 23-30. The scientists who first discovered the coins over the eyes were John P. Jackson, Eric J. Jumper, and R. W. (Bill) Mottern; Jackson, Jumper, Mottern, and Stevenson, "The Three-Dimensional Image on Jesus' Burial Cloth," *Procedings of the 1977 United States Conference of Research on the Shroud of Turin* (Albuquerque,, N.M.: Holy Shroud Guild, March 1977), 74-94; Rex Morgan, "Filas in the News Again," *Shroud News*, no. 8, August 5, 1981: 4, *Shroud of Turin Website*, http://www.shroud.com/pdfs/sn008Aug81.pdf, Dr. Robert Haralick, *Analysis of Digital Images of the Shroud of Turin* (Blacksburg, VA: Spatial Data Analysis Laboratory, Virginia Polytechnic Institute and State University, 1983): 2; Kenneth E. Stevenson and Gary R. Habermas, *The Shroud and the Controversy* (Nashville, TN: Thomas Nelson Publishers, 1990), 36-37.

[90] Rex Morgan, "Filas in the News Again," *Shroud News*, no. 8, August 5, 1981: 4-5, *Shroud of Turin Website*, http://www.shroud.com/pdfs/sn008Aug81.pdf; Kenneth E. Stevenson and Gary R. Habermas, *The Shroud and the Controversy* (Nashville,

TN: Thomas Nelson Publishers, 1990), 36-37,67; the letters are about 1.5 millimeters high, Dr. Alan and Mary Whanger, *The Shroud of Turin: An Adventure of Discovery* (Franklin, TN: Providence House Publishers, 1998), 24-26.

[91] Rex Morgan, "Filas in the News Again," *Shroud News*, no. 8, August 5, 1981: 4, *Shroud of Turin Website*, http://www.shroud.com/pdfs/sn008Aug81.pdf.

[92] Francis L. Filas, "Shroud of Turin From Coins of Pontius Pilate," second edition (updated to June, 1982), *Shroud of Turin Website*, https://www.shroud.com/pdfs/FilascoinsJune1982.pdf where on page 23 (page 25 of the PDF) you can see how existing extant Pontius Pilate coins bore the UCAI misspelling; Dr. Alan and Mary Whanger, *The Shroud of Turin: An Adventure of Discovery* (Franklin, TN: Providence House Publishers, 1998), 24-25; Kenneth E. Stevenson and Gary R. Habermas, *The Shroud and the Controversy* (Nashville, TN: Thomas Nelson Publishers, 1990), 36-37, 66-67; Mark Antonacci, *Test the Shroud* (*n.p.*: Forefront Publishing Co.: 2015), 69-72; Bernard A. Power, "Scientific Facts on the Holy Shroud," http://www.shroudscience.info/index_files/THE%20SCIENTIFIC%20FACTS%20Word.htm; Dr. Alan Whanger, "Whanger – Coin Images," https://www.youtube.com/watch?v=8Jyd7kwzO08.

[93] Mark Antonacci, *Test the Shroud* (*n.p.*: Forefront Publishing Co.: 2015), 75.

[94] Mark Antonacci, *Test the Shroud* (*n.p.*: Forefront Publishing Co.: 2015), 69-70; Mark Antonacci, *The Resurrection of the Shroud* (New York: M. Evans and Company, Inc., 2000), 102-105. Since its use by Pontius Pilate, the lituus (staff) symbol was never again used anywhere in the Roman empire as an official government symbol; it has only occasionally appeared as a small side decoration, but nothing more than that.

[95] Dr. Alan and Mary Whanger, *The Shroud of Turin: An Adventure of Discovery* (Franklin, TN: Providence House Publishers, 1998), 27-28.

[96] Mark Antonacci, *Test the Shroud* (*n.p.*: Forefront Publishing Co.: 2015), 69-70.

[97] Mark Antonacci, *The Resurrection of the Shroud* (New York: M. Evans and Company, Inc., 2000), 102-103.

[98] Mark Antonacci, *The Resurrection of the Shroud* (New York: M. Evans and Company, Inc., 2000), 102.

[99] Mark Antonacci, *The Resurrection of the Shroud* (New York: M. Evans and Company, Inc., 2000), 102-104.

[100] Mark Antonacci, *The Resurrection of the Shroud* (New York: M. Evans and Company, Inc., 2000), 103-104.

101 Mark Antonacci, *The Resurrection of the Shroud* (New York: M. Evans and Company, Inc., 2000), 103-104; Mark Antonacci, *Test the Shroud* (*n.p.*: Forefront Publishing Co.: 2015), 71.

102 The probability given was one in eight million. Professor Francis Filas, S.J., *The Dating of the Shroud of Turin from Coins of Pontius Pilate* (Cogan Productions, a division of ACTA Foundation, January, 1984), 5, cited by John C. Iannone, *The Mystery of the Shroud of Turin: New Scientific Evidence* (New York: Alba House, 1998), 37-38, 204n9; Mark Antonacci, *The Resurrection of the Shroud* (New York: M. Evans and Company, Inc., 2000), 104.

103 Dr. Alan and Mary Whanger, *The Shroud of Turin: An Adventure of Discovery* (Franklin, TN: Providence House Publishers, 1998), 26; Dr.Alan D. Whanger's peer response to Willian Meacham, "The Authentication of the Turin Shroud: An Issue in Archaeological Epistemology," *Current Anthropology* 24, no. 3 (June 1983), *Shroud of Turin Website*, http://shroud.com/meacham2.htm.

104 Dr. Alan D. Whanger and Mary W. Whanger, "Revisiting the Eye Images: What are They?", Ohio Shroud Conference, August 2008, http://www.ohioshroudconference.com/papers/p31.pdf; Dr. Alan and Mary Whanger, *The Shroud of Turin: An Adventure of Discovery* (Franklin, TN: Providence House Publishers, 1998), 26; Dr. Alan D. Whanger's peer response to Willian Meacham, "The Authentication of the Turin Shroud: An Issue in Archaeological Epistemology," *Current Anthropology* 24, no. 3 (June 1983), *Shroud of Turin Website*, http://shroud.com/meacham2.htm.

105 Mark Antonacci, *The Resurrection of the Shroud* (New York: M. Evans and Company, Inc., 2000), 105-108; Mark Antonacci, *Test the Shroud* (*n.p.*: Forefront Publishing Co., 2015), 72-75.

106 For more information about the Shroud coins, see Council for Study of the Shroud of Turin, Dr. Alan and Mary Whanger, http://people.duke.edu/~adw2/shroud/jewish-coins.html.

107 Kenneth E. Stevenson and Gary R. Habermas, *The Shroud and the Controversy* (Nashville: Thomas Nelson Publishers, 1990), 65; *The Encyclopedia Americana International Edition* (Danbury, CT: Grolier, 2001), s.v. "Pollen"; *The Forensics Library*, "Forensic Palynology," http://aboutforensics.co.uk/forensic-palynology/.

108 *The Encyclopedia Americana International Edition* (Danbury, CT: Grolier, 2001), s.v. "Pollen"; *The Forensics Library*, "Forensic Palynology," http://aboutforensics.co.uk/forensic-palynology/.

109 Mark Antonacci, *Test the Shroud* (*n.p.*: Forefront Publishing Co.: 2015), 76.

[110] W. Bulst, "The Pollen Grains on the Shroud of Turin," *Shroud Spectrum International* 10 (March, 1984): 20-28, https://www.shroud.com/pdfs/ssi10part4.pdf; Mark Antonacci, *Test the Shroud* (*n.p.*: Forefront Publishing Co., 2015), 78.

[111] Ian Wilson and Barry Schwortz, *The Turin Shroud: The Illustrated Evidence* (New York: Barnes and Noble, Inc., 2000), 90.

[112] Avinoam Danin (citing Dr. Uri Baruch, palynologist with Israel Antiquities Authority), "The Origin of the Shroud of Turin from the Near East as Evidenced By Plant Images and By Pollen Grains," *Shroud of Turin Website*, http://shroud.com/danin2.htm. Dr. Danin is Professor of Botany at The Hebrew University of Jerusalem, Israel.

[113] Ian Wilson and Barry Schwortz, *The Turin Shroud: The Illustrated Evidence* (New York: Barnes and Noble, Inc., 2000), 89. Avinoam Danin, "The Origin of the Shroud of Turin from the Near East as Evidenced By Plant Images and By Pollen Grains," *Shroud of Turin Website*, http://shroud.com/danin2.htm.

[114] Dr. Alan and Mary Whanger, *The Shroud of Turin: An Adventure of Discovery* (Franklin, TN: Providence House Publishers, 1998), 84-85.

[115] Avinoam Danin, "The Origin of the Shroud of Turin from the Near East as Evidenced By Plant Images and By Pollen Grains," *Shroud of Turin Website*, https://shroud.com/danin2.htm.

[116] XVI International Botanical Congress. "Botanical Evidence Indicates "Shroud Of Turin" Originated In Jerusalem Area Before 8th Century." *ScienceDaily*, 3 August 1999, www.sciencedaily.com/releases/1999/08/990803073154.htm (accessed June 29, 2019). https://www.sciencedaily.com/releases/1999/08/990803073154.htm.

[117] Dr. Alan and Mary Whanger, *The Shroud of Turin: An Adventure of Discovery* (Franklin, TN: Providence House Publishers, 1998), 71-85.

[118] Avinoam Danin, "The Origin of the Shroud of Turin from the Near East as Evidenced By Plant Images and By Pollen Grains," *Shroud of Turin Website*, http://shroud.com/danin2.htm; Dr. Alan and Mary Whanger, *The Shroud of Turin: An Adventure of Discovery* (Franklin, TN: Providence House Publishers, 1998), 71-85.

[119] Dr. Alan and Mary Whanger, *The Shroud of Turin: An Adventure of Discovery* (Franklin, TN: Providence House Publishers, 1998), 83-84. The Greek word *aroma* in John 19:40 is often translated with the assumption that it means "spices." However, the actual Greek word *aroma* literally means "sending off scent, aroma" and refers to items that gives off *aromatic* effect. That could include spices, oils, or floral plants (which are found on the Shroud).

[120] Avinoam Danin, "The Origin of the Shroud of Turin from the Near East as Evidenced By Plant Images and By Pollen Grains," *Shroud of Turin Website,* http://shroud.com/danin2.htm.

[121] Mark Antonacci, *Test the Shroud* (*n.p.*: Forefront Publishing Co.: 2015), 358-359.

[122] Mark Guscin, "The Sudarium of Oviedo: Its History and Relationship to the Shroud of Turin, *Shroud of Turin Website,* http://www.shroud.com/guscin.htm.

[123] Ian Wilson and Barry Schwortz, *The Turin Shroud: The Illustrated Evidence* (New York: Barnes and Noble, Inc., 2000), 76-79.

[124] Mark Guscin, "The Sudarium of Oviedo: Its History and Relationship to the Shroud of Turin," *Shroud of Turin Website,* http://www.shroud.com/guscin.htm.

[125] Cesar Barta, Rodrigo Alvarez, Almudena Ordonez, Alfonso Sanchez, and Jesus Garcia from the University of Oviedo, Spain, and the Research Team of Spanish Center of Sindonology (EDICES), "New Discoveries on the Sudarium of Oviedo," *Shroud of Turin Website,* http://www.shroud.com/pdfs/stlbartapaper.pdf ; Mark Antonacci, *Test the Shroud* (n.p.: Forefront Publishing Co.: 215), 76.

[126] Mark Antonacci, *Test the Shroud* (n.p.: Forefront Publishing Co.: 215), 80; Mark Antonacci, *The Resurrection of the Shroud* (New York: M. Evans and Company, Inc., 2000), 113; A. Danin, A. U. Baruch, A. Whanger, M. Whanger, *Flora of the Shroud of Turin* (St. Louis, MO: Botanical Garden Press, 1999, 14-15, 24; XVI International Botanical Congress. "Botanical Evidence Indicates 'Shroud of Turin' Originated in Jerusalem Area Before 8th Century," *ScienceDaily,* August 3, 1999, www.sciencedaily.com/releases/1999/08/990803073154.htm. https://www.sciencedaily.com/releases/1999/08/990803073154.htm.

[127] Ian Wilson and Barry Schwortz, *The Turin Shroud: The Illustrated Evidence* (New York: Barnes and Noble, Inc., 2000), 85, 92.

[128] Avinoam Danin, "The Origin of the Shroud of Turin from the Near East as Evidenced By Plant Images and By Pollen Grains," *Shroud of Turin Website,* http://shroud.com/danin2.htm.

[129] Avinoam Danin, "The Origin of the Shroud of Turin from the Near East as Evidenced By Plant Images and By Pollen Grains," *Shroud of Turin Website,* http://shroud.com/danin2.htm; Avinoam Danin, *Botany of the Shroud: The Story of Floral Images on the Shroud of Turin* (?: Danin Publishing, 2010); Diana Fulbright, "Review – Botany of the Shroud: The Story of Floral Images on the Shroud of Turin," by Avinam Danin, https://www.shroud.com/pdfs/FulbrightBotanyReview.pdf ; Ian Wilson and Barrie Schwortz, *The Turin Shroud: The Illustrated Evidence* (New York: Barnes &

Noble, Inc., 2010), 92; Anthony Brach, Jerusalem's Month of Flowers: Plants for Lent and Easter, http://www.people.fas.harvard.edu/~brach/Jerusalem_Flowers/.

[130] Avinoam Danin, "The Origin of the Shroud of Turin from the Near East as Evidenced By Plant Images and By Pollen Grains," *Shroud of Turin Website*, http://shroud.com/danin2.htm.

[131] John C. Iannone, *The Mystery of the Shroud of Turin: New Scientific Evidence* (New York: Alba House, 1998), 54, 65. Dr. Alan and Mary Whanger, *The Shroud of Turin: An Adventure of Discovery* (Franklin, TN: Providence House Publishers, 1998), 85; Mark Antonacci, *The Resurrection of the Shroud* (New York: M. Evans and Company, Inc., 2000), 120.

[132] Dr. Michael S. Cooper, "How Palynology and Aldehydes Affect Allergy Treatment: History Leads Us to an Experimental Drug that Degrades the Aldehyde Complex," *OptometryTimes.com*, August 2016, https://www.deepdyve.com/lp/ubm-advanstar/how-palynology-and-aldehydes-affect-allergy-treatment-jkrbcp0deT; Vaughn M. Bryant, Gretchen D. Jones, "Forensic Palynology: Current Status of a Rarely Used Technique in the United States of America," *Forensic Science International*, 163, no. 3, November 22, 2006: 183-197, https://www.sciencedirect.com/science/article/pii/S0379073805006225; Ferwin, "Brief History of Palynology," *Letters from Gondwana (Paleontology, books and other stuff)*, 03/31/2013, https://paleonerdish.wordpress.com/2013/03/31/brief-history-of-palynology-3/.

[133] Ian Wilson, *The Turin Shroud* (Penguin Books, 1979); Museum of the Holy Shroud, "History of the Shroud," http://www.museumoftheholyshroud.net/History.htm.

[134] Mark Antonacci, *The Resurrection of the Shroud* (New York: M. Evans and Company, Inc., 2000), 109, 121; Mark Antonacci, *Test the Shroud* (n.p.: Forefront Publishing Co.: 2015), 76; Ian Wilson and Barry Schwortz, *The Turin Shroud: The Illustrated Evidence* (New York: Barnes and Noble, Inc., 2000), 93.

[135] Mark Antonacci, *The Resurrection of the Shroud* (New York: M. Evans and Company, Inc., 2000), 156.

[136] Mark Antonacci, *Test the Shroud* (n.p.: Forefront Publishing Co.: 2015), 311.

[137] John C. Iannone, *The Mystery of the Shroud of Turin: New Scientific Evidence* (Staten Island, NY: Alba House, 1998), 154-155; Ian Wilson and Barry Schwortz, *The Turin Shroud: The Illustrated Evidence* (New York: Barnes and Noble, Inc., 2000), 24, 115-116, 152.

[138] Quotation with permission from Prof. William Meacham, Research Fellow 1980-2012, Center of Asian Studies, University of Hong Kong, "Radiocarbon Measurement and the Age of the Turin Shroud: Possibilities and Uncertainties," from the Proceedings of the Symposium *"Turin Shroud – Image of Christ?"* Hong

Kong, March 1986, *Shroud of Turin Website*,
http://www.shroud.com/meacham.htm.

[139] Mark Antonacci, *The Resurrection of the Shroud* (New York: M. Evans and Company, Inc., 2000), 157.

[140] Prof. William Meacham, Research Fellow 1980-2012, Center of Asian Studies, University of Hong Kong, "Radiocarbon Measurement and the Age of the Turin Shroud: Possibilities an Uncertainties," from the Proceedings of the Symposium *"Turin Shroud – Image of Christ?"* Hong Kong, March 1986, *Shroud of Turin Website*, http://www.shroud.com/meacham.htm; Mark Antonacci, *The Resurrection of the Shroud* (New York: M. Evans and Company, Inc., 2000), 157-158.

[141] Quotation with permission from Prof. William Meacham, Research Fellow 1980-2012, Center of Asian Studies, University of Hong Kong, "Radiocarbon Measurement and the Age of the Turin Shroud: Possibilities an Uncertainties," from the Proceedings of the Symposium *"Turin Shroud – Image of Christ?"* Hong Kong, March 1986, *Shroud of Turin Website*, http://www.shroud.com/meacham.htm.

[142] Quotation with permission from Prof. William Meacham, Research Fellow 1980-2012, Center of Asian Studies, University of Hong Kong, "Radiocarbon Measurement and the Age of the Turin Shroud: Possibilities an Uncertainties," from the Proceedings of the Symposium *"Turin Shroud – Image of Christ?"* Hong Kong, March 1986, *Shroud of Turin Website*, http://www.shroud.com/meacham.htm.

[143] Ian Wilson and Barry Schwortz, *The Turin Shroud: The Illustrated Evidence* (New York: Barnes and Noble, Inc., 2000), 140.

[144] Many historic depictions of Shroud expositions illustrate the Shroud as being held at the very corner that was eventually used for the 1988 C-14 testing. This would inevitably result in contamination of that area of the Shroud which could result in inaccurate carbon-14 dating results. Ian Wilson and Barry Schwortz, *The Turin Shroud: The Illustrated Evidence* (New York: Barnes and Noble, Inc., 2000), 100.

[145] Remi Van Haelst, "Radiocarbon Dating the Shroud of Turin - The Nature Report," from *Shroud of Turin Website*, https://www.shroud.com/vanhels5.pdf; Mark Antonacci, *The Resurrection of the Shroud* (New York: M. Evans and Company, Inc., 2000), 168; Mark Antonacci, *Test the Shroud* (*n.p.*: Forefront Publishing Co.: 2015), 154.

[146] Mark Antonacci, *Test the Shroud* (*n.p.*: Forefront Publishing Co.: 2015), 298-299; R. Burleigh, M. Leese, and M. Tite, "An Intercomparison of Some AMS and Small Gas Counter Laboratories," *Radiocarbon* 28, no. 2A (1986): 571-577.

[147] Quotation from Mark Antonacci, *The Resurrection of the Shroud* (New York: M. Evans and Company, Inc., 2000), 178-179.

[148] J. Raloff, "Controversy Builds as Shroud Tests Near," *Science News*, 133 (April 16, 1988), quoted in Mark Antonacci, *The Resurrection of the Shroud* (New York: M. Evans and Company, Inc., 2000), 176.

[149] "About the Conference," 18 December, 2015, "Conference Presentation," https://www.matec-conferences.org/articles/matecconf/abs/2015/17/contents/contents.html. Then click on PDF for "About the Conference," 18 December, 2015. There are many other peer-reviewed papers about the conference available as well.

[150] *Introductory Paper: Scientific Results on the Turin Shroud Coming from a Paduan University Research Project*, Giulio Fanti, MATEC Web of Conferences 36 (2015) 00001, DOI: https://doi.org/10.1051/matecconf/20153600001, CC-BY-4.0 copyright license https://creativecommons.org/licenses/by/4.0/. Professor Giulio Fanti and Pierandrea Malfi list ten reasons supporting why the 1988 radiocarbon dating results are dubious within their book *The Shroud of Turin: First Century After Christ!* (Singapore: Pan Stanford Publishing Pte. Ltd., 2015), 160-161. Professor Giulio Fanti and Pierandrea Malfi also cite observations from professors M. Riani (at Parma), A. Atkinsons (London), and F. Crosilla (at Udine) (published in the *Italian Society of Statistics*) and maintain that the 1988 radiocarbon dating was "unreliable and scientifically meaningless." They also reference a "prestigious international statistics review" which suggests environmental bias. Mark Antonacci gives a thorough review of the political and devious behind-the-scenes controversies underling the 1988 radiocarbon dating process in his book *Test the Shroud* (*n.p.*: Forefront Publishing Co.: 2015), 297-319.

[151] Giulio Fanti and Pierandrea Malfi, *The Shroud of Turin: First Century After Christ!* (Singapore: Pan Stanford Publishing Pte. Ltd., 2015) , from back cover.

[152] Mechanical ond opto-chemical dating of the Turin Shroud, Guilio Fanti, Pierandrea Malfi and Fabio Crosilla, MATEC Web of Conferences, 36 (2015) 01001, DOI: https://doi.org/10.1051/matecconf/20153601001, CC-BY-4.0 copyright license https://creativecommons.org/licenses/by/4.0/.

[153] Concerning threads from the original radiocarbon material: in 2001 and 2005, STURP chemist Raymond Rogers publish some research that the 1988 carbon-14 dating of the Shroud may have been taken from a sample location of the Shroud which was not part of the original Shroud, but rather consisting of fabric used to make a later repair to the Shroud. If this were true, it could explain why the 1988 carbon-14 dating results gave such a recent date for the Shroud of 1260-1390 A.D./C.E. Since Rogers last published his papers in 2005, further research has indicated that his hypothesis is unlikely. For those who desire in-depth

information concerning this matter, please see chapter 9 of *Test the Shroud* by Mark Antonacci. Here I will list just a few items that contradict the Rogers hypothesis. Photo microscopy (which far exceeds what any medieval restorer could see with the naked eye) did not reveal any trace of such repair on the C-14 samples. Photographs taken with numerous wavelengths and techniques, X-ray radiographs, and UV fluorescent tests did not reveal any evidence of repair to the C-14 test samples. Relative concentrations of elements of calcium, strontium, iron, and other elements of the C-14 samples also matched the Shroud, whereas medieval knowledge at that time would have been oblivious to try to match this. Mark Antonacci, *Test the Shroud* (n.p., Forefront Publishing Co., 2015), 168-186.

154 Mark Antonacci, *The Resurrection of the Shroud* (New York: M. Evans and Company, Inc., 2000), 60.

155 Arthur C. Lind and Mark Antonacci, "Hypothesis that Explains the Shroud's Unique Blood Marks and Several Critical Events in the Gospels, *Shroud of Turin Website*, 2014, http://www.shroud.com/pdfs/stllindpaper.pdf; Mark Antonacci, *Test the Shroud* (n.p., Forefront Publishing Co., 2015), 233-276; Mark Antonacci, *The Resurrection of the Shroud* (New York: M. Evans and Company, Inc., 2000), 222-232.

156 Mark Antonacci, *Test the Shroud* (n.p., Forefront Publishing Co., 2015), 233; Mark Antonacci, *The Resurrection of the Shroud* (New York: M. Evans and Company, Inc., 2000), 232.

157 Test the Shroud Foundation, https://www.testtheshroud.org/.

158 Arthur C. Lind and Mark Antonacci, "Hypothesis that Explains the Shroud's Unique Blood Marks and Several Critical Events in the Gospels, *Shroud of Turin Website*, 2014, http://www.shroud.com/pdfs/stllindpaper.pdf, Mark Antonacci, *The Resurrection of the Shroud* (New York: M. Evans and Company, Inc., 2000), 216-232; Mark Antonacci, *Test the Shroud* (n.p.: Forefront Publishing Co.: 2015), 99-102, 233.

159 Mark Antonacci, *The Resurrection of the Shroud* (New York: M. Evans and Company, Inc., 2000), 222; Mark Antonacci, *Test the Shroud* (n.p.: Forefront Publishing Co.: 2015), 234.

160 Mark Antonacci, *Test the Shroud* (n.p.: Forefront Publishing Co.: 2015), 98.

161 Mark Antonacci, *Test the Shroud* (n.p.: Forefront Publishing Co.: 2015), 98, 166, 234.

162 Mark Antonacci, *Test the Shroud* (n.p.: Forefront Publishing Co.: 2015), 235.

163 Mark Antonacci, *Test the Shroud* (n.p.: Forefront Publishing Co.: 2015), 100-101. Low energy radiation protons do not travel more than about 3 cm (1.18 inches) in air and 30 microns (two or three fibers) in linen. Jean-Baptiste Rinaudo, "Protonic

Model of Image Formation on the Shroud of Turin," *Third International Congress on the Shroud of Turin*, Turin, Italy, June 5-7, 1998; J. Rinaudo, "A Sign for Our Time," *Shroud Sources Newsletter*, May/June 1996; K. Little, "The Formation of the Shroud's Body Image," *British Society for the Turin Shroud Newsletter*, No. 46, November/December 1997, 19-26; all cited by Mark Antonacci, *The Resurrection of the Shroud* (New York: M. Evans and Company, Inc., 2000), 161, 216, 222-224, 309n32, 309n50.

[164] John P. Jackson, "Is the Image on the Shroud Due to a Process Heretofore Unknown to Modern Science? *Shroud Spectrum International* 34 (March 1990); John P. Jackson, "An Unconventional Hypothesis to Explain All Image Characteristics Found on the Shroud Image," *History, Science, Theology and the Shroud*, A. Berard, ed. (St. Louis: Richard Nieman, 1991), 325-344; all foregoing cited in Mark Antonacci, *The Resurrection of the Shroud* (New York: M. Evans and Company, Inc., 2000), 218-224, 309n39 and *Test the Shroud* (*n.p.*: Forefront Publishing Co., 2015), 235-238.

[165] Mark Antonacci, *The Resurrection of the Shroud* (New York: M. Evans and Company, Inc., 2000), 161.

[166] Arthur Lind, "Image Formation by Charged Nuclear Particles," video "Image Formation by Protons," *International Conference on the Shroud of Turin, Pasco, Washington*, July 19-22, 2017, http://www.shrouduniversity.com/pasco17.php, and especially video https://www.youtube.com/watch?v=yANRGdYMhtA&feature=youtu.be.

[167] Frank Viviano, "Why Shroud of Turin's Secrets Continue to Elude Science," *National Geographic*, April 17, 2015, https://news.nationalgeographic.com/2015/04/150417-shroud-turin-relics-jesus-catholic-church-religion-science/; Nuclear engineer Robert Rucker, reviewed by Mark Antonacci, "Status of Research on the Shroud of Turin," *Shroud Research Network*, July 14, 2019, http://www.shroudresearch.net/hproxy.php/Status-of-Research-on-the-Shroud-of-Turin.pdf?lbisphpreq=1.

[168] Nuclear engineer Robert Rucker, reviewed by Mark Antonacci, "Status of Research on the Shroud of Turin," *Shroud Research Network*, July 14, 2019, http://www.shroudresearch.net/hproxy.php/Status-of-Research-on-the-Shroud-of-Turin.pdf?lbisphpreq=1. Physicist Aurther Lind, video "Image Formation by Charged Nuclear Particles," "Image Formation by Protons," *International Conference on the Shroud of Turin, Pasco, Washington*, July 19-22, 2017, http://www.shrouduniversity.com/pasco17.php, and especially the video https://www.youtube.com/watch?v=yANRGdYMhtA&feature=youtu.be, Heller 1981, Rogers 2002.

[169] J. Rinaudo, "Protonic Model of Image Formation on the Shroud of Turin," *Third International Congress on the Shroud of Turin*, Turin, Italy, June 5-7, 1998, p. 4; J. Rinaudo, "A Sign for Our Time," *Shroud Sources Newsletter*, May/June 1996 cited by Mark Antonacci, *The Resurrection of the Shroud* (New York: M. Evans and Company, Inc., 2000), 217; Mark Antonacci, *Test the Shroud* (*n.p.*: Forefront Publishing Co., 2015), 101.

[170] Mark Antonacci, *Test the Shroud* (*n.p.*: Forefront Publishing Co., 2015), 100; Dr. Kitty Little, "The Formation of the Shroud's Body Image," *British Society for the Turin Shroud Newsletter*, No. 46, November/December 1997, 19-26, 20.

[171] Physicist Aurther Lind, "Image Formation by Charged Nuclear Particles," video "Image Formation by Protons," *International Conference on the Shroud of Turin, Pasco, Washington*, July 19-22, 2017, http://www.shrouduniversity.com/pasco17.php, and especially video; https://www.youtube.com/watch?v=yANRGdYMhtA&feature=youtu.be,

[172] Arthur Lind, "Image Formation by Charged Nuclear Particles," video "Image Formation by Protons," *International Conference on the Shroud of Turin, Pasco, Washington*, July 19-22, 2017, http://www.shrouduniversity.com/pasco17.php, and especially video https://www.youtube.com/watch?v=yANRGdYMhtA&feature=youtu.be.

[173] Mark Antonacci, *The Resurrection of the Shroud* (New York: M. Evans and Company, Inc., 2000), 216, 224; and *Test the Shroud* (*n.p.*: Forefront Publishing Co., 2015), 235-237.

[174] Mark Antonacci, *The Resurrection of the Shroud* (New York: M. Evans and Company, Inc., 2000), 224.

[175] Mark Antonacci, *The Resurrection of the Shroud* (New York: M. Evans and Company, Inc., 2000), 41.

[176] Source from Mark Antonacci, *Test the Shroud* (*n.p.*: Forefront Publishing Co, 2015), 102.

[177] As quoted in Mark Antonacci, *Test the Shroud* (*n.p.*: Forefront Publishing Co., 2015), 100; Dr. Kitty Little, "The Holy Shroud and the Miracle of the Resurrection," *Christian Order* (April 1994), 218-231, 221.

[178] Mark Antonacci, *The Resurrection of the Shroud* (New York: M. Evans and Company, Inc., 2000), 41, 213-214, 245.

[179] Mark Antonacci, *The Resurrection of the Shroud* (New York: M. Evans and Company, Inc., 2000), 234.

[180] Mark Antonacci, *The Resurrection of the Shroud* (New York: M. Evans and Company, Inc., 2000), 213, 215.

181 As quoted in W. McDonald, "Science and the Shroud, *The World and I* (Oct. 1986): pp. 420-428, 426 from Mark Antonacci, *Test the Shroud* (*n.p.*: Forefront Publishing Co., 2015), 9.

182 Mark Antonacci, *The Resurrection of the Shroud* (New York: M. Evans and Company, Inc., 2000), 224.

183 Mark Antonacci, *The Resurrection of the Shroud* (New York: M. Evans and Company, Inc., 2000), 224, 230; Mark Antonacci, *Test the Shroud* (*n.p.*: Forefront Publishing Co.: 2015), 159-160, 238, 245.

184 Dr. Alan and Mary Whanger, *The Shroud of Turin: An Adventure of Discovery* (Franklin, TN: Providence House Publishers, 1998), 28-29.

185 Ian Wilson and Barrie Schwortz, *The Turin Shroud: The Ilustrated Evidence* (New York: Barnes & Noble, Inc., 2000), 128. Authors cite Harvard physicist Dr. Thomas J. Phillips who explained that the radiation could both explain the cause of the Shroud's image and the skewing of the carbon 14 content. If radiation emanated from the body during the formation of the image, it could create new C-14 from existing C-13, making the Shroud's C-14 dating readily appear a thousand years younger; Mark Antonacci cites a number of references supporting this, including an experiment on Egyptian linen from 3400 BCE that altered the C-14 dating into the future, five hundred centuries forward in time, *The Resurrection of the Shroud* (New York: M. Evans and Company, Inc., 2000), 159-161, 229, 303n7, 303n8, 303n11, 303n14, 303n17. A few of the references cited by Anonacci are the following: Dr. Jean-Baptiste Rinaudo, "Protonic Model of Image Formation," pp. 5-6; J. Rinaudo, "A Sign for Our Time," *Shroud Sources Newsletter*, May/June 1996, pp. 2-4, J. Rinaudo, in *BSTS Newsletter*, No 38, August/September 1994, pp. 13-16 and /*BSTS Newsletter*, No 39; T. Phillips, "Shroud Irradiated with Neutrons? *Nature* 337 (1989): 594; R. Hedges, "Hedges Replies," *Nature* 337 (1989): 594.

186 Mark Antonacci, *Test the Shroud* (*n.p.*: Forefront Publishing Co., 2015), 33, 166, 236-238, 269, 272.

187 Ian Wilson and Barry Schwortz, *The Turin Shroud: The Illustrated Evidence* (New York: Barnes and Noble, Inc., 2000), 75-77; Mark Antonacci, *The Resurrection of the Shroud* (New York: M. Evans and Company, Inc., 2000), 29-30.

188 Various skeletal features have been identified from the Shroud image such as: carpal and metacarpal bones, 22 teeth, eye sockets, left femur, left thumb flexed under the hand, the backbone, and possibly more. August D. Accetta MD, Kenneth Lyons MD, and John Jackson PhD., "Nuclear Medicine and its Relevance to the Shroud of Turin," *Shroud of Turin Website*, http://www.shroud.com/pdfs/accett2.pdf; Physicist Dr. J. P. Jackson, "Is the Image on the Shroud Due to a Process Heretofore Unknown to Modern Science?

Shroud Spectrum International 34 (March 1990): 3-29, 18; J..P. Jackson , "An
Unconventional Hypothesis to Explain All Image Characteristics Found on the
Shroud Image," *History, Science, Theology and the Shroud,* A. Berard, ed. (St. Louis:
Richard Nieman, 1991), 325-344,333-335; Mark Antonacci, *The Resurrection of the
Shroud* (New York: M. Evans and Company, Inc., 2000), 213; Mark Antonacci,
Test the Shroud (*n.p.*: Forefront Publishing Co., 2015), 54-55; Michael Blunt,
Professor of Anatomy, University of Sydney in I. Wilson, *The Blood and the Shroud*
(New York: The Free Press, 1998), 29; Dr.Alan Whanger, in M. and A. Whanger,
The Shroud of Turin: An Adventure of Discovery (Franklin, TN: Providence House
Publishers, 1998), 111-115; Dr. A. D. Accetta, "Nuclear Medicine and Its
Relevance to the Shroud of Turin," *"Sindone 2000" Orvieto Worldwide Congress,*
Italy (August, 2000); Dr. A. D. Accetta, "Experiments with Radiation as an Image
Formation Mechanism," *Shroud of Turin International Research Conference,*
Richmond, VA, June 18-20, 1999; Dr. Carter, "Formation of the Image," 433-434;
Dr. A and M Whanger, *The Shroud of Turin.* 117-118.

[189] Mark Antonacci, *Test the Shroud* (*n.p.*: Forefront Publishing Co., 2015), 54-55.

[190] Mark Antonacci, *The Resurrection of the Shroud* (New York: M. Evans and Company,
Inc., 2000), 8-9.

[191] Giulo Fanti, *Introductory Paper: Scientific Results on the Turin Shroud Coming from a
Paduan University Research Project,* MATEC Web of Conferences 36, 2015, Article
00001, DOI: https://doi.org/10.1051/matecconf/20153600001. Creative Commons
License Attribution 4.0 International (CC by 4.0)
https://creativecommons.org/licenses/by/4.0/.

[192] Mark Antonacci, *Test the Shroud* (*n.p.*: Forefront Publishing Co., 2015), 277.

[193] The following are various factors regarding the ultraviolet radiation hypothesis of
the Shroud image formation. PhD Physicist John Jackson presented what is
called the *Cloth Collapse Model* to propose the how the image was formed by
ultraviolet radiation. This was a brilliant contribution addressing many questions
pertaining to the formation of the Shroud's image. It postulated that the Shroud
collapsed only downward by gravity at the moment of the resurrection and that
ultraviolet radiation induced the image on the Shroud. Mark Antonacci has high
regard for this hypothesis but cites various shortcomings of the proposition
(which aspects, in turn, may be accounted for by the *Historically Consistent
Hypothesis*). For example, the *Cloth Collapse Model* does not account for the *pristine
quality* of the transition of the Shroud's 130 blood marks onto the cloth which
could be accounted for by the *Historically Consistent Hypothesis*. If the cloth only
collapsed by gravity, how would this account for the dorsal (rear) image of the
body where such aspects of the body were not in contact with the cloth—for
example, the rear of the upraised leg and heel? Nor would it account for the
three-dimensional encodement of the dorsal (rear) side of the body. Ultraviolet

light cannot encode potential coin and flower images. Ultraviolet radiation would not be able to irradiate the cloth without also leaving a white discoloration on cloth (a feature which does not exist on the Shroud). The ultraviolet light experiments did not claim to modify the molecular structure of the linen cloth producing conjugated carbonyl groups which exist with the image fibers of the Shroud and which, in contrast, did result from the *proton* radiation experiments by Dr. Rinaudo. (Be sure to review chapter 23 part 1 regarding the various impressive results from Dr. Rinaudo's *proton* radiation experiments which deal with this matter.) The only way that ultraviolet light could impact the Shroud in a straight-line vertical path between each pin point part of the body to the corresponding vertical pin point location on the Shroud is if the ultraviolet light was "collimated" into a straight-line path. Collimated ultraviolet light does not happen naturally. Ultraviolet light can only become collimated by artificial manual intervention by use of a collimator device, lenses and mirrors, etc. Without artificial intervention, ultraviolet light diffuses in many directions (not in a straight-line path), similar to diffusion of light from a lamp into a dark room. The UV light spreads out in various directions. (*Encyclopaedia Britannica*, s.v. "Collimator" (by the Editors of Encyclopaedia Britannica), https://www.britannica.com/technology/collimator. Collimated UV Light Source System, Wageningen University and Research, https://www.wur.nl/en/product/Collimated-UV-light-source-system.htm). Unlike the effects resulting from ultraviolet light, the *Historically Consistent Hypothesis* also helps to explain the continuing red color of the blood, the strengthening of the cloth material, even an artificially younger C14 dating result, as well as explain the image of internal skeletal features, cf. Mark Antonacci, *Test the Shroud* (*n.p.*: Forefront Publishing Co., 2015), 274-275; Mark Antonacci, *The Resurrection of the Shroud* (New York: M. Evans and Company, Inc., 2000), 220-221.

[194] *A Summary of STURP's Conclusions,* from the STURP Final Report, distributed at the press conference held after their final meeting in October 1981, quoted from *Shroud of Turin Website,* http://www.shroud.com/78conclu.htm.

[195] Martin Abegg, Jr., Peter Flint, and Eugene Ulrich, *The Dead Sea Scrolls Bible: The Oldest Known Bible Translated for the First Time into English* (New York: HarperCollins Publishers Inc, 1999), 267.

[196] Adrian Schenker, *The Earliest Text of the Hebrew Bible: The Relationship between the Masoretic Text and the Hebrew Base of the Septuagint Reconsidered,* ed. Adrian Schenker (Atlanta: Society of Biblical Literature, 2003), 137-144.

[197] Martin Abegg, Jr., Peter Flint, and Eugene Ulrich, *The Dead Sea Scrolls Bible: The Oldest Known Bible Translated for the First Time into English* (New York: HarperCollins Publishers Inc, 1999), 360. Some people may wonder why various

Bible translations differ. In some cases, the Hebrew words may have a variety of
definitions. Also, various Hebrew texts have been used for translating the
Hebrew, and these texts sometimes have different Hebrew words in their texts.
In this case, we have cited one of the oldest Hebrew texts uncovered from the
Dead Sea Scrolls. Scholars estimate that this Dead Sea Scroll Hebrew text 1QIsa-a
MT was copied around 125 B.C.E. which is more than a thousand years earlier
than the oldest Hebrew texts available before the discovery of the Dead Sea
Scrolls.

[198] Isaiah chapter 53 was the Scripture most cited by the first century followers of
Yeshua. Since many Greek speaking Jews and Gentiles had come to faith, the
Greek Septuagint also became a favorite text of *Yeshua's* followers. As the
followers of *Yeshua* continued to multiply, they became the top competition for
the *P'rushim* (Pharisees') influence over the Jewish community. After the Temple
was destroyed in 70 A.D/C.E., the Pharisees pressed ahead with a major project
to convert, edit, and redact all Masoretic Hebrew texts of Scriptures into a unified
recension Pharasaic/Rabbinic harmonized, sanctified, authorized text, and also to
write a new Greek text compatible with this project as a replacement for the
Greek Septuagint. (See the excellent and scholarly treatment of this by Prof.
Menachem Cohen of Bar-Ilan University in "The Idea of the Sanctity of the
Biblical Text and the Science of Textual Criticism," from Australia National
University, http://cs.anu.edu.au/~bdm/dilugim/CohenArt/. Fortunately, with the
discovery of the Dead Sea Scrolls, we now have access to Scripture texts which
are more than one thousand years older than our previously oldest Masoretic
Hebrew texts. The discovery of these very ancient Dead Sea Scrolls (1QIsa-a,
1QIsa-b, 4QIsa-d, as well as the Septuagint) revealed something new in Isaiah
53:11; namely, that after the fatal suffering of Isaiah's righteous servant, that the
servant would *"see light"* or *"see the light of life"* (which information our former
Hebrew Masoretic Texts had not contained until the discovery of these far more
ancient Dead Sea Scrolls). This is cited in the footnotes of the NIV translation,
and also from Martin Abegg, Jr., Peter Flint, and Eugene Ulrich, *The Dead Sea
Scrolls Bible: The Oldest Known Bible Translated for the First Time into English* (New
York: HarperCollins Publishers, 1999), 360.)

[199] *Gesenius' Hebrew and Chaldee Lexicon to the Old Testament Scriptures*, H.W.F.
Gesenius, trans. Samuel Prideaux Tregelles, LL.D. (Grand Rapids, MI: Baker
Books, 1979), s.v. "24."

[200] Shawn Lichaa, Nehemia Gordon, Meir Rekhavi, *As it is Written: A Brief Case for
Karaism (n.p* : Hilkiah Press, 2006), 34-38; *Dr.* Irv Bromberg, University of
Toronto, Canada, "The Seasonal Drift of the Traditional (Fixed Arithmetic)
Hebrew Calendar,"
http://www.individual.utoronto.ca/kalendis/hebrew/drift.htm.

[201] The Biblical new moon refers to the *waxing crescent* new moon visible on the viewer's right-hand side of the moon in the northern hemisphere, or viewer's left-hand side in the southern hemisphere, whereas the last half of the month *waning crescent* moon is seen on the viewer's opposite side. The Biblical new moon is not the *astronomical new moon* (the completely *dark moon*) which is indicated on many calendars as the "new moon" but occurs on the day prior to the waxing crescent new moon. The Karaite Korner, "The New Moon in the Hebrew Bible," http://www.karaite-korner.org/new_moon.shtml; Talmud Yerushalmi, Rosh Hashanah 57d.

[202] *Gesenius' Hebrew and Chaldee Lexicon to the Old Testament Scriptures*, H.W.F. Gesenius, trans. Samuel Prideaux Tregelles, LL.D. (Grand Rapids, MI: Baker Books, 1979), s.v. "6153."

[203] Joseph Henry Thayer, D.D., *A Greek-English Lexicon of the New Testament Being Grimm's Wilke's Clavis Novi Testamenti*, trans. Joseph Henry Thayer, D.D. (Wheaton, IL, Martinsville, IL: Evangel Publishing Company, 1974), s.v. "**en**natos,1766," 216. The "ninth" hour by first century Jewish reckoning (Luke 23:44) was 3:00 pm according to our modern time reckoning.

[204] Flavius Josephus, *Wars of the Jews* (VI.9.3); *Josephus: Complete Works*, William Whiston, trans. (Grand Rapids, MI: Kregel Publications, 1960), 588.

[205] Joseph Henry Thayer, D.D., *A Greek-English Lexicon of the New Testament Being Grimm's Wilke's Clavis Novi Testamenti*, trans. Joseph Henry Thayer, D.D. (Wheaton, IL, Martinsville, IL: Evangel Publishing Company, 1974), s.v. "**en**natos,1766," 216. The "ninth" hour by first century Jewish reckoning (Luke 23:44) was 3:00 pm according to our modern time reckoning.

[206] David Instone-Brewer, *Jesus of Nazareth's Trial in the Uncensored Talmud* (n.p.: n.d), 275, http://www.tyndalehouse.com/Bulletin/62=2011/07_Instone_Brewer2.pdf.

[207] The first century Jews from Galilee did not pronounce the Hebrew letter *'ayin* at the end of a word. David Stern, *Jewish New Testament Commentary* (Clarksville, MD: Jewish New Testament Publications, Inc, 1996), 4-5; David Flusser, *Jewish Sources in Early Christianity* (Tel-Aviv: MOD Books, 1989), 15.

[208] The Hebrew gospel of Mattityahu (Matthew) consistently spells the name as "*Yeshu*" except in Matt. 1:21 where the angel formally assigned the name "*Yeshua.*" There the Shem-Tov Hebrew gospel of Mattityahu (1:21) fully spells out "*Yeshua.*" George Howard, *Hebrew Gospel of Matthew* (Macon, GA: Mercer University Press, 1995). Sometimes the subject comes up that the name "*Yeshu*" is a derogatory acronym meaning "may his name and memory be obliterated." It is highly dubious that this acronym originated from the first century. The earliest known reference to that acronym did not appear until medieval times during the tenth century from *Toldoth Yeshu* narratives (cf: Edman, L (1857). *Sefer Toledot*

Yeshu sive Liber de ortu et origine Jesu ex editione wagenseiliana transcriptus et explicatus [*Sefer Toledot Yeshu*: or *The Book of the rising and origin of Jesus from the Wagenseiliana edition: Transcription and Explanatiori*]; also, George Howard, *Hebrew Gospel of Matthew* (Macon, GA: Mercer University Press, 1995), 206-207.

[209] Quotation from David Instone-Brewer, *Jesus of Nazareth's Trial in the Uncensored Talmud* (n.p.: n.d), 275, from Tyndale Bulletin 62.2 (2011) used with permission granted verbally via phone at 011-44-1223-566601, http://www.tyndalehouse.com/Bulletin/62=2011/07_Instone_Brewer2.pdf. For those desiring more in-depth information concerning this quotation from the Talmud regarding the crucifixion of *Yeshua*, readers are encouraged to look up this URL where they may read the scholarly treatment of Sanhedrin 43a in b. Talmud from the PDF by David Instone-Brewer. He cites evidence of messy attempts to erase this from some Talmud manuscripts that existed prior to the invention of the printing press.

[210] *The International Standard Bible Encyclopaedia* (Grand Rapids, MI: Wm. B. Eerdmans Publishing Co., 1939, 1956), s.v. "Sanhedrin" (by Paul Levertoff).

[211] Leon Morris, *The Gospel According to John: The English Text with Introduction, Exposition and Notes* (Grand Rapids: Wm. B. Eerdmans Publishing Co., 1971), 779.

[212] Jonathan Ben-Dov, *Head of All Years: Astronomy and Calendars at Qumran in Their Ancient Context*, Studies on the Texts of the Desert of Judah vol. 78 (*n.p.*: Brill Academic Pub, 2008).

[213] Talmud Yerushalmi, Rosh Hashanah, Mishnah 2:6-7; 2:8-3:1; Jacob Neusner, William Scott Green, and Calvin Goldscheider, eds., *The Talmud of the Land of Israel: A Preliminary Translation and Explanation*, trans. Edward A. Goldman., vol. 16 (Chicago and London: The University of Chicago Press, 1988), 6-7.

[214] In limited situations (or interpretations) where *Torah Moshe* (the Law of Moses) was unclear, only then did *Torah Moshe* authorized that the court (i.e. which was the Bet Din court during the days of *Yeshua*), its judges, or the Levite priests, at the place that God would choose (i.e. Jerusalem) would be authorized to make halakhic decisions or verdicts pertaining to unclear situations (Deut. 17:8-13).

[215] David Daube, *He that Cometh* (1966), a lecture given by Professor David Daube October, 1966, p. 6. Daube (raised as an orthodox Jew) has been hailed on two continents as one of the world's foremost biblical scholars. He states that the tradition of the Passover *Afikoman* is *universally found* in *all* versions of the Passover eve liturgy found as far back as any records exist; therefore, it must be very ancient. Daube shows that the *Afikoman* tradition was used for lambless Passover suppers where a piece of *matzah* was symbolically substituted for the missing Passover lamb.

216 Leon Morris, *The Gospel According to John: The English Text with Introduction, Exposition and Notes* (Grand Rapids: Wm. B. Eerdmans Publishing Co., 1971), 782-785.

217 Talmud Yerushalmi, Rosh Hashanah, Mishnah 2:6-7; Jacob Neusner, William Scott Green, and Calvin Goldscheider, eds., *The Talmud of the Land of Israel: A Preliminary Translation and Explanation*, trans. Edward A. Goldman., vol. 16 (Chicago and London: The University of Chicago Press, 1988), 6.

218 Talmud Yerushalmi, Rosh Hashanah Mishnah 2:1, (Gemara 57d-58a); Jacob Neusner, William Scott Green, and Calvin Goldscheider, eds., Edward A. Goldman, trans., *The Talmud of the Land of Israel: A Preliminary Translation and Explanation*, trans. Edward A. Goldman., vol. 16 (Chicago and London: The University of Chicago Press, 1988), 56-62.

219 Talmud Yerushalmi, Rosh Hashanah, Mishnah 2:8,12; 3:1; Jacob Neusner, William Scott Green, and Calvin Goldscheider, eds., Edward A. Goldman, trans., *The Talmud of the Land of Israel: A Preliminary Translation and Explanation*, vol. 16 (Chicago and London: The University of Chicago Press, 1988), 6-7.

220 This note explains why there would be a lambless Passover supper the day before the official Temple sacrifice of the Passover. But first, there are two verses which may be misconstrued to be saying that the Passover lambs were sacrificed prior to the Last Supper—the day before *Yeshua* was crucified. They are found in Luke 22:7 and Mark 14:12. "Then came the Day of Unleavened Bread, when the Passover **must be killed**. And He [*Yeshua*] sent Peter and John, saying, 'Go and prepare the Passover for us, that we may eat'" (Luke 22:7 NKJV, emphasis added). Also in Mark 14:12 (NKJV): "Now on the first day of Unleavened Bread, **when they killed the Passover** *lamb*, His disciples said to Him, 'Where do You want us to go and prepare, that You may eat the Passover?'" At first glance, these references sound as if the Passover was sacrificed just prior to the Last Supper, on the day before *Yeshua* was crucified. However, in *both passages*, the Greek text is using the customary *imperfect tense*. Kenneth S. Wuest, *Wuest's Word Studies From the Greek New Testament*, vol. 1 (Grand Rapids, MI, 1973), p. 258 clarifies that: "The customary imperfect is used meaning 'when they were **accustomed** to kill the *to pascha*'" (emphasis added, Mark 14:12). In other words, the Greek text is not saying that the Passover had actually been killed that day, but rather that customarily they would have been killed that day. Wuest then provides his own translation of Mark 14:12 for the purpose to clarify the understanding of the customary *imperfect tense*: "*And on the first day of the unleavened loaves, when it was* **THE CUSTOM** *to kill the Passover, His disciples say to Him, Where do you desire that we go and prepare to eat the Passover?*" (Emphasis added.) The Greek customary *imperfect tense* is used to describe a custom or something that has been routinely done in the past. It is not used to refer to a specific action or event that occurred.

This tense is distinctly in contrast to the Greek *aorist indicative tense* (which references a past action as simply having taken place). These passages (Luke 22:7 and Mark 14:12) therefore, are not describing an event that took place (the Passover sacrifice), but rather they are referencing what would have been the normal custom. These peculiar references from Mark and Luke are reflective of a dispute between the Pharisees versus the Boethusians, the Sadducees and the Bet Din Court which would occur from time to time pertaining to an occasional debate as to which day the new moon appeared. The official confirmation of the new moon initiated the start of a new Jewish month. This, in turn, would impact which day the Passover was to be sacrificed at the Temple. The history of disputes, as to which day the new moon appeared, is documented in the Talmud Yerushalmi (The Jerusalem Talmud), Rosh Hashanah Mishna 2:1 (57d-58a) and described in *The Talmud of the Land of Israel: A Preliminary Translation and Explanation*, trans. Edward A. Goldman, eds. Jacob Neusner, William Scott Green, and Calvin Goldscheider, vol. 16, Rosh Hashanah (Chicago and London: The University of Chicago Press, 1988), 6-7. Whatever day the new moon appeared, it in turn, would effect what day the Passover was to be sacrificed at the Temple. Mark and Luke could have simply stated that it was the day when the Passover *"was* killed." They expressly did not say that because the sacrifice did not happen that day. Instead, not merely one of the two Gospels, but *both* of these Gospels deliberately used the customary *imperfect tense* to indicate only the custom, rather than to cite an actual event of the Passover sacrifice. Most significantly, the fact that *Yeshua* used the *Afikoman* tradition during the Last Supper (which represented a symbolic substitute for a missing Passover lamb) *clearly confirms* that the Passover had not yet been sacrificed at the time of the Last Supper—otherwise *Yeshua* would have sinned by not eating a Passover lamb while residing in Jerusalem. Both gospels cite many Passover traditions throughout the Last Supper, but all gospels completely omit any mention of the Passover lamb which was the central purpose for a Passover supper. So why did this controversy exist? It was the Bet Din Court that held the official authority authorized by the Law of Moses (Deut. 17:8-13) to render verdict decisions on questionable matters, such as when the new moon was officially sanctified (recognized) for the Temple activities (Talmud Yerushalmi, Rosh Hashanah, Mishnah 2:8). This commandment (Deut. 17:8-13) made such court decisions final and binding. Furthermore, this court authority was duly recognized and adhered to during this Temple period—even if the new moon assessment was later *proven* to be wrong(!)—as reported in Talmud Yerushalmi, Rosh ha-Shanah, Mishnah 2:12 and Mishnah 3:1. Once the proclamation of the new moon sanctification occurred, the news of it would immediately begin to be disseminated to Jews throughout the nations so that they could begin to prepare for the Passover— some Jews making distant pilgrimages to Jerusalem. The Pharisees would have to abide by the Bet Din Court verdict—even if they disagreed with the sanctified day of the new moon sighting. However, they could still celebrate a lambless Passover on whatever day they considered to be the correct day. Since the Pharisees controlled the synagogues, much of the Jewish community would have been aware of their opinion. All this worked to *Yeshua's* advantage because he could then celebrate a lambless Last Supper Passover with his disciples according to the Pharisees' opinion of the date of the new moon, and then the next day he would be crucified on the official date and hour when the Passover lambs were actually sacrificed at the Temple according to the official sanctification ruling of the new moon by the *Bet Din* Court (Deut. 17:8-13). The ancient Talmud Yerushalmi (Pesahim 10:8A) reports that when a Passover offering [lamb] was eaten, the *Afikoman* tradition was omitted. Accordingly, Yeshua's utilization of the Afikoman tradition during his Last Supper Passover is confirmation that the Passover lambs had not yet been sacrificed at the time of the Last Supper.

[221] Surprisingly, the summation of evidence indicates that *Yeshua* was actually crucified on a Thursday (not Friday). A Thursday crucifixion is the *only* scenario that harmonizes with all the details recorded by *Yeshua's talmidim* (disciples). It resolves at least four misunderstood contradictions in the gospels! The following facts introduce how this scenario fits together. The ancient Jerusalem Talmud Yerushalmi (Mishnah Rosh Hashanah 2:1 – 3:1) deals extensively with frustrations between the Pharisees and the Boethusians over various false witnesses of the new moon. Official recognition of the waxing crescent new moon was important because it indicated the first day of a new month. This, in turn, would effect which day of the week the Passover (14th of the month) would occur, as well as other festival days of the first month. The text in dispute was Lev. 23:5-16. All parties (Pharisees, Boethusians, and Sadducees) agreed from verse 5 that the Passover was to be observed on the 14th day of the first month (*Aviv*). All parties also agreed that the next day (the 15th day of the month) was to be the first day of a seven day Feast of Unleavened Bread (Lev. 23:6). The next verse (Lev. 23:7) is where disputes began to arise. That text states: "On the first day [i.e. the first day of the Feast of Unleavened Bread, which began on the 15th day of the first month] you are to have a holy convocation [*mikra kodesh*, i.e. a sacred assembly]; **don't do any kind of ordinary work**" [*mlechet avodah lo* ("no labor of work)"] (Lev. 23:7 CJB, emphasis added). The Pharisees taught that this day of "no work" was to be a *Festival Sabbath*. However, the Boethusians and the Sadducees taught that it was a day of rest but not a "Sabbath" because the text did not specifically label it as a "*Shabbat*" (like the text did twice for the Day of Atonement a few verses later—Lev. 23:32). This disagreement, in turn, led to another dispute about the date for the next event during the Feast of Unleavened Bread: namely, the waving of the *omer reishiyt* (the *sheaf of first fruits* of the barley harvest). The text states that the priest was "to wave the sheaf before *ADONAI* [the LORD, *YHVH*], . . . on the **day AFTER the Shabbat**." (Lev. 23:11 CJB,

emphasis added). What "Shabbat" day was this referring to? The Pharisees taught that it referred to the 15th of the month—the day of "no ordinary work" (Lev. 23:7)—and this would mean that the Pharisee's barley first fruits should be offered on the next work day—(which most always was the 16th of the month). The Boethusians and the Sadducees, contrary to the Pharisees, taught that the first fruits barley wave offering on the "**day AFTER the Shabbat**" was referring to the day after the normal weekly Sabbath day during the week of Unleavened Bread (which might fall on any of a variety of dates during the week of Unleavened Bread, but would *always* fall on the day after the weekly Sabbath during the week of Unleavened Bread.) This infrequently might match the Pharisee's date of the 16th of the month. But usually it would be several dates apart from the 16th, depending on which date the weekly Sabbath day happened to fall on.

There is but one circumstance out of a variety of situations which perfectly matches the Gospel narrative, and, at the same time, it harmonizes with both the Pharisee interpretation and the Boethusian / Sadducean interpretation. This happenstance is when the Temple Passover sacrifice (and the crucifixion) occurred on a Thursday—the 14th day of the first month *Aviv*. But why would the Pharisees observe a lambless Passover on the day before that? It was sometimes difficult (not having telescopes in those days, and perhaps also due to problems with cloud cover) to identify precisely which day the waxing crescent new moon appeared—which would indicate the first day of the new month *Aviv*. The Pharisees evidently disagreed with which day the Bet Din court sanctified as the day of the new moon. (See prior endnote.) But, according to Talmud Yerushalmi and (Deut. 17:8-13), the Pharisees would have to abide by the Bet Din court decision. However, the Pharisees could still observe a *lambless* Passover supper on whatever day they thought to be consistent with their assessment of the new moon—their lambless Passover thus falling on the 13th, instead of the 14th of the month. The official Temple Passover sacrifice would, however, fall on a Thursday (the official 14th of the month according to the Bet Din Court ruling) and all parties would have to adhere to this Bet Din Court decision. Friday would be the 15th of the month, which was the date for the Pharisees' festival Sabbath (in conformance with the Bet Din new moon sanctification). And Saturday (the 16th) would be the normal weekly Sabbath. This would effectuate the rare situation where the Pharisees would face two back-to-back Sabbaths (Friday, their Festival Sabbath, and Saturday the weekly Sabbath). The Pharisees would normally consider the 16th of the month to be their *omer reishiyt*/first fruits date. But since this 16th of the month fell on the day of the weekly Sabbath, the Pharisees would have to postpone their *omer reishiyt* until *after* both back-to-back Sabbaths (namely, after their 15th of the month Festival Sabbath as well as after the weekly Sabbath. They would therefore deem their *omer reishiyt* day to be on Sunday the 17th of the month (which was the same day when the Temple, the Boethusians, and the Sadducees would offer their *omer reishiyt*/barley first fruits). **Ultimately, this scenario indicates that Yeshua was crucified on a Thursday Passover, the 14th of the month *Aviv*.**

A Thursday crucifixion (5th day of the Jewish week) *resolves four misunderstood inconsistencies* within the Gospels:

(1) **The first contradiction this resolves is found in John19:31-32 concerning the reason why there was a rush to get the bodies off the crosses before sunset.** The answer to this provides solutions to several questions related to Passover events. John 19:31 (TLV) reads: "The **next day** [i.e. the approaching day following the crucifixion] **was a festival *Shabbat*.** So that the bodies should not remain on the execution stake during *Shabbat*, the Judean leaders asked Pilate to have the legs broken and to have the bodies taken away" (John 19:31 TLV, emphasis added). People naturally assume this approaching Sabbath after the coming sunset was the normal weekly Sabbath. It was not! The rush to get the bodies off the crosses *before sunset* on the day of the crucifixion was *not* due to an approaching weekly Sabbath, but rather due to the approaching Pharisee's 15th of the month *festival Shabbat*. This also indicates that Yeshua was crucified on the 14th of *Aviv*—the day of the Passover offering at the Temple, and the day *before* the Pharisee's 15th of the month *festival Shabbat*—which is why there was the rush to get the bodies off the cross before sundown. It also establishes that the Temple Passover sacrifice did not occur prior to *Yeshua's* Last Supper. Had the 14th of the month Passover been sacrificed just prior to *Yeshua's* Last Supper, then that would have meant that the crucifixion occurred during the 15th of the month –the day of the Pharisees' festival *Shabbat*—but that was the very day when they specifically **did not want bodies hanging on crosses**. This is another confirmation that the Passover was not sacrificed prior to Yeshua's Last Supper.

(2) **The second contradiction this resolves is found in Matthew 12:40 where *Yeshua* prophesied that he would be buried during "three days and three nights."** For this scenario, keep in mind that our modern days begin at midnight (12:00 a.m.). This means that each modern day [Saturday for example] would have two nighttimes; namely, (1) after 12:00 a.m., the beginning of Saturday, and (2) the other nighttime from sundown until midnight (which is the end of Saturday). In contrast, the Jewish Biblical day only had one nighttime each day beginning immediately after sunset—the start of the Biblical day. Now, if *Yeshua* was crucified on a Friday, it is not possible to fit in even so much as a *part* of a third day's daytime time, nor any *part* of a third nighttime between *Yeshua's* burial and the resurrection. **Thus, with a "Friday" crucifixion, this would leave not three, but *only two nighttime dates*, and *only two daytime dates* in the tomb.** With a "Friday" crucifixion, (1) the first nighttime date in the tomb would begin *after* the sunset of the "Friday" crucifixion which initiated the evening of the 7th Jewish day of the week (modern Saturday). (Keep in mind that the beginning of evening

was the start of a new Biblical Jewish day.) (2) The second nighttime date in the tomb would begin after sundown (of modern Saturday) which would introduce the first Jewish day of the week (modern Sunday)—but there would be no further evenings available after that. This leaves only two nighttime dates in the tomb. Likewise, a Friday crucifixion would only leave two daytimes dates in the tomb—not three. The first daytime being the final daylight of a Friday crucifixion when the body was placed in the tomb, and (2) the second daylight day would be the full daylight of the 7th day of the week—our modern Saturday. This only leaves two daylight days in the tomb (not three) because *Yeshua* was resurrected while it was still dark before daylight on the first day of the week (modern Sunday, John 20:1). However, if *Yeshua* was crucified on a Thursday (instead of Friday) this provides precisely a part of three daylight dates and a part of three nighttime dates in the tomb. Quoting *Yeshua* from Matt. 12:40 (TLV): "For just as Jonah was in the belly of the great fish for three days and three nights, so the Son of Man will be in the heart of the earth for three days and three nights." Just as *Yeshua* had prophesied (Matt 12:40), the Greek texts indicate that *Yeshua* spent a *part* of three daylight dates and a part of three nighttime dates in the tomb **but the total hours in the tomb was likely somewhere approximating 48 hours (which fits very well with the stage of rigor mortis found on the Shroud--Mark** Antonacci, *Test the Shroud* (*n.p.*, Forefront Publishing Co., 2015), 283). Thus, with a Thursday crucifixion, the three daylight days in the tomb would be (1) a part of Thursday afternoon when the body was placed in the tomb until the close of sunset, (2) full daylight on Friday (the 6th Jewish day of the week, and (2) full daylight on Saturday—the Jewish 7th day of the week, but no daylight on Sunday the 1st day of the Jewish week because *Yeshua* was resurrected while it was still dark before daylight on the first day of the week (John 20:1). The three evenings in the tomb for a Thursday crucifixion would be: (1) a full evening after the Thursday crucifixion, (2) a full evening after Friday's sunset (which would be the beginning of the weekly *Shabbat*), and (3) only a partial evening after Saturday's sunset (which initiated the first Jewish day of the week) because Yeshua was resurrected while it was still dark on the first day of the week (John 20:1). A Thursday crucifixion therefore provides precisely a part of three daylight dates and three nighttime dates in the tomb, fulfilling *Yeshua's* prophecy of Matt. 12:40. This points to a Thursday crucifixion.

(3) **The third contradiction this clarification unriddles is found in Luke 24:13-21 where two disciples on the road to Emmaus met *Yeshua* on the day of the resurrection and told him during the first day of the week (modern Sunday) that today (Sunday) was the third day since/after the crucifixion.** They said to *Yeshua*: "Today is the **third day since** these things happened" (i.e. the third day since the crucifixion, Luke 24:1,13,21 KJV, emphasis added). Sunday is not the "third day" *after* Friday; but Sunday is the "third day" *after* Thursday.

(4) **The fourth contradiction that this clarification solves is found in Matthew 28:1. There, the Greek text states the women discovered the empty tomb after the Sabbaths (plural Sabbaths!) on the first day of the week.** Most translations render something similar to the King James Version: "In the end of the sabbath, as it began to dawn toward the first *day* of the week, came Mary Magdalene and the other Mary to see the sepulcher" (Matt. 28:1). There they discovered the empty tomb of *Yeshua*. The actual Greek text of this passage uses the *plural* word "Sabbaths" (*sabbaton*); not the singular (*sabbatou*). It is literally translated "After the Sabbath*s*" **(plural)**, not "After the Sabbath" (singular). Some Bible scholars have noted this: James Montgomery Boice, *The Gospel of Matthew: Volume 1,* (Grand Rapids: Baker Books, 2001), 222; also, the International Standard Version (ISV), and the Young's Literal Translation (YLT) do correctly translate this as "Sabbaths" (plural) from the original Greek. Boice comments how this plurality of Sabbaths puzzled most translators who then **altered** their translation to the **singular** Sabbath. If *Yeshua* was crucified on a Thursday, then after sunset that evening would have initiated the next Jewish day (Friday) which was the Pharisee's *"festival Sabbath"* on the 15th of the month (their interpretation of Lev 23:5-7), which then would be followed by the weekly 7th day Sabbath. Accordingly, the first day of the week (Sunday, the day of the resurrection) would have followed two consecutive days of Sabbath observance—precisely as stated in the Greek text of Matthew 28:1. This points again to a Thursday crucifixion, followed by **two Sabbaths** (the Pharisee's Friday *festival Sabbath*, followed by the 7th day weekly Sabbath), followed by the resurrection on the first day of the week (Sunday) when the women found the empty tomb.

[222] David Daube, *He That Cometh* (1966), Lecture given by Professor David Daube October 1966, pp 9-10; *Encyclopaedia Judaica: CD-ROM Edition* (Jerusalem: Keter Publishing House, *n.d.*), s.v. "Afikoman," (by Dov Nov/Editorial Staff Encylopedia Judaica; *Encyclopaedia Judaica: CD-ROM Edition* (Jerusalem: Keter Publishing House, *n.d.*), s.v. "Passover," "The Seder" (by Louis Jacobs).

[223] David Daube cites various evidence indicating that the *Afikoman* originated from the Jews of the Diaspora (and perhaps more specifically from the Jews of Alexandria). One example, is the wise son's question which is based from the Greek Septuagint (rather than a Hebrew text) of scripture. David Daube, *He That Cometh* (1966), Lecture given by Professor David Daube October 1966 held in the Crypt of St. Paul's Cathedral, London, 9-11.

[224] David Daube cites that Sephardic Jews still use the *Afikoman* to represent the final piece of the missing Passover lamb. David Daube, *He That Cometh* (1966), Lecture given by Professor David Daube October 1966, pp 9-10; also the *Encyclopaedia Judaica* informs that with the destruction of the Temple, the *Afikoman* continued to represent a reminder of the Paschal sacrifice eaten at the end of the Passover seder, and also that some Jews still use the *Afikoman* to anticipate *the coming* of

the Messiah, *Encyclopaedia Judaica:* CD-ROM Edition (Jerusalem: Keter Publishing House, *n.d.*), s.v. "Passover," "The Seder" (by Louis Jacobs) and also s.v. "Afikoman" (by Dov Noy/Editorial Staff Encyclopaedia Judaica).

[225] The Jewish Greek word *Afikoman* is derived or coined from the Greek word *aphikomenos.* (David Daube, *New Testament Judaism: Collected Works of David Daube,* Calum Carmichael, ed., vol. 2 [Berkley: Robbins Collection Publications, 2000], 425.) The use of a Greek word *Afikoman* is indicative that the *Afikoman* tradition originated from the Jews of the Diaspora whose primary language was Greek. Modern Rabbinic Judaism claims the word means "that which comes after," or "dessert," or "after-dinner revelry." Renowned Jewish Scholar David Daube asserts that such translations are "far-fetched, tortuous" for which there is no evidence whatever in the whole of Greek literature. Daube clarifies that *Afikoman* is the Greek *aphikomenos* or *ephikomenos* (a term similar to the more common word *erchomenos*) and translates as "The Coming One," or "He that cometh." The term *Afikoman* was used by the Jews of the Diaspora as a reference to the Messiah ("The Coming One"). David Daube, *He That Cometh* (1966), Lecture given by Professor David Daube October 1966, p 8,14.

[226] Eminent Jewish scholar David Daube has been acclaimed as "one of the greatest legal scholars in the world" during the 20th century. He grew up in an orthodox Jewish home in Germany, and escaped NAZI Germany. Three of his fields of scholarship were Roman law, Biblical law, and Hebraic law. Concerning the *Afikoman,* Daube wrote that the *earliest* reference to the word *Afikoman* is found in the Passover liturgy. He states that the word *Afikoman* properly translated means "he that comes." Daube notes that the *Afikoman* tradition is "a universal rite, found in **all** versions of the Passover eve liturgy, **so must be considered very old**" (emphasis added). The *Afikoman* first appears near the start of the Passover in the Seder order titled *Yachaz* ("let him divide") where the *Afikoman* is broken in half and hidden away. It then appears again near the close of the Seder (after the supper) within the Seder order titled *Tzafun* ("that which is hidden") where it is retrieved from its hidden location, and passed around to the participants to break off their own piece from it to be eaten as the final morsel of the supper. The *Afikoman* therefore prominently (and significantly!) bridges nearly the entire span of the Passover ceremony. David Daube suggests that due to its theological implications pertaining to *Yeshua,* Rabbis deliberately offered tortuous definitions of the word *Afikoman*—which Daube describes as wide off the mark and perhaps deliberately so, as though to obscure its implications with *Yeshua* during his final Passover last supper. Daube cites that sometime after 300 C.E./A.D., changes were made to the Passover ceremony so that questions posed about the meaning of the Passover rituals were re-arranged and moved senselessly to the beginning of the liturgy *before any* of the Passover rituals could have been observed by four young sons. Why would children ask questions

about rituals which have not yet been observed during the ceremony? Daube suggests that the purpose for this rearrangement served to disassociate the significance of the Passover rituals from *Yeshua's* application of the *Afikoman*. There are four types of sons having questions about the Passover Seder. It is the wise son who asks the important question: "What is the meaning of these Passover rituals (its testimonies, decrees, and ordinances)?" Daube points out that here the wise son is asking the important question as to what the is meaning of these Passover rituals, but the Rabbinic definitions of the word *Afikoman* provides the son's question with a variety of widely conflicting, unsuitable translations concerning trifling little meal customs as the answer to the wise son's meritorious question: such as "that which comes after," "desert," "after diner revelry," "entertainment." Is that what the Passover liturgy is all about? A wise son would be disappointed with that answer. Daube indicates that this Jewish Greek word was coined off by the Jews from the actual Greek word *aphikomenos* ("the coming one"). Daube concludes that as soon as it is realized that the Jewish/Greek meaning of the hidden *Afikoman* means "he that comes" (i.e. the Messiah) it becomes clear why it is addressed to the wise son as the full answer to his question and sums up the significance of the rituals attached to the Passover. Daube also cites the Didache as an early first century document of the Passover tradition (from the *Natzratim* Jews, the Jewish sect of the Nazarenes, who were the followers of *Yeshua*) wherein the "hidden" *Afikoman* matzah is then "revealed" (unhidden) and then reunited with its former broken half of matzah while reciting: "As this broken bread was scattered on the mountains and, being gathered together, became one, so may your congregation be gathered together." It is evident how this tradition appears to reflect back to the prophetic hope recorded by *Yesha'yahu*/Isaiah 11:10-16 pertaining to a future "prophetic Passover" wherein Messiah will become revealed ("unhidden") and will "come" to reunite the Diaspora Jews back together as one body with the Israeli Jews into the Promised Land. (It would seem obvious that Diaspora Jews might regard this prophesy, which specifically pertains to Diaspora Jews, as something very special and personal for them.) This futuristic "prophetic Passover" of Isaiah 11 specifically foretells how God would one day "recover the **second time** with His hand the remnant of His people, who will remain . . . and will assemble the banished ones of Israel, and will gather the dispersed of Judah [i.e. Diaspora Jews] from the four corners of the earth . . . and . . . will utterly destroy the tongue of the Sea of Egypt; and He will wave His hand over the River with His scorching wind . . . and make *men* walk over dry shod . . . just as there was for Israel in the day that they came up out of the land of Egypt" (Isaiah 11:11-12,15-16 NASB). This prophesy concerning the Diaspora Jews certainly alludes to a future prophetic exodus event. The Didache concludes its Passover ritual of the *Afikoman* ("The Coming One") with a similar Aramaic exclamation: "*Maranatha!*" (Translated: "Our Lord *COMES*," i.e. "the Coming One"). *Sha'ul/Paulos* also referenced the *Afikoman* tradition in much the same manner as the Didache (where just prior to partaking of the *Afikoman*, it is first reunited together with its former broken half to represent God's people being united together as one body): "The bread which we break—isn't it a sharing of Messiah's body? Since there is one bread, we who are many are one body—for we all partake of one bread" (1 Cor. 10:16-17 TLV). One of the most common first century references to the Messiah was "the Coming One" as cited in variety of passages: (Matt. 11:3; Luke 7:19; John 6:14; 11:27; 12:13; Heb. 10:37; Dan. 7:13; Ps. 118:26). David Daube, *He That Cometh* (1966), Lecture given by Professor David Daube October 1966 held in the Crypt of St. Paul's Cathedral, London, 6-13; David Daube, *New Testament Judaism: Collected Works of David Daube,* Calum Carmichael, ed., vol. 2 (Berkley: Robbins Collection Publications, 2000), 425-440.

[227] David Daube, *New Testament Judaism: Collected Works of David Daube,* "The Significance of the *Afikoman,*" Calum Carmichael, ed., vol. 2 (Berkley: Robbins Collection Publications, 2000), 425-427; David Daube, *He That Cometh* (1966), Lecture given by Professor David Daube October 1966 held in the Crypt of St. Paul's Cathedral, London , 6,13.

[228] When *Yeshua* broke bread during the Last Supper Passover, the Greek word for "bread" is *artos* (Matt 26:26; Mark 14:22; Luke 22:19; 1 Cor. 10:16-17; 11:23. The Jewish-Greek definition of *artos* (as used in the Septuagint) is a generalized Greek word which applies to all types of bread (including matzah) and was often used to translate the Hebrew word *lechem* ("bread"), but there was no Greek word to translate the Hebrew word *matzah*("unleavened bread"), *The Complete Biblical Library* (The New Testament Greek-English Dictionary) Thoralf Gilbrant, Intl ed., vol. 11 (Springfield, MO: The Complete Biblical Library, 1990), 446. This word *artos* was used in the Greek Septuagint to describe the Passover unleavened bread (Heb. *matzah*) for example in Deut. 16:3: "you shall eat it with unleavened (Gr. *azuma*) bread (Gr. *artos*) of affliction."

[229] "David Daube was one of the greatest legal scholars in the world," said Robert Cole, a professor emeritus of law at UC Berkley. He was a scholar of Roman law, Biblical law, Hebraic Law, Talmudic and Jewish Law, Rabbinic Judaism, New Testament, and ethics. He published something nearly every year from 1932 through 2000. He was raised an orthodox Jew. He escaped NAZI Germany in 1933 at the age of 24. At that time, he was fluent in six languages (German, French, Latin, Ancient Greek, Hebrew, and Aramaic, and later in English). He obtained degrees from many universities among which were the University of Freiburg, the University of Gottingen, Cambridge University, and Oxford University, and others. He quickly attained the highest levels of academia in the fields of Roman and Biblical law at Cambridge. He also was a professor at Oxford, and then ultimately relocated as a professor of Roman and Hebraic law

at U.C. Berkeley's Boalt Hall School of Law.
https://www.jweekly.com/1999/03/12/noted-bible-scholar-david-daube-dies/.

[230] David Daube, *He That Cometh* (1966), Lecture given by Professor David Daube October 1966, held in the Crypt of St. Paul's Cathedral, London, p 13.

[231] B. Talmud – Mas. Pesachim 108b. The Passover wine was required to be specifically "red" wine.

[232] David Daube, *New Testament Judaism: Collected Works of David Daube*, Calum Carmichael, ed., vol. 2 (Berkley: Robbins Collection Publications, 2000), 441-442; B. Talmud – Mas. Pesachim 117b-118a; *The Family Haggadah*, Rabbis Nosson Scherman and Meir Zlotowitz, eds., Rabbi Nosson Scherman, trans. (Brooklyn, NY: Mesorah Publications, Ltd., 1994), 69-77.

[233] David Daube, *He That Cometh* (1966), Lecture given by Professor David Daube October 1966, pp 9-10. David Daube notes that Sephardic Jews still use the Afikoman to represent a piece of the Passover lamb. Other references cite this same tradition of using the Afikoman to symbolically represent the missing Passover lamb: *Encyclopaedia Judaica: CD-ROM Edition* (Jerusalem: Keter Publishing House, *n.d.*), s.v. "Afikoman," (by Dov Nov/Editorial Staff Encylopedia Judaica; *Encyclopaedia Judaica: CD-ROM Edition* (Jerusalem: Keter Publishing House, *n.d.*), s.v. "Passover," "The Seder" (by Louis Jacobs).

[234] Talmud Yerushalmi, Rosh Hashanah, Mishnah 2:8,12; Jacob Neusner, William Scott Green, and Calvin Goldscheider, eds., Edward A. Godman, trans., *The Talmud of the Land of Israel: A Preliminary Translation and Explanation*, vol. 16, (Chicago and London: The University of Chicago Press, 1988), 6-7.

[235] Talmud Yerushalmi, Rosh Hashanah, Mishnah 2:12; 3:1; Jacob Neusner, William Scott Green, and Calvin Goldscheider, eds., Edward A. Godman, trans., *The Talmud of the Land of Israel: A Preliminary Translation and Explanation*, vol. 16, (Chicago and London: The University of Chicago Press, 1988), 7.

[236] Flavius Josephus, *Wars of the Jews* (VI.9.3); *Josephus: Complete Works*, William Whiston, trans. (Grand Rapids, MI: Kregel Publications, 1960), 588.

[237] Quotation with permission from David M. Rohl, *Pharaohs and Kings: A Biblical Quest* (New York: Crown Publishers, Inc., 1995), 278-286. Egyptologist David Rohl is citing Egyptian priest Manetho via Josephus. For further research and details see other books by David Rohl, such as: *Exodus: Myth or History*, and *A Test of Time: The Bible—From Myth to History* volume one.

[238] Quotation from David Instone-Brewer, *Jesus of Nazareth's Trial in the Uncensored Talmud* (n.p.: n.d), 275, provided by Tyndale Bulletin 62.2 (2011), used with permission granted verbally via phone at 011-44-1223-566601, http://www.tyndalehouse.com/Bulletin/62=2011/07_Instone_Brewer2.pdf. For

those desiring more in-depth information concerning this quotation from the Talmud regarding the crucifixion of *Yeshua,* readers are encouraged to look up the foregoing URL where they may read the scholarly treatment of b. Sanhedrin 43a in a PDF by David Instone-Brewer.

[239] *The Internatioonal Standard Bible Encyclopaedia* (Grand Rapids, MI: Wm. B. Eerdmans Publishing Co., 1939, 1956), s.v. "Sanhedrin" (by Paul Levertoff).

[240] Exodus 13:14-15; 1 Chronicles 17:21.

[241] No one today can claim to know the Gregorian date when *Yeshua* was crucified because it involves two variables which cannot be known today; namely, (1) what day was the new moon physically observed (which was not legally permitted to be declared if skewed by cloud cover), and (2) concomitant with that, the barley crop must also be found to be in the stage of *aviv* ripeness.

[242] https://www.myjewishlearning.com/article/i-was-redeemed-from-egypt/.

[243] 1906 Jewish Encyclopedia, JewishEncyclopedia.com, s.v. "Sadducees" (by Kaufmann Kohler), http://www.jewishencyclopedia.com/articles/12989-sadducees.

[244] Dr. Alan and Mary Whanger, *The Shroud of Turin: An Adventure of Discovery* (Franklin, TN: Providence House Publishers: 1998), 85.

[245] Martin Abegg, Jr., Peter Flint, and Eugene Ulrich, *The Dead Sea Scrolls Bible: The Oldest Known Bible Translated for the First Time into English* (HarperCollins Publishers: NY, 1999), 267, 360.

[246] Mark Antoacci, *The Resurrection of the Shroud* (New York: M. Evans and Company, Inc, 2000), 109.

[247] Mark Antoacci, *The Resurrection of the Shroud* (New York: M. Evans and Company, Inc, 2000), 113.

[248] XVI International Botanical Congress. "Botanical Evidence Indicates "Shroud Of Turin" Originated In Jerusalem Area Before 8th Century." ScienceDaily, 3 August 1999; https://www.sciencedaily.com/releases/1999/08/990803073154.htm.

[249] Mark Antonacci, *Test the Shroud* (n.p., Forefront Publishing Co., 2015), 11, 101-102; Mark Antonacci, *The Resurrection of the Shroud* (New York: M. Evans and Company, Inc, 2000), 37, 42. The image is due exclusively to molecular changes, not paints, pigments, or other substances, Giulio Fanti, Pierandrea Malfi, *The Shroud of Turin: First Century After Christ!* (Singapore: Pan Stanford Publishing Pte. Ltd, 2015), 21.

[250] Mark Antonacci, *Test the Shroud* (n.p., Forefront Publishing Co., 2015), 11, 101-102; J. Rinaudo, "Protonic Model of Image Formation on the Shroud of Turin," *Third*

International Congress on the Shroud of Turin, Turin, Italy, June 5-7, 1998, p. 4; J. Rinaudo, "A Sign for Our Time," *Shroud Sources Newsletter*, May/June 1996 cited by Mark Antonacci, *The Resurrection of the Shroud* (New York: M. Evans and Company, Inc., 2000), 161, 217.

[251] Mark Antonacci, *Test the Shroud* (n.p., Forefront Publishing Co., 2015), 170; ; J. Rinaudo, "Protonic Model of Image Formation on the Shroud of Turin," *Third International Congress on the Shroud of Turin*, Turin, Italy, June 5-7, 1998, 4-5.

[252] Mark Antonacci, *Test the Shroud* (n.p., Forefront Publishing Co., 2015), 100.

[253] Libb Thims, *Human Chemistry*, vol. 1 (Morrisville: NC: Lulu Enterprises, USA, 2007), 24.

[254] Aaron Saenz, "Microscope Sees Molecules for the First Time," *SingularityHub* [from Singularity University], September 01, 2009, https://singularityhub.com/2009/09/01/microscope-sees-molecules-for-first-time/ .

[255] Mark Antonacci, *Test the Shroud* (n.p., Forefront Publishing Co., 2015), 99.

[256] The Hungary Page, "Dr. Dennis Gabor: What is Holography," *HipCat@Hungary.org*, http://www.americanhungarianfederation.org/FamousHungarians/gabor.

[257] Ian Wilson and Barrie Schwortz, *The Turin Shroud: The Illustrated Evidence* (New York: Barnes and Noble, 2000), 10.

[258] Frank Viviano, "Why Shroud of Turin's Secrets Continue to Elude Science," *National Geographic*, April 17, 2015, https://news.nationalgeographic.com/2015/04/150417-shroud-turin-relics-jesus-catholic-church-religion-science/.

[259] Dr.Alan and Mary Whanger, *The Shroud of Turin: An Adventure of Discovery* (Franklin, TN: Providence House Publishers, 1998), 53-55.

[260] Dr.Alan and Mary Whanger, *The Shroud of Turin: An Adventure of Discovery* (Franklin, TN: Providence House Publishers, 1998), 10, 53-55, 71-72.

[261] Victor Tunkel, lecture 'A Jewish View of the Shroud' to the British Society for the Turin Shroud, 12 May, 1983.

[262] This quotation within quotation is from Solomon Gansfried, *Code of Jewish Law* (*KitzurShulchan Aruch*), trans. Hyman E. Goldin, vol. iv (New York: Hebrew Publishing Company, 1927), Ch. CXCVII. Laws relating to Purification (Tahara) nos 9 & 10 (pp. 99-100).

[263] Entire quotation from Ian Wilson, *The Blood and the Shroud: New Evidence That the World's Most Sacred Relic Is Real* (New York: The Free Press, 1998), 55. Used with permission.

[264] *Jewish Virtual Library*, s.v. "Jewish Holy Scriptures: The Shulkhan Arukh," http://www.jewishvirtuallibrary.org/the-shulkhan-arukh from Joseph Telushkin, *Jewish Literacy* (New York: William Morrow and Co., 1991).

[265] Bonnie B. Lavoie, Gilbert R. Lavoie, Daniel Klustein and John Reagan, "Jesus, the Turin Shroud, and Jewish Burial Customs," *The Biblical Archaeologist* 45, no. 1 (Winter, 1982), 5-6.

[266] Bonnie B. Lavoie, Gilbert R. Lavoie, Daniel Klustein and John Reagan, "Jesus, the Turin Shroud, and Jewish Burial Customs," *The Biblical Archaeologist* 45, no. 1 (Winter, 1982), 5-6.

[267] Leon Morris, *The Gospel According to John: The English Text with Introduction, Exposition and Notes*, General ed. F. F. Bruce (Grand Rapids, MI: Wm. B. Eerdmans Publishing Co., 1971), 824.

[268] Sizes: The Online Quantinary,"Litra," https://sizes.com/units/litra.htm.

[269] Dr. Alan and Mary Whanger, *The Shroud of Turin: An Adventure of Discovery* (Franklin, TN: Providence House Publishers, 1998), 71-72, 83.

[270] *The International Standard Bible Encyclopaedia*, (Grand Rapids, MI: Wm. B. Eerdmans Publishing Co., 1974), s.v. "Myrrh" (by E. W. G. Masterman). Dr. Marzia Boi cites that the Jewish sacred incense of Exodus 30:34-38 included "estacte" or "stacte" (myrrh). He also indicates that incense aromas were used to ward off carrion-eating insects. Dr. Marzia Boi, "The Ethnocultural significance for the use of plants in Ancient Funerary Rituals and its possible implications with pollens found on the Shroud of Turin," *Shroud of Turin Website*, https://www.shroud.com/pdfs/boiveng.pdf.

[271] Encyclopaedia Britannica, s.v. "Mina: Unit of Weight" (by The Editors of Encylopaedia Britannica), https://www.britannica.com/science/mina-unit-of-weight. The minah was a basic standard unit of weight among ancient Hebrews estimated to be 18 ounces. A pound is 16 ounces. Hence, more than 80 minas would be more than 90 pounds. Many English translations state that the weight of the myrrh and aloes brought by Nicodemus was 100 pounds.

[272] H. L. Strack und P. Billerbeck: *Kommentar zum Nuen Testament aus Talmud und Midrash*, 4 vols. (Munchen, 1922-28). Leon Morris, *The Gospel According to John: The English Text with Introduction, Exposition and Notes*, General ed. F. F. Bruce (Grand Rapids, MI: Wm. B. Eerdmans Publishing Co., 1971), 825.

[273] *New World Encyclopedia*, s.v. "Gamaliel," http://www.newworldencyclopedia.org/entry/Gamaliel.

[274] Luke 23:54. A.T. Robertson, *Word Pictures in the New Testament*, vol. 2 (Nashville, TN: Broadman Press, 1930), 289. This same word *epiphosko* is also used in

Matthew 28:1 (ASV): "Now late on the Sabbath day, as it began to dawn [*epiphoskousei*] toward the first *day* of the week . . . ." A.T. Robertson cites that Luke 23:54 and Matt. 28:1 employ the Jewish-Greek usage of the Greek word *ephiphosko* meaning (with its Jewish-Greek definition) the twilight transition period leading to a new 24 hour Jewish day which begins once evening arrives. Unfortunately, there is no translation of the Messianic Writings (New Testament) in existence which translates the Greek using the Jewish-Greek definitions of the Greek words. The Jewish Septuagint (LXX) would be an ideal source for this by reverse engineering its Greek words to extract their definitions from the original Hebrew word definition (which the Septuagint was trying to translate from Hebrew). The Jews also coined some their own new Greek words; A.T. Robertson, *Word Pictures in the New Testament*, vol. 1 (Nashville, TN: Broadman Press, 1930), 240. J.A.T. Robinson, "The Shroud of Turin and The Grave—Clothes of the Gospels," in *Proceedings*; A. Feuillet, "The Identification and the Disposition of the Funerary Linens of Jesus' Burial According to the Data of the Fourth Gospel," *Shroud Spectrum International* 4 (September 1982) 13-23, reprint from *La Sindone E La Scienze*, II Congresso Internazionale di Sindonologia, Turin, Italy, 1978.

[275] Mark Antonacci, *Test the Shroud* (*n.p.*, Forefront Publishing Co., 2015), 60; Mark Antonacci, *The Resurrection of the Shroud* (New York: M. Evans and Company, Inc., 2000), 98.

[276] Martin Abegg, Jr., Peter Flint, and Eugene Ulrich, *The Dead Sea Scrolls Bible: The Oldest Known Bible Translated for the First Time into English* (New York: HarperCollins Publishers Inc, 1999), 360.

[277] Many actual Roman census records have been found among Egyptian papyri, and they employ the same Greek word for "enrollment" recorded in the book of Luke 2:2. Jack Finegan, *Light from the Ancient Past: The Archaeological Background of the Hebrew-Christian Religion*, Volume II (Princeton: Princeton University Press, 1969), 258.

[278] *The Jewish Encyclopedia*, (Funk & Wagnalls Company, 1901), s.v. "Pseudo-messiahs," (by Kaufmann Kohler, H.G. Friedmann), http://jewishencyclopedia.com/articles/12416-pseudo-messiahs.

[279] Robert A. Rucker, "Status of Research on the Shroud of Turin," April 18, 2019, *Shroud Research Network*. To find this paper, visit the website at http://www.shroudresearch.net/home.html,

[280] Mark Antonacci, *Test the Shroud* (*n.p.*, Forefront Publishing Co., 2015), 114.

[281] Mark Antonacci, *Test the Shroud* (*n.p.*, Forefront Publishing Co., 2015), 115-116.

[282] Mark Antonacci, *Test the Shroud* (*n.p.*, Forefront Publishing Co., 2015), 112, 115, 131-132.

[283] Mark Antonacci, *Test the Shroud* (*n.p.*, Forefront Publishing Co., 2015), 123, 127, 140, 147; P. Jennings,"Still Shrouded in Mystery," *30 Days in the Church and in the World* 1.7 (1988): 70-71, 71.

[284] Quotation with permission from nuclear engineer Robert A. Rucker, "Testing the Neutron Absorption Hypothesis," April 18, 2019. To find this paper, visit the website at http://www.shroudresearch.net/home.html, then click the RESEARCH tab at the top, then scroll to find this paper. It is listed as paper number 20. You may visit Robert Rucker's website *Shroud Research Network* to follow recent updates and developments pertaining to the Neutron Absorption Hypothesis, at http://www.shroudresearch.net/home.html.

[285] Mark Antonacci, *Test the Shroud* (*n.p.*, Forefront Publishing Co., 2015), 125, 130, 139.

[286] Mark Antonacci, *Test the Shroud* (*n.p.*, Forefront Publishing Co., 2015), 137.

[287] Mark Antonacci, *Test the Shroud* (*n.p.*, Forefront Publishing Co., 2015), ii.

Printed in the USA
CPSIA information can be obtained
at www.ICGtesting.com
LVHW080418071123
763186LV00005B/287